Foundations of
INTELLIGENT
TUTORING
SYSTEMS

Edited by

Martha C. Polson
J. Jeffrey Richardson
University of Colorado

Advisory Editor

Elliot Soloway
Artificial Intelligence Project
Yale University

LAWRENCE ERLBAUM ASSOCIATES PUBLISHERS

1988   Hillsdale, New Jersey   Hove and London

Lawrence Erlbaum Associates, Inc., Publishers
365 Broadway
Hillsdale, New Jersey 07642

Production and interior design: Lori L. Baronian
Cover design: Beth Ann Schmalz and Lori L. Baronian

Library of Congress Cataloging-in-Publication Data

Foundations of intelligent tutoring systems / edited by Martha C. Polson, J. Jeffrey Richardson.
    p.   cm.
    Bibliography: p.
    Includes index.
    Contents: Foundations of intelligent tutoring systems / Hugh L. Burns and Charles G. Capps—The expert module / John R. Anderson—The student modeling module / Kurt VanLehn—Curriculum and instruction in automated tutors / Henry M. Halff—The environment module of intelligent ttuoring systems / Richard R. Burton—The role of human-computer interaction in intelligent tutoring systems / James R. Miller—Pragmatic considerations in research, development, and implementation of intelligent tutoring systems / William B. Johnson—Evaluating ITS / David C. Littman and Elliot M. Soloway—Directions for research and applications / J. Jeffrey Richardson.
    ISBN 0-8058-0053-0.   ISBN 0-8058-0054-9 (pbk.)
    1. Computer-assisted instruction.   I. Polson, Martha C. (Martha Campbell)   II. Richardson, J. Jeffrey.
    LB1028.5F634 1988
    371.3′9445—dc19   87-22455
                                                                              CIP

Printed in the United States of America
10 9 8 7 6 5 4 3 2 1

Contents

3

Student Modeling 55
Kurt VanLehn

4

Curriculum and Instruction in Automated Tutors 79
Henry M. Halff

5

The Environment Module
of Intelligent Tutoring Systems 109
Richard R. Burton

6

The Role of Human–Computer Interaction in Intelligent Tutoring Systems   **143**
James R. Miller

7

Pragmatic Considerations in Research, Development, and Implementation of Intelligent Tutoring Systems   **191**
William B. Johnson

8

Evaluating ITSs: The Cognitive Science Perspective   **209**
David Littman and Elliot Soloway

9

Contributors and Editors

John R. Anderson, *Carnegie-Mellon University.* Dr. Anderson is Professor of Psychology, Carnegie-Mellon University, holding the Walter Van Dyke Bingham Chair of Cognitive Science. Having received his Ph.D. in psychology from Stanford University in 1972, his current research is centered on ACT, a production-system capable of simulating intelligence behavior. His numerous research interests are now being brought together in a major new project at Carnegie-Mellon to develop intelligent computer-based tutors, with tutors for high-school geometry and introductory college LISP having been developed already.

Hugh L. Burns, *United States Air Force.* Hugh Burns, as a Lieutenant Colonel in the U.S. Air Force, serves as Chief, Intelligent Systems Branch, Air Force Human Resources Laboratory (AFHRL) Brooks AFB, San Antonio, Texas. He earned his Ph.D. at the University of Texas at Austin investigating rhetorical theory, computer-assisted instruction, and instructional discourse. Lt. Col. Burns participated in the Air Force's Project Forecast II-A "Think Tank" to identify the critical technologies for the next generation of Air Force needs and capabilities.

Richard R. Burton, *Xerox Palo Alto Research Center.* Dr. Burton is a Member of the Research Staff of the Xerox Palo Alto Research Center, working in the Intelligent Systems Laboratory. Dr. Burton's long involvement in intelligent tutoring systems began prior to the receipt of his Ph.D. in information and computer science from the University of California, Irvine, in 1976. He was collaborator on three foundational intelligent tutoring systems: BUGGY, WEST, and SOPHIE.

Charles G. Capps, *United States Air Force.* Charles Capps is a Lieutenant assigned to the Air Force Human Resources Laboratory (AFHRL) at Brooks AFB, Texas. He received his undergraduate degree from the University of Alabama and his Master's degree in clinical psychology at Michigan State University. Since being assigned to the Intelligence Systems branch at AFHRL, his research activities have focused on projects investigating student performance and instructional expertise within intelligent instructional systems.

Henry M. Halff, *Halff Resources, Inc.* Dr. Halff is well known in scientific, military, and government communities for his management of research programs in the rapidly advancing fields of educational technology and cognitive science, work performed as scientific officer of the Office of Naval Research. Recently, Dr. Halff founded Halff Resources, where he is currently involved in applications of artificial intelligence to computer-aided instruction. Dr. Halff received his Ph.D. in psychology in 1969 from the University of Texas.

William B. Johnson, *Search Technology, Inc.* Dr. Johnson is Senior Scientist, Search Technology, Inc., where he manages training research for the military, nuclear power, and aviation industries. Dr. Johnson is currently the knowledge engineer for the Office of Naval Research project on intelligent maintenance training. Holding a Ph.D. in education, 1980, from the University of Illinois, Dr. Johnson is also a certified private pilot, airframe and powerplant mechanic, and designated mechanical engineer. He served as consultant to the 1985 National Academy of Science Air Force Summer Study on Fault Isolation in Air Force Weapons and Support Systems. He is an expert in simulation-oriented computer-based instruction for fault diagnosis.

David C. Littman, *Yale University.* Dr. Littman is currently a doctoral candidate in the Artificial Intelligence Program of the Department of Computer Science. Dr. Littman received his first Ph.D. in Experimental Psychology from Cornell University in 1976. Dr. Littman has been involved in evaluating educational technology since 1977. His main interests are intelligent tutoring systems and artificial intelligence approaches to scientific reasoning.

James R. Miller, *Microelectronics Computer Corporation.* Dr. Miller is team leader of the MCC Human Interface Program where question answering and coaching are being investigated in order to enable the computer user and system to cooperate in achieving tasks stated by the user. Prior to joining MCC, Dr. Miller was Director of Sponsored Research, Computer-Thought Corporation, where he was responsible for the student model, on-line documentation system, and user interface of a knowledge-based training system for the Ada programming language. Dr. Miller holds a Ph.D. in Psychology from the University of California, Los Angeles, granted in 1978.

Martha Campbell Polson, *University of Colorado.* Dr. Polson is Assistant Director of the Institute of Cognitive Science at the University of Colorado, Boulder. Since receiving her Ph.D. from the University of Indiana in 1968, her research interests have spanned a number of areas. Prior to assuming her current position, she was a visiting scientist at the Training Systems Division of the Air Force Human Resources Laboratory where she became involved in the intelligent tutoring systems program and this project.

J. Jeffrey Richardson, *University of Colorado.* Dr. Richardson is Executive Director of the Center for Applied Artificial Intelligence, College of Business, University of Colorado. This center pursues AI applications in business, equipment maintenance, intelligent tutoring systems, and operations research. Dr. Richardson also heads the Colorado Institute for Artificial Intelligence, a state-wide university–industry consortium dedicated to enhancing the technology and human resources foundation for AI in Colorado. His principle research interests include AI applications in equipment maintenance and in training. Dr. Richardson received his Ph.D. in education from the University of Colorado in 1981 and worked at Denver Research Institute prior to moving to the University of Colorado.

Elliot M. Soloway, *Yale University.* Dr. Soloway is Associate Professor of computer science and psychology at Yale University where he is Director of the Cognition and Programming Project. Having received his Ph.D. in computer and information science at the University of Massachusetts in 1978, his work focuses on the cognitive modeling of computer programming. An important application of this is the development of intelligent tutorial systems for college-level programming instruction. Dr. Soloway is also Vice President of Computer-Teach, Inc., an educational software company.

Kurt VanLehn, *Carnegie-Mellon University.* Dr. VanLehn is Assistant Professor in the Department of Psychology at Carnegie-Mellon University, having recently moved there from his position as Research Associate at Xerox Palo Alto Research Center. Having received his Ph.D. in computer science from the Massachusetts Institute of Technology in 1983, Dr. VanLehn is a major contributor to the cognitive science literature pertaining to human skill acquisition, including pioneering work in acquiring procedural skills from lesson sequences and "felicity conditions" for human skill acquisition. Further contributions include the formulation, as a product of the BUGGY project, of repair theory: a generative theory of bugs in procedural skills.

Preface

This book provides a synthesis of the field of Intelligent Tutoring Systems (ITSs). It is neither a collection of project reports nor a survey of ITS systems, but rather a coordinated set of essays, written at the general foundational level, each treating an integral aspect of the field. Each essay defines its topic, its relationship to other topics, the state-of-the art, basic research issues, and near-term applications projects.

The genesis of this book is a planning process set into motion by the Air Force Human Resources Laboratory (AFHRL) to develop its research agenda in ITSs. Acknowledged leaders in the field were contacted and agreed to participate in this process. The authors, editors, and sponsors held a meeting and agreed on the logical organization of the field reflected in the chapters and on the assignment of ITS topics to each chapter. Outlines for each chapter were developed and presented in a workshop held by the sponsor. Based on feedback from the workshop, the outlines were refined and draft papers were written. These were circulated among the authors, editors, and sponsors, critiqued and revised. The revised papers were presented at the AFHRL Research Planning Forum for Intelligent Tutoring Systems, held September 3-4, 1986 in San Antonio, Texas. The papers presented in San Antonio form the chapters of this book, augmented by the introductory and concluding chapters. The findings in this book regarding research and applications opportunities provided input to AFHRL's ITS research agenda.

We would like to acknowledge Lt. Col. Hugh L. Burns, Chief of the Intelligent Systems Branch, Training Systems Division, AFHRL for his role in sponsoring this work. Thanks to Lt. Charles G. Capps of AFHRL and to Dr. Matthew J. Wayner, Director of the Division of Life Sciences, University of Texas at San Antonio and his assistant, Janie Ramos, for their support in organizing the meetings, workshop, and conference associated with this work. Funding was through the

Air Force Office of Scientific Research, Grant Number AFSOR-86-0144, monitored by Dr. Alfred R. Fregley. Special acknowledgments are due to Janet L. Grassia, who did the copyediting for this book, and Marjorie J. DeFries, who edited and managed the copyright releases for the figures and to Tania M. Sizer, who prepared the glossary.

Martha C. Polson
Institute for Cognitive Science
University of Colorado

J. Jeffrey Richardson
Center for Applied Artificial Intelligence
Graudate School of Business Administration
University of Colorado

Foundations of Intelligent Tutoring Systems:
An Introduction

Hugh L. Burns
Charles G. Capps
United States Air Force

Artificial intelligence in education comes of age in systems now called "intelligent tutors," a step beyond traditional computer-assisted instruction. Computer-assisted instruction evolves toward intelligent tutoring systems (ITSs) by passing three tests of intelligence. First, the subject matter, or domain, must be "known" to the computer system well enough for this embedded expert to draw inferences or solve problems in the domain. Second, the system must be able to deduce a learner's approximation of that knowledge. Third, the tutorial strategy or pedagogy must be intelligent in that the "instructor in the box" can implement strategies to reduce the difference between expert and student performance. At the foundation of ITSs, therefore, one finds three special kinds of knowledge and problem-solving expertise programmed in a sophisticated instructional environment. This book examines these knowledge foundations—expert knowledge, student diagnostic knowledge, and the instructional or curricular knowledge—in detail. This book also describes (a) how these kinds of knowledge are embodied in computer-assisted instructional environments; (b) how these systems accrue the advantages of advanced computer interface technologies; (c) how ITSs will emerge in the real world of complex problem solving; and finally (d) how researchers must learn to evaluate the effectiveness and overall quality of these dynamic systems in a world where one day machine tutoring will be taken for granted.

The purpose of this chapter is to introduce the major research issues and development themes that the primary authors—John Anderson, Kurt VanLehn, Henry Halff, Richard Burton, James Miller, William Johnson, David Littman, and Elliott Soloway—explore and amplify. At the core of this book is a simple notion that an ITS has an anatomy (see Figure 1.1), an anatomy that creates convenient classifications of the research and development dimensions.

The expert module contains the domain knowledge. The student diagnostic module diagnoses what the student knows. The instructor module identifies which deficiencies in knowledge to focus on and selects strategies to present that knowledge. The instructional environment and human-computer interface channel tutorial communication. In addition to these components, implementation and evaluation issues are most important. When, where, and how should these ITSs be used? How effective is the ITS and how is its quality understood? ITSs are hard to design and the field requires further study. Consequently, as the research community moves toward more and better ITSs, the need for integration of the "distinct" modules should be obvious. It should come as no surprise that in a complex, knowledge-based, problem-solving, computer-assisted tutoring system, the whole necessarily becomes more than the sum of its parts.

THE EXPERT MODULE

John Anderson, whose current research is in the architecture of cognition and in production systems capable of simulating intelligent human behavior, identifies the concepts and challenges of designing the expert module, that part of a tutor which provides the domain knowledge. The major lesson that the artificial intelligence community has learned from all of the research in expert systems is that any expert module must have an abundance of specific and detailed knowledge derived from people who have years of experience in a particular domain. Consequently, much effort is expended in discovering and codifying the domain knowledge, thus distilling years of experience into a knowledge representation. The enormous amount of knowledge in complex domains as well as the interrelationship of that knowledge means that designing and developing the expert module may be the most demanding chore in building an ITS. Authoring systems for intelligent tutors, alone, are unlikely to discover and codify all of the necessary domain knowledge. Thus, investigating how to encode knowledge and how to represent such expertise in an ITS remains the central focus of developing an expert module.

How does a research team explicitly go about encoding the knowledge in the ITS data structure? Three approaches are common, each moving toward a more cognitively faithful representation of the content expertise. The first is finding a way to encode the knowledge

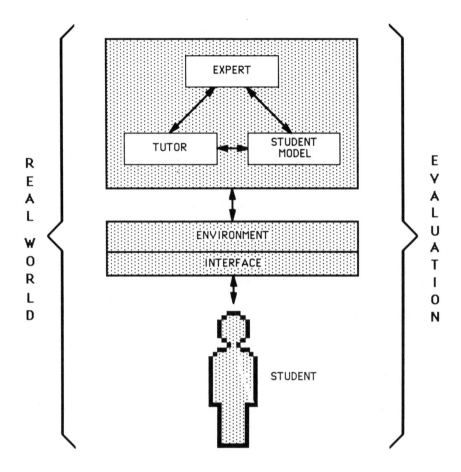

FIGURE 1.1

without actually codifying the underlying human intelligence. The literature often refers to these as "black box" expert systems. The simple input-output information available from a black box system is not suitable for instruction. One method of enhancing these models is to employ a methodology called "issue-based tutoring" (Burton & Brown, 1982). In other words, a programmer attaches instructions to specific issues observable in the behavior of both the expert and the student within the learning environment. Thus, when a student chooses (or fails to choose) a behavior, he or she may receive feedback about the particular behavior. The examples in the artificial intelligence canon include systems that use a mathematical equation-solving process in place of the symbolic human processing. SOPHIE (which stands for Sophisticated Instructional Environment) and

Steamer (Brown, Burton, & deKleer, 1982; Hollan, Hutchins, & Weitzman, 1984) perform their calculations through such techniques. Although the architectures of these systems have not represented human knowledge, they do produce outputs that are useful in recognizing differences between student and expert performance.

The second approach involves the building of a "glass box model" to influence the tutorial mechanisms of the system. To do this, a researcher must use knowledge-engineering techniques. A knowledge engineer interviews an expert and designs a computational representation for delivering the knowledge, usually a rule-based formalism. This implementation does not necessarily correspond to the way the human expert reasons, especially in novel, unfamiliar situations or when providing explanations. Thus, this glass box model allows only for explanations of the information process inherent in the rules of its knowledge base. The rules are typically more strategically aligned with performance rather than explanation, limiting their utility in an instructional setting. However, knowledge-engineering tools and techniques, that is, ways of extracting and codifying information, are becoming more and more useful for ITS development as attention is paid toward making representations more faithful to the breadth and depth of expert reasoning.

Nevertheless, because so much effort is expended in the knowledge acquisition process, turning preexisting expert systems into ITSs is a fond ambition. Clancey's (1982) GUIDON tried to implement MYCIN (Buchanan & Shortliffe, 1984)—an expert system for diagnosing bacterial infections—as the expert model within an ITS. MYCIN's representation of knowledge was highly "compiled." By analogy, a computer program's source code (high-level programming instructions written in languages such as FORTRAN, PASCAL, or COBOL) is compiled into object code (the primitive hardware instructions that the computer responds to). The source code is relatively easy to read, but not executable by a computer. The object code is "machine readable"—the computer can run it, but it is extremely difficult for people to understand. Extending the analogy even further, the "readability" of the source code itself depends on the extent to which the programmer followed structured programming practices. Similarly, the "readability," or utility in explanation, of a knowledge base depends on the principledness of the knowledge engineer's approach to representing the domain knowledge in the rule base (Clancey, 1981). The more principled and well-structured, the better the expert system serves for explanation and instruction. Clancey's research illustrates how limited expert systems can be in instructional settings.

The third approach to encoding the domain knowledge simulates not only the knowledge but also the way a human uses that knowledge. Here, in this area of cognitive modeling, the cognitive science community sees the greatest payoff for the design and development of ITSs. If the goal of cognitive modeling is to develop as realistic a simulation of human problem-solving processes as possible, many research questions must be answered. These questions include: (a) which psychological components are essential for tutoring, (b) at what level should they be represented, and (c) how should different types of knowledge be treated—procedural, declarative, and qualitative. One way of classifying the psychological components is according to problem-solving models as articulated by Newell and Simon (1972), among others. These problem-solving models should have the highest cognitive fidelity, that is, correspondence to an actual human through processes, as possible.

Because the three types of knowledge dictate the strategies of instruction, they need clear definition. Procedural knowledge is knowledge about how to perform a task and is well represented in the literature on expert systems as rule-based, production systems. Many artificial intelligence researchers believe that production rules with their recognize-act cycle capture the basic character of human cognition and, consequently, offer exciting possibilities for ITSs. Declarative knowledge contrasts with procedural knowledge in that it is fact-like, not specialized for a particular use. Finally, qualitative knowledge is the causal understanding that allows a human to reason about behavior using mental models of systems. One of the most challenging issues will be constructing a metatheory that unifies and shows the relationships between procedural, declarative, and qualitative knowledge. John Anderson concludes that research investigating expert modules for tutoring systems will be a unique test of the sufficiency of cognitive theories. Conversely, the design of an ITS will contribute to the discovery of more accurate theories of cognition.

THE STUDENT DIAGNOSIS MODULE

Kurt VanLehn describes the essential problems of student modeling in ITSs. Many ITSs infer a model of the student's current understanding of the subject matter and then use that understanding to adapt the instruction to the student's particular needs. The knowledge structure that depicts the student's current state is the student model, and the reasoning process to develop it is called "student diagnosis." Outputs from student diagnostic modules can be used for a variety of purposes, such as advancing through selected curriculums, coaching or offering unsolicited advice, generating new problems, and adapting sets of explanations. VanLehn describes the research issues in terms of three dimensions and discusses the need for: (a) improving the bandwidth of available knowledge about the student, (b) distinctly identifying types of knowledge to be learned, and (c) assessing differences between students and experts.

How much of the learner's activity is available to the diagnostic program? This is the bandwidth question, according to VanLehn. Most programs work on the low end of the information band where only the final state, that is, the student's answer to a question, is available to the system. Access to an intermediate state allows the diagnostic module to assess the observable physical activity, for example, key strokes or scratch work. The bandwidth of potentially the greatest value allows ITSs access to the learner's mental state, step by step as reasoning proceeds. Because the student diagnostic module needs reliable knowledge about the learner's mental state, bandwidth is critical in designing ITSs.

The second dimension of the student diagnostic module is the target knowledge type. VanLehn classifies knowledge types into two types of procedural knowledge, flat and hierarchical, and declarative knowledge. Specialized strategies for using (or interpreting) knowledge are paired with each type of knowledge. This interpretation process is more difficult to implement for declarative knowledge than for procedural. The interpreter for hierarchical procedural knowledge is more difficult than for flat procedural knowledge. Because the difficulty of the student diagnostic process is closely related to the difficulty of the interpretation process, a flat procedural knowledge base makes the student modeling process the easiest, whereas a declarative knowledge base presents the most difficult student modeling problem.

Assessing differences between students and experts is the third dimension VanLehn discusses. In programming a student diagnostic module, most ITS designers use the same knowledge representation scheme as was used in the expert module so that the expert and student modules actually share the same knowledge base. This is called the overlay method of student modeling, where the student's knowledge is represented as a subset of the expert's. Hence, missing conceptions are represented, but not misconceptions.

The next level of complexity in student modeling is to represent misconceptions, erroneous and incorrect knowledge, as opposed to simply incomplete knowledge. In this approach, the overlay model is augmented by a bug library. Bugs, that is, misconceptions or misunderstandings, must typically be collected empirically, but can be generated computationally from the target procedure, as is done in repair theory (Brown & VanLehn, 1980). To reduce the empirical work required for obtaining an exhaustive set of bugs, bugs are sometimes generated from bug part libraries, where bug parts, fragments of production rule clauses, are assembled into bugs. This represents the highest degree of sophistication in student modeling. Success in this is critically tied to the bandwidth issue.

Designing the student diagnostic module is a high-risk venture and, consequently, presents a wide range of issues to be investigated. How detailed do the descriptions of the student's knowledge have to be? What models of learning can be designed as a superstructure for the diagnostic algorithms? How much should the artificial intelligence research community push expert systems technology toward ITS technology? Of course, a variety of studies of bandwidth, knowledge type, and student-expert differences could be executed. This research promises many useful outcomes.

THE CURRICULUM AND INSTRUCTION MODULE

Henry Halff describes how the instructional module and curriculum issues give form and meaning to ITS research and development as instructional systems. An ITS should have three tutoring character-istics: (a) controls over the representation of the instructional knowledge for selecting and sequencing the subject matter; (b) capabilities for responding to students' questions about instructional goals and content; and (c) strategies for determining when students need help and for delivering the appropriate help. The goal of the instructional module is to circumscribe the nature of teaching and to implement teaching as a solution to the educational communication problem. Separating instructional and content expertise—or the "dancer from the dance," as William Butler Yeats once wrote—is the challenge in designing the instructional module. Obviously, the types of knowledge and the nature of the learning process interrelate with the teaching act. Less obvious is the interaction between content specifics and instructional strategy.

Specific knowledge necessary for learning but not necessary for proficient performance is called "propaedeutics," or enabling knowledge. Often this kind of knowledge is not represented in designing a tutor, when the focus is more on the knowledge in the expert module. In such cases, the required instructional background knowledge often comes about as an afterthought, once the building process has begun. This is the danger that lies in building an expert system first, then enhancing that expertise with explanations or instructional sequences designed to foster an effective learning experience for the ITS user.

Mitigating against this problem somewhat, Halff contends that there are families of instructional knowledges which could transfer from one tutor to another, for example, diagnostic tutorial routines and simulation tutorial routines. Instructional knowledge routines should allow a student to relate theory to practice, to propose solutions, to develop more effective problem-solving strategies. They should also minimize the load on the student's working memory while new concepts are being internalized.

Thus, the instructional module should and can be more than just a by-product of the expert and student modules, and some instructional principles should be robust and explicit enough to generalize across domains. The available literature on instructional theory provides instructional methodologies and can help designers decide such questions as what information to present in what sequence.

If a lesson can be found in curriculum design, it is simply that the overall goals of a tutor must be clear and well communicated. To that end, an ITS must appropriately manage the content and size of the content, conveying that structure to a learner and insuring that the instructional goals are within the learner's reach.

Presentation techniques all depend on the instructional objective. Elicitation and explanation help lead learners to an understanding of facts and concepts. Case presentations and simulated entrapment induce learners to formulate rules and to understand relations. Exercises, drills, and examples allow learners to generalize from subskills to the performance of the full task. Seeing the required skills prepares the student for the real-life situation. All of these strategies should be encompassed in an ITS design when the instructional module is laid out. The instructional engine that propels the presentation, Halff contends, must be investigated more fully.

Achieving any dynamic flexibility at the instructional level requires designing specific instructional states and means of transitioning from one state to another. Here is where artificial intelligence techniques may be the most useful in the instructional module. Meno-tutor (Woolf & McDonald, 1985) is one example of an attempt to achieve this flexibility by manipulating 27 interrelated instructional states. The ITS community is thus articulating needs for meta-rules to accommodate this dynamic reformulation of the tutor at the instructional level.

Another challenge to artificial intelligence involves understanding instructional discourse. Such understanding, for example, would include strategies appropriately intervening in the course of a student's problem-solving activity. Intervention, on the one hand, allows the

ITS control of the tutorial process, but it is also important in keeping a learner on the right track by preventing inappropriate or incorrect learning. Beyond intervention, that is, offering advice, hints or guidance, other strategies are needed for answering questions and providing explanations. These kinds of abilities must be incorporated in the design of an adequate instructional module and depend on further progress in the artificial intelligence field of natural language comprehension. Attempts to use templates (Carbonell, 1970) or semantic networks (Brown et al., 1982) have been tried; however, a comprehensive theory of explanation that would make automation possible has yet to be proposed.

As computer-assisted instruction becomes more intelligent in itself and more intelligently used in the classroom, educators will contribute models for properly shaping an automated instructional process. The fields of instruction and curriculum design can supply guidelines for the general support of ITS design and specifications for developing tool kits for certain educational applications. However, many of the tougher issues of ITS design are, so far, beyond the reach of these guidelines and tools. Still lacking, Halff points out, are (a) the design principles that determine whether a deductive or inductive approach is taken for the ITS instructional module, (b) precise theories that account for instructional effectiveness, and (c) explicit instructional principles in particular domains. Recognizing these deficiencies, however, is a sign of real progress. The effort to construct an instructional module—that explicit computational model of an instructor—ought to unravel some of the pedagogical paradoxes in the human tutoring process. Instructional knowledge acquisition promises to be a rich area for research and development—both for theory and for practice.

THE INSTRUCTIONAL ENVIRONMENT

An instructional environment consists of those elements of an ITS that support what the learner is doing: situations, activities, and tools provided by the system to facilitate learning. Richard Burton explores the issues pertaining to the instructional environment by establishing a pedagogical foundation, by carefully examining some of the more successful "microworlds," and by presenting near-term and long-term research agendas.

The activities and tools presented to the learner in an ITS always reflect an underlying educational philosophy. The trend, as computers get faster and as ITS researchers and educators become more creative and clever, is clearly to create a more open, more robust, more fulfilling, and more effective educational experience. Several principles for building instructional environments have emerged from this trend. An instructional environment should prove that there is more in an ITS than meets the eye. It should foster constructive learning through activities—tools, games, worlds—designed to use students' prior knowledge and to present students with new information and experiences from which they can construct new knowledge. The environment should emphasize conceptual understanding, not rote procedures. It should attempt to connect in-school and outside-school knowledge. It should be designed so that students feel self-monitored, allowing effective learners to assume responsibility for their own learning. The environment should also be developed in the premise that education is a life-long pursuit. From such principles, the educational technology community generally believes that computerized instructional environments become self-contained worlds that can enhance and motivate learning—even if the environments themselves are not intelligent.

Among research considerations pertaining to instructional environments are: (a) levels of abstraction, (b) fidelity, (c) sequences, and (d) help routines. Level of abstraction means what features of the real world are represented in the design of the environment. Fidelity means how closely the simulated environment matches the real world. Important here are considerations of the different types of fidelity; for example, physical fidelity, display fidelity, mechanical fidelity, and cognitive fidelity. Sequences refers to the framework a designer constructs for learning complex skills. A learner progresses through a sequence of increasingly complex microworlds, each providing new challenges and new sets of achievable goals. By means of help routines the designer takes into account additional information learners may need for operating the ITS. But there are different degrees of help. For example, help tells a learner what to do. Assistance or active help actually does the task for the user. In addition to help and such active assistance are empowering tools, reactive help systems, modeling, and—finally—tutoring itself.

The several instructional environments Burton examines share a sophistication in educational design. Burton's own research in sophisticated instructional environments is well known in the intelligent tutoring heritage. In the electronic troubleshooting environment of SOPHIE I, the learner must find a fault in a broken piece of equipment. The tools are the measurement devices, which receive their commands in English. The instructional environment of SOPHIE provides circuit simulation, a natural language program, and routines for judging the adequacy of student actions and for offering advice. Foundational research like Burton's research on SOPHIE opened many doors for ITS designers.

Research opportunities in instructional environments exist in the near term and long term. Generally, Burton sees near-term opportunities in taking advantage of new technologies; the long-term focus of research will be more on basic scientific issues concerning human conceptual problems. In the near future, studies that investigate the power of various simulation kits or ITS design tools should give the research community several environments to explore. The next generation of LISP processing machines should also spur development of ITSs as well as experimental testing of various intelligent tutors. Instructional environments will be enhanced to take advantage of innovations in computer hardware—graphics chips, for example. The ITS design community should also make advances based on new technologies such as read-write optical disks, speech processing input/output, and faster parallel machines.

The long-term issues center on scientific assessments of the ways environments are conceptualized by experts, learners, and instructors. For example, what tradeoffs must be made among the various environmental properties? What are the stages of conceptualization in a problem-solving environment? How can an ITS use information that the environment provides? Do we need color graphics? animation? natural language processing? speech synthesis? Instructional environments must also support the transformation from incorrect concepts to correct ones. How should that be accomplished?

Additionally, the research community should carry out studies to articulate appropriate fidelity requirements and to identify meta-skills useful in dynamic, instructional environments. It will also be necessary to study environments to support the teaching of social skills as well as intellectual skills. Simulation kits provide several exciting possibilities. Medium-scale testing of these in the classroom environment will also be necessary. Empowering tools that enable learners to design more explicit problem-solving settings for themselves should provide some exciting research.

Creativity and cleverness mark the design of the few environments that have been expressly designed for ITSs; creativity and cleverness will continue to be well exercised in the design and development of future intelligent tutors. But success in building instructional environments will largely depend on how well designed the ITS's human-computer interface is.

THE HUMAN-COMPUTER INTERFACE

When considering human-computer interactions in ITSs, James Miller emphasizes making appropriate tradeoffs in the design of ITS interfaces. The learner working with an ITS generally has two problems. First, the learner must learn some subject matter that he or she may not understand. Why else would an ITS be used? The other problem is that the learner must use the technology itself in order to learn and is very likely not an expert user. If the human-computer interaction is poorly designed, a training session will probably be ineffective. Simply put, if the learner has to spend significant intellectual energy working the computer, then the learner has less intellectual and emotional energy for learning what is supposedly being taught.

The goal of interface design, therefore, is to make the interface transparent. The research community is beginning to think of the human-computer interaction as a communication problem and to design this interaction as a system of semantic and contextual processes built on a solid conceptual model. The knowledge embedded in this component of an ITS thus evolves from knowledge of previous computer systems, from human interface research, from the real world objects that are being imitated in the computer system, and from knowledge of the entire range of the communication process—perceiving, understanding, and creating meaning.

The state of the art in interface research and development, Miller points out, allows for two basic styles of design. The first allows users to become direct participants in the domain; the second allows them to control the domain by instructing the system to carry out desired actions. First-person interfaces, or direct manipulation interfaces as they are sometimes called in the literature, are familiar as the icons in the images of the Apple Macintosh personal computer. The soul of these interfaces is the icon whose manipulation is intended to map directly to a desired outcome. The breakthrough for this kind of interaction has been large bit-mapped displays and the mouse, a pointing and selecting device. One of the advantages of iconic interaction is that learners do not have to remember names of documents, commands, and so forth, because all of this information is intrinsically part of the icon data structure. The strength of the first-person interface is its self-evident properties; its weakness is extensibility. In the second-person interface, an ITS user commands the system. Command languages are fairly well understood and can powerfully interact with a system. The general thrust of endeavor in the intelligent tutoring community, however, will be to minimize research on new command languages and concentrate on more direct manipulation and interaction in the actual delivery of the tutor.

Where are the promising research opportunities for the interface design team in an ITS project? First, the overall goal is to make the domain semantics visible. Studies that illustrate ways of constructing models of complex domains with special support for learners' acquisition of these representations and for special recognition of learners' corresponding conceptual models should be especially valuable. Investigation of the various graphical techniques for presenting models also offers a large payoff, especially if the graphical models are linked to various stages of the conceptualization. This direction points research of interfaces toward a few of the issues pertinent to the instructional environment, for example, level of abstraction and fidelity.

Another interesting research issue will be developing tool kits for interface development. Such kits would include direct manipulation techniques, natural language interfaces, speech processing, videodisks, touch screen technologies, and combinations of these. How these technologies will evolve for intelligent systems users is difficult to predict. When Miller speculates about the arrival of tomorrow's technology—three-dimensional graphics, continuous speech recognition, mammoth displays—he doubts that it will be immediately clear how to use this technology wisely. Finally, although many of the interface technologies could help integrate the separate ITS modules, developers must still suit the content to the interface and the interface to the content. If the interface is overdone and calls attention to itself, then the communication between the student and the instructional system will be impaired.

ITS PRAGMATICS

William Johnson reminds developers of intelligent tutors that the day will come when their systems—built in the laboratories—must make the transition to the real world. This generates a number of pragmatic considerations. The individual modules, the environments, and the interfaces must be integrated into a working entity. An ITS must be used in its educational, technical, or industrial setting. If the jury is still out on the success and promise of the ITS as a mode of instruction, then answers to many implementation questions have not been forthcoming either. Certainly it is true that nothing is as practical as good theory; nevertheless, there are pragmatic issues beyond good theory. Who are the users? What are the expectations? How can intelligent tutors be effectively implemented? Suffice it to say that a person does not simply decide in a vacuum that an ITS is the most appropriate means of instruction for a given domain—certain practical matters must be considered.

The willingness of the sponsors and the users to adapt this technology is an important practical consideration. Support must be generated across several levels of the affected organization. Initially, someone must have a desire to implement the ITS. Whether it is to introduce a new curriculum, to improve an old one, or perhaps to supplement existing courses, someone in a position of authority must see a need to institute intelligent tutoring. Then, that person must provide the necessary support both throughout the full research and development cycle and during the implementation of the system.

Five considerations are crucial to determining whether implementation of an ITS is currently feasible. First, ITSs are ready for trial application but admittedly are in their infancy at this time. Second, the programming tools developed in artificial intelligence for knowledge engineering and intelligent authoring as well as the necessary "field" hardware are not sufficient. Third, hardware and software are constantly changing—and with increasing speed. Fourth, the demand for various personnel resources within the development team is quite drastic—subject matter experts, students, instructors, computer engineers, computer scientists, managers of advanced technology programs are all needed. Fifth, evaluation of intelligent tutoring, or for that matter any evaluation of artificial intelligence systems, is expensive in terms of both money and time.

This initial picture may seem bleak but it is important to note these deficiencies. ITS developers must present their research fairly. Researchers in artificial intelligence have good reason to avoid publicity hype; it damages the credibility of the entire scientific community. Naturally, implementation issues will change rapidly during the next few years, but this state of flux justifies bringing the systems to the demonstration stage. Until the scientists are more aware of the real-world demands placed upon ITSs, many of the limitations cannot be reduced. Research must therefore be conducted in appropriate educational or training settings. The emphasis should be on evaluating some phases of these emerging tutors in the real world and on measuring their effect on their intended users.

The demands placed upon ITS developers are extensive. However, the science is indeed in its early years, and as more systems are built and implemented, the skills of the designers will improve drastically. Obviously, the technology will be ever changing and the development of ITSs will continue to require the effort of knowledge engineers, subject matter experts, computer programmers, and specialists in the science of human factors. These people ensure the efficacy of a necessarily complex system. Johnson offers a word of advice: "Keep the need for active involvement of the domain expert throughout the research and development cycle." Many times, the domain expert may not feel or understand the need for some alien, automated teaching machine; yet much of the success of an entire ITS project depends on the cooperation between the domain expert and the knowledge engineer.

Providing valuable information is only one of the contributions domain experts make to an ITS project. They can also identify criteria for selecting appropriate ITS instructional objectives. Johnson presents several characteristics that help identify candidates for applications areas: (a) high flow of students, (b) low availability of instructors, (c) expensive real equipment, (d) remote site training, (e) unavailable real equipment, (f) high public visibility, (g) unsafe real equipment, (h) high recurrent training volume.

These criteria for selecting appropriate applications for tutoring suggest domains that are complex and technical by nature. For example, maintenance of expensive, dangerous, and sensitive equipment is an excellent proving ground for ITSs. The intelligent components of the system allow learners to explore the environments and use the information conveyed by their instructors. Military technical schools are also prime candidates for ITSs. No other organization can furnish the sheer numbers of students who are available for relatively short periods of time. Not only are the requirements for the trainees quite rigorous, but also the obligations and course demands felt by the instructors are overwhelming—the task being to teach students from a myriad of backgrounds the competencies and skills for a particular occupation. Training in personnel, procurement, logistics, and space operations are all important domains for demonstrating that artificial intelligence approaches to training are both needed and effective. Finally, industrial settings also present an excellent opportunity for testing ITSs in the real world, and especially for testing computer-assisted, on-the-job tools in which the "intelligent coach" is an embedded feature, not an independent entity.

Johnson's bottom line is simply this: If ITSs are to reach their promise, then the laboratory systems must operate and survive in the real world.

ITS EVALUATION

David Littman and Elliot Soloway describe what has emerged as a serious gap in the ITS literature—evaluation methods and quality control. Obviously, an intelligent tutor must be evaluated so that one knows how good it truly is, and the evaluator must be able to articulate why such systems are good or bad. To date, designers and evaluators have yet to establish guidelines for use in judging a system's worth. In fact, evaluation is the aspect of the intelligent tutoring methodology least written about. Science calls for empirical testing of systems, theories, and models. Intelligent tutors have not, for the most part, met this requirement of the experimental method.

Both formative and summative evaluations are important in evaluating instructional products. Since the instructional impact of an ITS, that is, its summative evaluation, is critically dependent on how well it was designed and built, Littman and Soloway properly place primary emphasis on formative evaluation and a strategy for formative evaluation specifically suited for ITSs.

Formative evaluations take place during the development of a system. As data are collected and feedback received, scientists make changes. This ongoing process can involve any of the modules in an ITS. Advice may come from the knowledge engineers, the subject matter experts, and from early trials with potential users of the system. The system engineer can circumvent bugs that would have occurred and anticipate other undesirable behavior throughout the program.

Littman and Soloway emphasize the need for developing a systemic approach to formative evaluation of ITSs, and they outline a two-part methodology for performing formative assessments. The first part, external evaluation, focuses on the impact of the ITS on students' problem-solving processes and is based on explicit models of how students solve problems. Student modeling techniques are used to identify the kinds of problems students should find hard to solve and easy to solve. An ITS can then be evaluated according to how well it teaches students the specific skills they need to solve problems. The effectiveness of the system is determined through measurement of observable phenomena that occur during the learning process. Instructional experts should be able to recognize these overt signs and determine whether or not the intended outcome was achieved. External evaluation can make rigorous testing possible. Because student modeling techniques capture how students solve problems, those techniques can be used to predict the ease or difficulty of additional problems and the knowledge necessary to solve them. The performance of students actually solving these problems can be compared to the predictions.

The second formative evaluation method, internal evaluation, addresses the question of why the ITS behaves as it does. It involves analysis of the architectural components of the ITS and the way these components respond to input values. Littman and Soloway recommend that their internal evaluation answer three questions. First, what does the ITS know? Second, how does the ITS do what it does? Third, what should the ITS do?

Littman and Soloway discuss many of the lessons their research group learned in applying ideas for external and internal evaluation to an ITS called PROUST, a LISP program that finds the nonsyntactic bugs in PASCAL programs written by students, and then tutors the students about these errors. During the external evaluation, the PROUST research group used its cognitive model of novice programming to determine whether PROUST helped students acquire programming skills. One conclusion drawn from that evaluation effort was that simply counting the number of answers a student got right or wrong did not provide a useful measure of the effects of PROUST on novice programmers. It appeared that a more fine-grained analysis was necessary. Therefore the evaluation focused on PROUST's impact on specific "micro" problem-solving skills, such as students' ability to determine whether a computer program is protected against certain invalid input data.

The kind of evaluation Littman and Soloway propose has some intriguing implications. One is that evaluation can help designers identify the kinds of reasoning capacities their tutorial systems must have. For example, the PROUST evaluation uncovered a need for the system to reason about how students name variables in their programs. Without this reasoning capacity, the program was unable to completely understand programs that humans find very easy to understand. When this capability was added to PROUST, its tutorial performance was noticeably improved. Thus, evaluation can have a very real impact on the design of tutorial systems.

TOWARD KNOWLEDGE-BASED EDUCATIONAL SYSTEMS

With more than 20 ITSs scattered throughout the literature (see Table 1.1), a well-understood technology for ITS development cannot be expected. More experience is needed and more ITSs need to be built in exploration of the possibilities. However, the education and training communities can expect high payoffs only when an ITS technology does formally emerge. So, more ITSs need to be built not only for exploration, but for determining a generalizable body of knowledge about how to build ITSs. This development will not be a simple task. What is clearly understood, however, is that such systems will require seven kinds of expertise, at least. This expertise pertains to the components that must be integrated as the foundation for ITSs:

1. content expertise in the expert module,
2. diagnostic expertise (determining what learners know and need to learn) in the student diagnostic module,
3. instructional and curriculum expertise in the instructor module,
4. expertise in creating instructional environments,
5. human-computer interface expertise,
6. implementation expertise, and
7. evaluation expertise.

These components comprise the anatomy of ITSs and together provide the educational community with a basic conceptual model for designing, developing, deploying, and evaluating machine tutors.

It is not easy to integrate all of this knowledge in a single delivery system. The hope of achieving, through artificial intelligence, a rich, interactive, flexible, real-time capacity to support learning is the basic motivation for research and development in ITSs. ITSs promise not only to help people learn how to perform complex tasks better, but also to reveal how people learn. This collection of essays examines the ITS's anatomy and proposes two things: (a) achievable ITS capabilities for the near term and (b) fundamental research questions that must be answered along the way toward more robust and effective, knowledge-based educational systems.

REFERENCES

Brown, J. S., Burton, R. R., & deKleer, J. (1982). Pedagogical, natural language and knowledge engineering techniques in SOPHIE I, II, and III. In D. Sleeman & J. S. Brown (Eds.), *Intelligent tutoring systems* (pp. 227–282). New York: Academic Press.

Brown, J. S., & VanLehn, K. (1980). Repair theory: A generative theory of bugs in procedural skills. *Cognitive Science, 4,* 389–426.

Buchanan, B. G., & Shortliffe, E. H. (1984). *Rule-based expert systems: The MYCIN experiments of the Stanford Heuristic Programming Project* (p. 576). Reading, PA: Addison–Wesley.

Burton, R. R., & Brown, J. S. (1982). An investigation of computer coaching for informal learning activities. In D. Sleeman & J. S. Brown (Eds.), *Intelligent tutoring systems* (pp. 79–98). New York: Academic Press.

Carbonell, J. R. (1970). AI in CAI: An artificial intelligence approach to computer-assisted instruction. *IEEE Transactions on Man–Machine Systems, 11,* 19–202.

Clancey, W. J. (1981). *The epistemology of a rule-based expert system: A framework for explanation* (Report No. STAN-CS-81-896). Stanford, CA: Department of Computer Science, Stanford University.

Clancey, W. J. (1982). Tutoring rules for guiding a case method dialogue. In D. Sleeman & J. S. Brown (Eds.), *Intelligent tutoring systems* (pp. 201–225). New York: Academic Press.

Hollan, J. H., Hutchins, E. L., & Weitzman, L. (1984). Steamer: An interactive inspectable simulation-based training system. *AI Magazine, 5,* 15–27.

Newell, A., & Simon, H. (1972). *Human problem solving.* Englewood Cliffs, NJ: Prentice-Hall.

Woolf, B., & McDonald, D. D. (1985). Building a computer tutor: Design issues. *AEDS Monitor, 23,* 10–18.

The Expert Module

John R. Anderson
Carnegie-Mellon University

Intelligent tutoring systems, by their name, are supposed to bring intelligence in some way to the task of computer-based instruction. There are two key places for intelligence in an ITS. One is in the knowledge the system has of its subject domain. The second is in the principles by which it tutors and in the methods by which it applies these principles. Clearly, human tutors are effective only when they possess both kinds of intelligence; lack of either component leads to instructional ineffectiveness. Humans cannot tutor effectively in a domain in which they are not expert, and there are also inarticulate experts who make terrible instructors.

The focus of this chapter is the expert module of a tutor that provides the domain intelligence. In my view, this is the backbone of any ITS. A powerful instructional system cannot exist without a powerful body of domain knowledge. Frequently, and perhaps typically, the expert modules in ITSs are incomplete, and as a consequence, they can provide only part of the instruction required in the domain. All existing ITSs need to be supplemented by human teachers. So, for instance, Steamer (Hollan, Hutchins, & Weitzman, 1984), which is used to train engineers about steam propulsion plants, knows a great deal about the mathematical properties of steam but rather little about how to operate a steam plant. As a consequence, Steamer provides only part of the instruction necessary to operate such plants. Nonetheless, it is judged to provide an important component of the instruction.

A powerful expert module must have an abundance of knowledge.

This is certainly the lesson from the expert system's work in artificial intelligence. It is also the lesson from the study of human expertise, where experts are invariably people with many years of experience. Hayes (1985) investigated what it takes to achieve levels of performance commonly ascribed to geniuses in areas ranging from mathematics to music. He determined that no genius produced a truly exceptional work without at least 10 years of experience. Presumably, these 10 years of experience were required for enough knowledge to accumulate to permit the exceptional performance.

It should be emphasized that a great deal of effort needs to be expended to discover and codify the domain knowledge. The sheer amount of knowledge required in most complex domains ensures that developing the expert module will always be labor-intensive. As techniques of intelligent tutoring evolve, authoring systems might be expected to assume much of the work involved in tutoring. However, authoring systems will never do the work of discovering and codifying the domain knowledge. Already, we estimate that in our applications to programming and mathematics, over 50% of our effort goes into encoding the domain knowledge. This proportion will only increase as other components become more automated.

Having decided that we need to encode into the system a large body of knowledge, we must confront the problem of how to encode that knowledge. There are basically three options. The first is to try to find some way of reasoning about the domain that does not require our actually codifying the knowledge that underlies human intelligence. For instance, a system can use mathematical equation-solving, which produces through numerical processes what humans achieve through symbolic processes. SOPHIE (Brown, Burton, & deKleer, 1982), for example, used the SPICE simulator for electronic circuits. This system performs its calculations by mathematical relaxation techniques. It does not have human knowledge of electronic currents, but it can still reason about them by simulating them with its mathematical model. This first kind of model is called a "black box model."

The second possibility is basically to go through the standard stages of developing an expert system. This involves extracting knowledge from a human expert and devising a way of codifying and applying that knowledge. Although the knowledge comes from a human, the way it is applied does not have to correspond to the way the human expert applies it.

The third possibility is to go one step further and make the expert module a simulation, at some level of abstraction, of the way the human uses the knowledge. This is clearly the most demanding approach to developing an expert module, but I will argue that

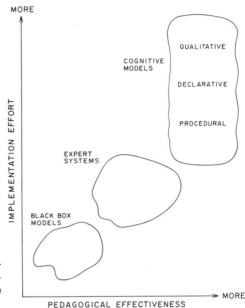

FIGURE 2.1 The tradeoff between the pedagogical effectiveness of an expert module and the effort of constructing it.

·experience shows this approach to be essential to producing high-performance tutoring systems.

In general, expert modules cannot be reviewed in the abstract. It is necessary to understand how they will fit into an overall tutoring system. It certainly is the case that what is easy for the expert module considered in isolation is not easy for the tutoring system in total. Thus using a set of mathematical equations, although expedient, would make it extremely difficult to generate articulate instruction. Figure 2.1 illustrates the relationship I perceive between ease of development and pedagogical effectiveness.

In what follows, the three approaches to the expert module will be reviewed, giving the greatest emphasis to the cognitive modeling approach, which lends itself most easily to powerful tutoring methods.

RELATIONSHIP OF EXPERT MODULES
TO EXPERT SYSTEMS

Before analyzing the different types of expert modules, it is worthwhile to consider their relationship to the expert systems of artificial intelligence (see Hayes-Roth, Waterman, & Lenat, 1983). The first issue is to define an expert system. There are two notions of expert systems, one that is tied to a certain methodology and a second that is criterion-based. A "knowledge-engineering" methodology has arisen for developing expert systems, and it involves deploying humanlike knowledge in nonhuman ways. When I refer to expert systems, I refer to products of this methodology. These are sometimes referred to as first-generation expert systems because they tend to be narrow and brittle. Another definition would be criterion-based: Any system that achieves high-quality performance could be classified as an expert system. Thus, because any kind of expert module in an ITS must be capable of doing a complex task proficiently, it would be considered an expert system by this criterion-based definition. In particular, cognitive models would be expert systems if they model complex, demanding problem solving. The reason I am not using the criterion-based definition is that it does not enable me to distinguish between the expert module and expert systems.

It is particularly important here to consider what have been referred to as second-generation expert systems. These systems have a more fundamental understanding of the domain and are not so narrow or brittle. One does not yet get the same practical performance from these systems, but they are often viewed as the hope of the future. Systems of this kind are discussed under the category of *qualitative process* models, a special kind of cognitive model. Qualitative process models are concerned with reasoning about the causal structure of the world. In actual fact, research in qualitative process models is only sometimes concerned with cognitive fidelity; however, the emphasis here is on research that does strive for cognitive fidelity.

Figure 2.2 illustrates some of the set relationships among the concepts we have defined so far: cognitive models, black box models, expert systems defined by methodology, expert systems defined by criterion, qualitative process models, and the expert module of an ITS. As can be seen, the criterion-based definition of an expert system is sufficiently encompassing to include everything except those cognitive models that concentrate on getting the details of some behavior correct. Black box models, methodologically defined expert systems, and cognitive models all intersect with the expert module of an ITS.

Work on expert modules for ITS systems could potentially increase the range of tasks that can be solved by computers. Given the criterion-based definition, fundamentally expanding the boundaries of what can be done by expert systems may be the long-range consequence of the cognitive modeling approach that I will be advocating. That is, it seems that a reasonable methodology for acquiring a working expert system is to make a running simulation of a human expert.

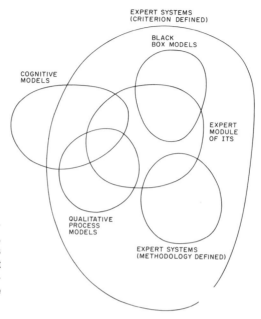

FIGURE 2.2 The set relationships among cognitive models, black box models, expert systems methodologically defined, expert systems criterion-defined, qualitative models, and the expert module of an ITS.

It must be pointed out, however, that no cognitive models to date have outperformed expert systems developed with the knowledge-engineering methodology. So far, the constraint of being true to human behavior has been more a burden than a stimulus.

By definition, intelligent tutoring systems can be built only for domains for which expert systems (criterion-defined) exist. This then poses an interesting question: Why build tutors to teach topics for which we already have expert systems to perform the task? Even if we are faced with a new domain requiring that a new expert module for our ITS be built, why not just quit at the expert module? There are three standard answers:

1. To satisfy the need for robustness. It is generally considered desirable that humans be able to perform functions that machines perform just in case these machines break down or are temporarily inaccessible. Thus, even though calculators are common, we teach our children basic arithmetic skills; and even though spelling correctors exist, it is considered valuable to know how to spell accurately. Presumably, this need for robustness is especially strong in military domains.

2. To establish prerequisite knowledge. Tutors can teach students knowledge that is often a prerequisite to learning skills that an expert system cannot emulate. Thus, we need to teach calculus problem-solving skills (Kimball, 1982) as a prerequisite to creating Ph.D. physicists. We need to teach basic LISP programming skills (Reiser, Anderson, & Farrell, 1985) as

a prerequisite to using LISP for artificial intelligence programming. In effect, tutors can facilitate students' mastery of basic skills before they learn advanced skills. Because the tutor cannot teach the advanced skill, a premium is placed on having a tutor that smooths the transition from the tutoring environment to learning on one's own.

3. To teach part of a skill. A corollary of the previous answer is that tutors can sometimes teach part of a skill if not all of it. So, for instance, the Geometry Tutor (Anderson, Boyle, & Yost, 1985) can tutor the generation of proofs but only if the proofs do not require constructions, because generating proofs is much more tractable than creating arbitrary constructions. We can therefore provide tutors for part of a high school geometry course. A variation on this is that we can use the partial expertise of a system to provide partial feedback. So for proof systems that are too complicated to build into a viable expert system, we can still tell a student whether a step in a proof is logically correct although we cannot suggest the proof itself.

BLACK BOX MODELS

A black box expert is one that generates the correct input-output behavior over a range of tasks in the domain and so can be used as a judge of correctness. However, the internal computations by which it provides this behavior are either not available or are of no use in delivering instruction. The classical example of a black box model is the original work on SOPHIE (Brown & Burton, 1975). It used a general-purpose electronic simulator called SPICE II (Nagel & Pederson, 1973) and was intended to teach students how to troubleshoot faulty electronic circuits. The tutor used its simulator to determine the reasonableness of various measurements that the student would make in troubleshooting the circuit. Because the SPICE simulator worked by solving a set of equations rather than by humanlike, causal reasoning, it was not possible for SOPHIE to explain its decisions in detail. Later versions of SOPHIE (Brown, Burton, & deKleer, 1982) utilized a causal model of circuits to deal with this deficiency. I discuss this causal model under the category of qualitative process models.

One could imagine a black box expert for the game of chess that found good moves by searching over millions of sequences of chess moves—something that human chess experts clearly do not do. Such a system could provide good advice about what move to make, but it could not explain why. A similar idea is used in the WEST program (Burton & Brown, 1982), in which a black box expert does an exhaustive search of the possible moves and determines the optimal move given a particular strategy.

Clearly, such an expert can be used in a simple reactive tutor that tells students whether they are right or wrong and possibly what the right move would be. Quite possibly such a reactive tutor is more pedagogically effective than no tutor. The notion of a black box plus reactive tutor is interesting because it suggests a cheap way of converting off-the-shelf expert systems into tutors. Note that it is not limited to black box experts but could be used with any type of expert system (criterion definition).

However, the intelligent tutoring paradigm is based on the belief that what a tutor says is critical and that it is helpful to say more than just "right," "wrong," and "do this." The question is how to build a more articulate tutor around an expert system when knowledge of that system is not accessible. One way to build such a tutor is with a methodology dubbed *issue-based tutoring* by Burton and Brown (1982). The basic idea is to make patterns defined on the students' behavior and the experts' behavior and to attach instruction to those patterns. For instance, one issue recognizer in WEST is evoked when the expert chooses to bump and the student does not. (See Figure 2.3.) It interrupts with an explanation of the usefulness of bumping. In WEST, the response of the issue-based recognizers not to single events but to patterns of events enables the system to respond in some fairly sophisticated ways.

Figure 2.4 illustrates the basic idea of issue-oriented tutoring based on observing the surface behavior of the expert and the student. Issue-oriented recognizers look for some configuration of the two surface behaviors that indicates that a tutorial issue is ripe for discussion. This idea of issue-based tutoring is very powerful and need not be restricted to black box modules. It is appropriate for other kinds of expert modules as well. So, for instance, in the Geometry Tutor (Anderson, Boyle, & Yost, 1985) an issue recognizer is invoked whenever the student uses an equality statement for a premise when a congruence statement is required. Attached to the issue recognizer is a dialogue that reinforces the difference between equality and congruence. Although this tutorial intervention could have been attached to the internal structure of our expert module (and some of the publications are written as if they were), it proves to be more economical and efficient to code this intervention as an issue recognizer defined on surface behavior.

However, as Brown and Burton recognized in their later versions of SOPHIE, there are things that cannot be tutored by such surface-level issue recognizers. Access to the internal structure of the expert is necessary for creating appropriate explanations. For instance, a standard mistake in geometry is to fail to use the reflexive rule of congruence when appropriate. (Because the reflexive rule can apply to every object in the diagram, there is a great potential for overusing

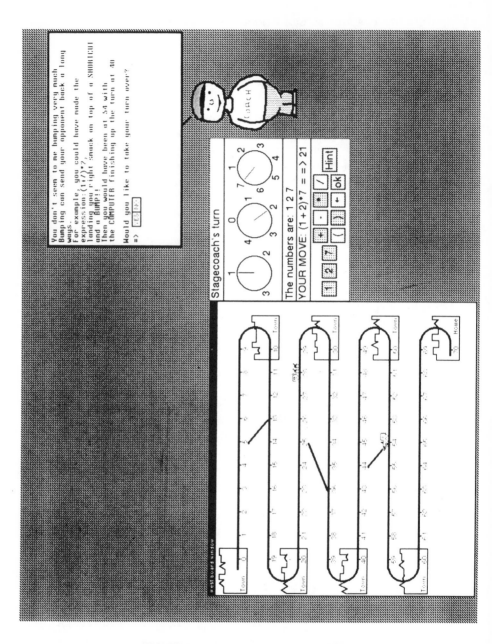

FIGURE 2.3 Tutoring of bumping in WEST.

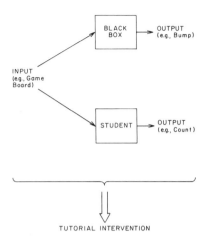

FIGURE 2.4 The pattern recognition that underlies issue-oriented tutoring.

it, and students appear to guard against overuse by never using the rule at all.) A tutoring system cannot explain to the student why the rule is appropriate in a particular context without access to the chain of reasoning that led the expert to conclude that the rule was appropriate.

Figure 2.5 illustrates the contrast between surface-level tutoring, which can be implemented with issue-oriented recognizers, and the kind of deep-level tutoring that can be implemented if there is access to the internal reasoning of the expert module. At the surface level we can note the legal problems with the student's response (a) and point to the correct behavior (b). However, if we model the student's error, we can explain the misconception to the student (c) and motivate the system's choice (d). Again, on the belief that explanation is helpful, deep-level tutoring should be more effective than surface-level tutoring.

GLASS BOX EXPERT SYSTEMS

A second category of expert modules is that of the expert systems that are prototypically generated in the knowledge-engineering tradition. The basic methodology of building these expert systems involves a knowledge engineer and a domain expert who can identify a problem area and its scope, enumerate and formalize the key concepts in the domain, formulate a system to implement the knowledge, and then iteratively test and refine that system. These systems are characterized by the great quantity and humanlike nature of knowledge that is articulated. The knowledge acquisition process is recognized

Surface Level versus
Deep Tutoring

Surface Level

(a) "The side-angle-side rule requires two congruent sides and a congruent angle; you have only given one congruent side and a congruent angle"

(b) "Try to prove $\overline{AB} \cong \overline{AB}$"

Deep Level

(c) "To apply the side-angle-side postulate you have to establish AB is congruent to itself. You cannot simply assume it"

(d) "Whenever you are trying to prove triangles congruent it is a good idea to prove that shared sides are congruent to themselves. This will give you a pair of corresponding parts"

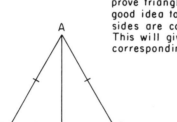

FIGURE 2.5 The contrast between surface-level tutoring and deep-level tutoring.

as the time-consuming component of building expert systems, and the one that great effort is being expended on in an attempt to automate.

By the very nature of the enterprise, the expert system that emerges from this exercise is going to be more amenable to tutoring than a black box model because a major component of this expert system is an articulate, humanline representation of the knowledge underlying expertise in the domain. The expert system methodology in its variations has been very successfully used to tackle a wide range of intellectual behaviors. There are expert systems for interpretation, prediction, diagnosis, design, planning, monitoring, debugging, repair, and control. Indeed, the expert system methodology is one way of incorporating tutoring expertise when the domain expert is also an expert teacher. This seems to be Stevens, Collins, and Goldin's (1982) approach, for instance, to the development of tutors.

Curiously, there have been relatively few examples of the classic expert systems being used as the expert modules of tutors. One example

IF
The infection which requires therapy is meningitis
Organisms were not seen in the stain of the culture
The type of infection is bacterial
The patient does not have a head injury defect
The age of the patient is between 15 and 55 years
THEN
The organisms that might have been causing the
infection are diplococus-pneumoniae(.75) and
neisseria-meningitidis(.74)

FIGURE 2.6   A typical MYCIN rule.

IF
The number of factors appearing in the domain
which need to be asked by the student is zero
The number of subgoals remaining to be determined
before the domain rule can be applied is equal to 1
THEN
Say: subgoal suggestion
Discuss the (sub)goal with the student in a
goal-directed   mode
Wrap up the discussion of the domain being considered

FIGURE 2.7   An example of GUIDON'S TUTORIAL RULES. *Note.* From "Tutoring Rules for Guiding a Case Method Dialogue" by W. J. Clancey, 1982. *Intelligent Tutoring Systems* (p. 218). Copyright 1982 by Academic Press. Reprinted by permission.

might be the use of MACSYMA by Genesereth (1982), although it is questionable whether MACSYMA is really an expert system, methodologically defined. The classic and well-analyzed case is GUIDON by Clancey (1982), which is based on MYCIN. MYCIN (Shortliffe, 1976), whose domain of expertise is the diagnosis of bacterial infections, is one of the best known of the expert systems. It consists of 450 if–then rules, such as the one in Figure 2.6, which encode bits and pieces of the probabilistic reasoning that underlies medical diagnosis.

The basic instruction in GUIDON is driven by t-rules, which are an extension of Burton and Brown's issue-oriented recognizers. T-rules (like the issue-oriented recognizers) are defined on a differential between the expert's behavior and the student's behavior, but they are also defined on the expert's reasoning processes. An example of a t-rule is given in Figure 2.7. Note that this rule refers to entities in the internal structure of the expert, such as rules and goals. The black box has been opened up.

Unfortunately, the actual reasoning process used by MYCIN to deploy its knowlege, an exhaustive backward search, is not the way the knowledge is deployed by humans. Figure 2.8 illustrates a fraction of that structure. This mismatch between the control structure of MYCIN and that of humans made an explanation of what to do next difficult. In addition, MYCIN's highly compiled rules of reasoning were difficult for GUIDON to justify. Also, many of the MYCIN rules, although appropriate for experts, were too complex to be directly taught to novices.

All of these difficulties led to the design of NEOMYCIN, in which an attempt was made to impose a different control structure on the domain knowledge. The control structure is now a domain-independent set of rules about how to use the domain rules. The currently active set of hypotheses is contained in a new data structure that is called a *differential* and that is designed to reflect some of the characteristics of human short-term memory. Also, a different data structure was used for the t-rules to facilitate explanation.

The fundamental lesson of GUIDON is that for tutoring systems to be truly effective, it is necessary to pay attention not only to the knowledge in the expert module but also to the way it is deployed. Many expert systems, although using humanlike knowledge, deploy that knowledge in the exhaustive manner so typical of computers. To be truly appropriate for tutoring, the expert module must deploy its knowledge according to the same restrictions as a human does. This principle leads us to the cognitive modeling approach.

Clancey's work was a watershed in the development of intelligent tutors because it illustrated that tutors were going to be seriously limited if they simply ported expert systems from artificial intelligence. Consequently, subsequent research has focused on the use of cognitive models. In many ways this research decision was a good one, but it has led to a neglect of practical issues, such as how off-the-shelf expert systems might be used. It would be comforting if there had been other projects besides Clancey's that explored extensively the use of expert systems for tutoring.

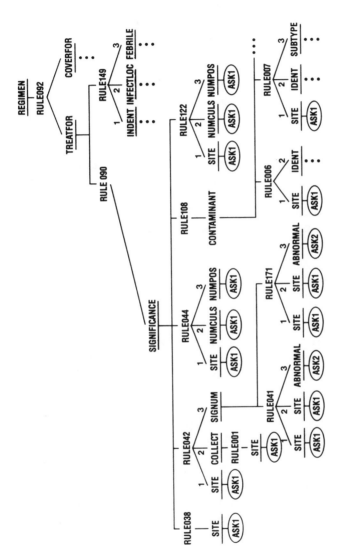

FIGURE 2.8 An illustration of the backward search structure generated by MYCIN. *Note.* From B. Buchanan & E. Shortliffe, *Rule-Based Expert Systems*, Copyright 1984, Addison-Wesley Publishing Company, Inc., Reading, MA. Figure 5–8. Reprinted with permission.

COGNITIVE MODELS

The goal of the cognitive modeling approach is to effectively develop a simulation of human problem solving in a domain in which the knowledge is decomposed into meaningful, humanlike components and deployed in a humanlike manner. The merit of this approach is that it gives us the expert module in the form that can be most easily and deeply communicated to the student. However, there are real costs in this approach. First of all, developing cognitive models is a more constrained and time-consuming task than simply developing expert systems. Fortunately, there have been dramatic improvements over the past 10 years in the ability of cognitive science to develop such models. These improvements have resulted at least in part from borrowing concepts from the expert systems work. A second difficulty is that running the computations of cognitive models can be quite computationally expensive. Fortunately, increasing computational power is diminishing this concern. Additional techniques for dealing with computational costs are addressed later in the chapter.

Another complexity is the issue of the amount of detail to be incorporated into a cognitive model. Many of the factors that are incorporated into some psychological simulations, such as the exact mechanisms of short-term memory search, seem irrelevant for tutoring. Faithfully modeling such phenomena in an expert module adds an unnecessary computational burden. The question arises of which psychological components are essential for purposes of tutoring and which are not. I have argued (Anderson, in press) that tutoring systems depend on cognitive assumptions at the algorithm level and not at the implementation level. The algorithm level refers to high-level specification of mental computation that ignores issues of neural implementation. The obvious analogy is to a program specified in a high-level programming language that does not address issues of machine implementation. The best exemplars of algorithm-level systems are the problem-solving models (e.g., Newell & Simon, 1972).

In discussing cognitive systems it is useful to distinguish between three types of knowledge that need to be tutored. There are domains like calculus problem solving where the main knowledge to be communicated is procedural, that is, knowledge about how to perform a task. There are domains like geography where the tutorial goal is to convey declarative knowledge in the form of a set of facts appropriately organized so that one can reason with them. Declarative knowledge contrasts with procedural knowledge in that it is more general and not specialized for a particular use. Third, there is causal knowledge, in the form of qualitative models, about a device that allows one to reason (in a task like troubleshooting) about the behavior of that device. I have listed these types of knowledge in the order that they are discussed. Coincidentally, the current success of our cognitive theories in dealing with these types has followed the same order. These classifications also have implications for the types of curriculum and instruction used to impart them, which is discussed by Halff (chapter 4).

PROCEDURAL KNOWLEDGE

Our relatively advanced ability to model the procedural knowledge underlying human problem solving probably owes a lot to the importation of ideas from expert systems. Almost uniformly, the standard representational formalism has been some kind of rule-based system just as in expert systems. This rule-based approach is taken in the LISP Tutor (Reiser, Anderson, & Farrell, 1985), the Geometry Tutor (Anderson, Boyle, & Yost, 1985). Algebra (Brown, 1983), BUGGY (Brown & VanLehn, 1980; Burton, 1982), and the LEEDS modeling system (Sleeman, 1982) among others. The dominant type of rule-based system takes the form of production systems, which arguably provide good models of human problem solving (Anderson, 1983; Newell & Simon, 1972). Although there are many variations on production system models, they all involve a set of if–then rules matched to a working memory of facts. The working memory embodies some of the basic short-term memory limitations of the human. The production rules with their recognize–act cycle capture the basic data-driven character of human cognition. One of the recent advances in production system models has been a set of ideas for modeling human learning within these models (Anderson, 1983; Holland, Holyoak, Nisbett, & Thagard, 1986; Laird, Rosenbloom, & Newell, 1986; Langley, 1985; VanLehn, 1983). This is an exciting potential for intelligent tutoring systems because of the prospect that the tutoring component can make its decisions by reference to the simulation of the student learning. Although this is an exciting possibility, no current tutoring systems actually use a learning simulation in this way. This is largely because these learning components are recent and tend to be very expensive computationally.

An exemplary set of procedural rules, shown in Figure 2.9, represents the skill underlying multiple-column subtraction in the Brown and VanLehn model of subtraction skills. They make the point that the underlying knowledge is very use-specific. Although this knowledge is derived from the basic properties of addition, the actual rules are quite specific to subtraction and would not generalize to addition. Thus, for instance, we have rules about borrowing rather

Constrained by both cognitive task analysis and general theory

Sub () SatisfactionCondition: TRUE
```
L1:    { } --- >              (ColSequence RightmostTOPCell
                                RightmostBottomCell RightmostAnswerCell)
```

COLSEQUENCE (TC BC AC) Satisfaction Condition: (Blank? (Next TC))
```
L2:    { } --- >              (SubCol TC BC AC)
L3:    { } --- >              (ColSequence (Next TC) (Next BC) Next AC))
```

SubCol (TC BC AC) Satisfaction Condition: (NOT (Blank? AC))
```
L4:    { (Blank? BC)} --- >    (WriteAns TC AC)
L5:    { (Less? TC BC)} --- >   (Borrow TC)
L6:    { } --- >              (Diff TC BC AC)
```

Borrow (TC) Satisfaction-Condition: FALSE
```
L7:    { } --- >              (BorrowFrom (Next TC))
L8:    { } --- >              (Add10 TC)
```

BorrowFrom (TC) Satisfaction Condition: TRUE
```
L9:    { (Zero? TC)} --- >      (BorrowFromZero TC)
L10:   { } --- >              (Decr TC)
```

BorrowFromZero (TC) Satisfaction Condition: FALSE
```
L11:   { } --- >              (Write9 TC)
L12:   { } --- >              (BorrowFrom (Next TC))
```

FIGURE 2.9 Production rule representation of the subtraction skill (Brown & VanLehn, 1980). *Note.* From "Repair Theory: A Generative Theory of Bugs in Procedural Skills," by J. S. Brown and K. VanLehn. *Cognitive Science, 4,* pp. 379–426. Reprinted with permission of Ablex Publishing Corporation.

than rules about carrying, even though borrowing and carrying are based on the same abstract rules of arithmetic. The choice of using a procedural knowledge representation involves deciding whether such a use-specific representation of the knowledge is appropriate. It certainly is the appropriate model in the case of human subtraction skills because they have very little to do with addition skills.

The Brown and VanLehn work illustrates one use to which we can put procedural representations. Brown and VanLehn propose that students make errors when they try to repair their procedures at the impasses created by missing production rules. By assuming that specific instances of these rules are missing, we can predict such students' errors. Extending a rule-based model to predicting errors puts an additional demand on its psychological reality. The rules in such a system now must capture the units of human knowledge because loss of the rules must correspond to human errors. If the rules were not the units of knowledge, then their loss would produce errors that are not seen in human behavior.

Their modularity is one of the major advantages of production rules for purposes of instruction: Each production rule is an independent piece of knowledge. This means that a rule can be communicated to the student independently of communicating the total problem structure in which it appears. This is not to say that production rules are context-free. Rather, they specify explicitly that part of the context that is relevant. So, for instance, if a production rule for using vertical angles in geometry makes reference to a goal of proving angles congruent, reference can be made to that feature of the problem and only that feature in explaining the rule:

> When you are trying to prove triangles congruent and they form vertical angles at one of their vertices, it is a good idea to prove these angles congruent by vertical angles. This will yield a pair of congruent corresponding angles which will help you prove the triangles congruent.

A frequent problem with earlier production rule models (Anderson, 1976; Newell, 1973) was that contextual constraints on the rules were not transparent. Rules had special tests built into their left-hand sides that constrained when they would apply; but it was difficult in looking at such rules to imagine when those tests would be satisfied. The current generation of goal-factored production systems (Anderson, 1983; Laird, Rosenbloom, & Newell, 1986) offer a substantial solution to this problem by making explicit reference in their conditions to goals that the production rules are relevant to. These goals, being structures with a well-defined semantics, facilitate the process of communicating to the student the relevant information about contextual constraints.

Another advantage of the modularity of production rules is that we can use the rules to represent the student's knowledge state. That is, the student's knowledge state can be diagnosed as a set of production rules. We can then use curriculum selection techniques, such as were pioneered with BIP (Barr, Beard, & Atkinson, 1975; Westcourt, Beard, & Gould, 1977), in which problems are selected to exercise instructional units that the student has not mastered. In contrast to BIP, however, the problem selection can be defined in psychologically real units rather than by somewhat arbitrary topics. In recent work with the LISP Tutor (Anderson, in press), we have found that the underlying production rules seem to be learned systematically and independently of one another. Selecting problems to exercise those productions diagnosed to be weak leads to improved learning.

Model Tracing

One of the major advantages of the rule-based approach is that it makes possible the implementation of a tutoring methodology called *model tracing*. This is a technique used in WUSOR (Goldstein, 1982), in Kimball's integration tutor (Kimball, 1982), in Spade (Miller, 1982), as well as in our own Geometry and LISP Tutors (Anderson, Boyle,

& Yost, 1985; Reiser, Anderson, & Farrell, 1985). In model tracing we try to place the student's surface behavior in solving a problem in correspondence with a sequence of productions that are firing in the internal student model. This correspondence then can be used to place an interpretation over the student's surface behavior. Clearly, the richness with which the student's behavior can be interpreted will map onto the richness of subsequent instruction. In our own research, which has a strong commitment to immediate feedback, the major function of such a model trace is to provide feedback on errors as close in time to the student's commission of these errors as possible. However, this is by no means the only function of model tracing, nor is it the only function for which model tracing has been used. Indeed, I would say our use of it for immediate feedback has been relatively unique.

Although it is nice to be able to interpret a student's thinking at every step through the problem solution, model tracing creates a number of demands that are quite stressful computationally. The major stress derives from the nondeterminism of the underlying student model. Typically, at each point there are a number of correct or incorrect productions that can fire. The combination of a few layers of production firings creates a space of thousands or millions of possible sequences of production firings. Managing this space of possible interpretations is naturally easier in the presence of a rich behavioral trace from a student. Ideally, if each production rule has an observable consequence, then the nondeterminism can be pared down at each cycle of the production system. Providing such a rich behavior trace creates an interesting demand on the interface design. Sometimes, however, efforts to obtain a rich behavior trace can lead to awkward and artificial interactions. For instance, in some of our endeavours we have tried to create a trace by interrogating students about their intentions at points of ambiguity. Students report this to be an annoying and distracting feature of our tutors.

Even in the best of all possible worlds, where each production has a behavioral consequence, there are problems of ambiguity in which multiple sequences of production actions will generate the same observed sequence of student behaviors. This is a problem particularly when some of these interpretations are correct and some are in error. The tutor must either delay feedback until the ambiguity is resolved or interrupt with distracting questions. For instance, suppose we have a student who is trying to code whether a is less than 2% of c and the student writes

$$(> (/ \ a \ c) \ .02)$$

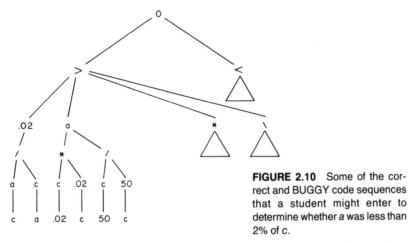

FIGURE 2.10 Some of the correct and BUGGY code sequences that a student might enter to determine whether *a* was less than 2% of *c*.

At what point can we tell the student that the choice ">" is inappropriate? Clearly, not when it is typed, because the student could be intending to reverse the arguments. As it turns out, the ambiguity is not resolved when the division sign is encountered either, because the student could have been intending

$$(> (/ \ c \ 50.0) \ a).$$

The ambiguity is resolved only when the *a* is entered. Figure 2.10 is an attempt to illustrate a small part of the problem space associated with this problem and the ambiguity in that problem space.

There are also serious problems with the efficiency of running production systems. Despite the recent advances in the OPS family of production systems, they are still not the world's most efficient computational formalism (Forgy, 1982). A critical feature of any expert module is that it run sufficiently rapidly so that the student is not left waiting too long during its computations. One solution is to build more efficient domain-specific production systems. In our own work we have had to build such domain-specific production systems that were optimized to take advantage of special domain features.

Compiling the Expert Out

Many formalisms for expert modules, including production systems, can be very expensive in terms of time and space. This makes it difficult to deliver tutorial instruction on economically feasible machines. One way of dealing with this problem is to perform in advance all the possible computations of the expert for a particular problem and to store them in some efficiently indexed scheme on disk. This method, which we call "compiling the expert out," has been used with success in some of our applications. The cost is that they can tutor only a specific set of problems on which the expert has been run. The dynamic ability to tutor any problem the student might enter is lost. However, in some applications this trade-off may be well worthwhile.

DECLARATIVE KNOWLEDGE

Both the weaknesses and strengths of procedural knowledge representations are derived from the fact that they are use-specific. In some instances more generalized declarative knowledge may be desired. In many cases we want the students to understand the basic principles and facts of a domain and how to reason with these generally, but are not concerned that the student become particularly facile at any one application of the knowledge. These are the situations that call for declarative knowledge representations.

It is not the case that the goals of procedural tutoring and declarative tutoring are mutually incompatible. We might well want a student to be both facile with the rules of a problem domain and articulate about the justifications for the rules. This seems to be the case in the domain of medical diagnosis, for instance (Clancey, 1982). Another need for declarative tutoring is illustrated in our LISP Tutor, for which we have created a special textbook (Anderson, Corbett, & Reiser, 1986) for teaching the declarative underpinnings of the procedural knowledge the LISP Tutor teaches. It clearly would have been better to have extended the LISP Tutor to cover what is in the textbook. In fact, it is part of our general theory of knowledge acquisition (Anderson, 1983) that knowledge must start in a declarative form before becoming proceduralized.

The SCHOLAR project (Carbonell, 1970) was an early example of a project whose goal was to communicate information, in this case about South American geography. It was Carbonell's belief that the semantic net representation of the knowledge base used in this project was close to the internal knowledge structure of humans. This belief was reinforced by a fair amount of contemporary experimental work (e.g., Collins & Quillian, 1972). Figure 2.11 shows a fraction of the semantic network Carbonell was working with. It consists of nodes representing various concepts, such as countries and products, linked by various relationships, such as part–whole or generalization hierarchy. These links were used to define certain fundamental inference processes on the network. For instance, the system can

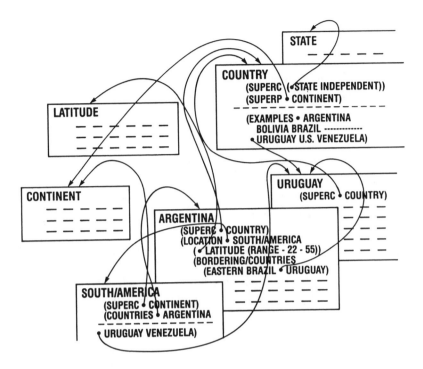

FIGURE 2.11 A portion of the semantic net in SCHOLAR. *Note.* From "AI in CAI: An AArtificial Intelligence Approach to Computer-Aided Instruction" by J. R. Carbonell, 1970, *IEEE Transactions on Man-Machine Systems, 11,* 190–202. Copyright 1970 IEEE. Reprinted by permission.

conclude that Santiago is in South America because Santiago is in Chile and Chile is in South America.

Subsequent to Carbonell's work, knowledge representations with semantic nets have become considerably more sophisticated and have evolved into frame and schema systems (Bobrow & Winograd, 1977; Brackman, 1978; Goldstein & Roberts, 1977; Minsky, 1975; Schank & Abelson, 1977; Stefik, 1980). However, the central idea has remained the same. We want hierarchical representations of knowledge structured such that flexible inference procedures on the knowledge base can be defined. Note that, in contrast to procedural representations, the knowledge base is separate from the inference procedures that are built on them. This clean distinction has been somewhat blurred by the use of "procedural attachments," in which various slots in the schema representations have procedures attached to them to define how they should be filled. But we still have a fundamental separation in a schema system between knowledge and control. This separation does not exist in procedural systems.

Carbonell's work has been continued by Collins (Collins, Warnock, & Passafiume, 1975; Stevens, Collins, & Goldin, 1982). Figure 2.12 illustrates one of the schema representations developed for evaporation, which is part of the knowledge base in the curriculum on rainfall. It is basically a schema representation consisting of various slots and fillers. In this case, there are slots for the actors in the evaporation schema, for the factors that influence the amount of evaporation, for the functional relationships among these factors, and for the result of evaporation. Bugs are created by various fallacious entries in these slots. So, for instance, many people believe that the sun is directly responsible for evaporation rather than that evaporation is a function of the temperature of the air mass and the water mass. This belief shows up as an erroneous filling in of the actor slot. Another bug involving the actor slot of this schema is what Collins calls the "small-moisture-source"—the idea that any body of water, including a small pond, is sufficient to produce rainfall.

The implicit presupposition in tutoring such knowledge bases is that the student already has the general inference procedures to be able to reason about the knowledge and that the real task is therefore to represent the knowledge in such a form that these inference procedures can be invoked. At some level this makes for a simple tutorial agenda, namely, to determine what a student has filled in at each slot and to fill in the missing information and debug the misconceptions. The major difficulty posed for tutoring systems is that declarative knowledge cannot be run the way procedural knowledge is, and so the criteria "if the student can use it he knows it" does not apply. For declarative knowledge tutors it is typical to fashion and interpret complex natural language dialogues. To understand these dialogues it is necessary to understand how students make inferences from their declarative data base, and a good deal of Collins's work has been devoted to just this (e.g., Collins, Warnock, Aiello, & Miller, 1975).

In contrast with tutoring procedural knowledge, tutoring declarative knowledge necessitates facing up to the full complexity of mixed initiative dialogues. The student says something that has to be clarified, which leads the tutor to ask a question, to which the student reacts with a question of his or her own, etc. One of the functions of the Socratic dialogues is to tame this process. Socratic dialogues really give the control to the tutor, who asks a series of questions to which the student is supposed to respond. In a true Socratic dialogue both instruction and knowledge assessment is supposed to be handled by asking questions. It might seem a bit unnatural to

Evaporation

Actors
Source: Large-body-of-water
Destination: Air-mass

Factors
Temperature(Source)
Temperature(Destination)
Proximity(Source, Destination)

Functional-relationship
Positive(Temperature(Source))
Positive(Temperature(Destination))
Positive(Proximity(Source, Destination))

Result
Increase(Humidity(Destination))

FIGURE 2.12 A schema representation of some of the knowledge underlying our understanding of evaporation. *Note.* From "Misconceptions in Student Understanding" by A. Stevens, A. Collins, & S. E. Goldin, 1982, *Intelligent Tutoring Systems* (p. 16). Copyright 1982 by The Academic Press. Reprinted by permission.

instruct by asking questions, but there are proven psychological benefits to knowledge that is generated rather than received (Bobrow & Bower, 1969). Moreover, asking questions enables the tutor to assess how well the instruction is being received. Figure 2.13 presents a piece of the Socratic dialogue with Collins's WHY system. Note that the discussion takes place with respect to specific cases. So, for instance, in Figure 2.13 WHY does not directly ask the student whether there is a positive functional relationship between the temperature of the source and evaporation. Instead, it probes the student's ability to apply this knowledge to the Amazon.

Collins formulated a set of tutoring rules for implementing the Socratic method. Figure 2.14 illustrates one that was involved in the question at the end of the sample dialogue. There are a couple of noteworthy features about such rules for Socratic tutoring. First, they have a family resemblance to the issue-based recognition rules we saw with the black box and expert models. Note, however, that the conditions of such rules refer to the underlying knowledge rather than to the surface behavior of the expert. Second, these rules involve a curious mix of knowledge assessment and instruction. The rule in Figure 2.14 could be used to determine that the student is aware of all the factors underlying rainfall but has just not mentioned them, or it could be used to make the student aware of a new factor. Evoking

WHY: Do you think the **AMAZON** jungle has heavy
  rainfall or light rainfall?
  (Ask for a prediction about a particular case)
STUDENT: Heavy rainfall

WHY: Why does the Amazon have heavy rainfall?
  (Ask for prior cause)
STUDENT: Because it's near the Atlantic

WHY: Yes, the Amazon jungle is near the equatorial
  Atlantic. How does that affect rainfall in the
  Amazon jungle?
  (Ask for intermediate cause)
STUDENT: The water in the current is warm.
  •
  •
  •
  •

WHY: Do you think that any place with mountains
  has heavy rainfall?
  (Form a general rule for insufficient cause)
STUDENT: Yes

WHY: Southern California has mountains. Why doesn't
  Southern California have heavy rainfall?
  (Pick a counter-example for an insuffient cause)

FIGURE 2.13 An example of a Socratic dialogue. *Note.* From "The Goal Structure of a Socratic Tutor" by A. Stevens & A. Collins, 1977, *Proceedings of ACM 1977.* Copyright 1977 by the Association for Computing Machinery, Inc. Reprinted by permission.

IF
The student gives an explanation of one or more
factors that are not sufficient
THEN
Formulate a general rule for asserting that the factors
given are sufficient
Ask the student if the rule is true

FIGURE 2.14 An example of a rule for Socratic tutoring. *Note.* From "Processing in Acquiring Knowledge" by A. M. Collins, 1976, *Schooling and the Acquisition of Knowledge,* p. 343–344. Reprinted by permission.

this rule does not entail a commitment to the intended pedagogical outcome.

It should be clear that understanding natural language is the Achilles' heel of any effort to do such declarative tutoring. There have not been a great many of these tutors. Collins's and Carbonell's work is the only notable instance, and I think the difficulty of the natural language problem is the principle reason why. This area of intelligent tutoring is certainly waiting for fundamental progress in natural language processing.

QUALITATIVE PROCESS MODELS

A third category of expert module is concerned with the knowlege that underlies our ability to mentally simulate and reason about dynamic processes. As noted earlier, this is an important component of the ability to engage in troubleshooting behavior, which involves reasoning through the causal structure of a device to find potential trouble spots.

Models of qualitative reasoning are in a relatively immature state compared to the schema and rule-based formalisms of artificial intelligence. A number of notable research efforts are developing such models (deKleer & Brown, 1984; Forbus, 1984; Kuipers, 1984), but there is hardly an established methodology for using them. DeKleer's work on envisionment is an interesting case in point because it evolved within the context of the SOPHIE project and the need to communicate to students the causal structure of an electronic circuit.

DeKleer and Brown divide the process of envisionment into constructing a causal model and then simulating the process in this causal model. Figure 2.15 illustrates their conception of this process. The causal structure of the device is inferred from its topology by examination of the local interactions among components. The assumption is that this causality can be understood locally, and it is called the "no function in structure" principle. When this principle is violated and description of a component makes reference to the functioning of the whole device, there is a danger that that component will assume the functioning of the device rather than explain it. Having this causal model, deKleer and Brown then use a calculus to propagate the behavior of the device through these components. Much of the current work on qualitative models is concerned with various calculi for such propagations.

Figure 2.16 illustrates one of the devices, a pressure regulator, which has been a focus of deKleer and Brown's work. It consists of a set of components, such as a valve, which operate on certain local

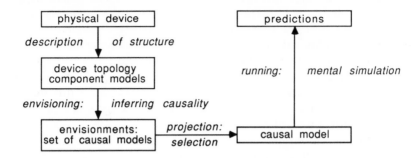

FIGURE 2.15 The development of a qualitative simulation according to deKleer & Brown. *Note.* Adapted from *Artificial Intelligence and Tutoring Systems: Computational and Cognitive Approaches to the Communication of Knowledge* by Etienne Wenger, 1987, Los Alto, CA: Morgan Kaufmann, Publishers, Inc. Adapted by permission.

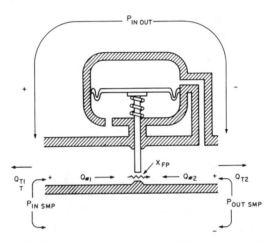

FIGURE 2.16 DeKleer & Brown's (1984) representation of a pressure regulator. *Note.* From "A Physics Based on Confluences" by J. deKleer & J. S. Brown, 1984, *AI Journal*, 24(1–3), pp. 7–83. Copyright 1984 by North Holland Publishing Co. Reprinted by permission.

inputs. So, for instance, the valve operates so that the amount of water flowing through it varies with the pressure and the position of the valve control. This relationship is expressed by what deKleer and Brown call a confluence, which is a constraint among variables. The confluence for the valve is

$$\delta P_{in,\ out} - \delta Q_{\#1(vv)} + \delta X_{FP} = 0$$

where $\delta P_{in,\ out}$ is the change in pressure,

$\delta Q_{\#1(vv)}$ is the change in flow,

and δX_{FP} is the position of the valve control.

The entire device is modeled by a set of such confluences. Reasoning about it involves tracing the constraints among the equations.

The psychological status of this work is quite ambiguous. As deKleer and Brown note, the no-function-in-structure principle is constantly violated in human reasoning. What they are trying to develop is more on the order of a prescriptive model of thinking. A constraint in this prescriptive model is apparently that it should be easy for humans to follow these prescriptions even if they normally do not. Such a prescriptive model is certainly appropriate as an expert module for an intelligent tutoring system.

It is not clear to me whether qualitative models really involve a category of knowledge fundamentally different from procedural and declarative knowledge. It might be argued that people have a set of declarative knowledge structures for representing the form and function of various devices and a set of procedures for reasoning about the causal interactions among these devices.

The real difference may not be in the knowledge type but in the indirectness of the knowledge so represented. The end goal in applications such as electronic troubleshooting is not to have the student correctly simulate the causal interactions in a circuit but to use that ability in service of the problem solving involved in troubleshooting. Thus, one of the issues that arises in a tutoring context is how to use the qualitative knowledge in a larger problem-solving context. This issue has largely not been addressed in the work on qualitative reasoning.

As a consequence, how to include qualitative simulations in a tutoring paradigm has yet to be worked out. Qualitative simulations can obviously be used in all the ways a black box model like SPICE can, but this hardly justifies their development. There is the obvious potential for using them in explanations in which the tutor would tell the student how it reasoned to a particular conclusion about circuit behavior. White and Fredericksen (1986) use such models to actually define the curriculum sequence. There is also a need for more psychological study on how such process models are actually used in troubleshooting. Although I think it is clear that such models are used and that systems such as deKleer and Brown's have at least a family resemblance to human qualitative reasoning, I think we know virtually nothing about how humans deploy these simulations to achieve their goals. Interestingly, there is a considerable body of negative results in getting students to bring mental models to tasks such as troubleshooting (Rouse & Morris, 1985).

The other possibility for qualitative models is to generate articulate simulations of a particular system, such as in the Steamer project or in SOPHIE. The simulation can illustrate the qualitative transformations assumed in the qualitative simulation. The assumption is that there is a pedagogical benefit to illustrating a process in the same terms as a student should use in reasoning about it.

BASIC RESEARCH ISSUES

Although there has certainly been dramatic progress in our understanding of how to build the expert module for a tutoring system, we need a great deal more basic research before construction of expert modules can progress as an engineering enterprise. As we saw in the work on expert systems, there are real limitations in using work from artificial intelligence, which has progressed without concern for cognitive fidelity. We still need to deepen our understanding of human cognitive processes and how they can be modeled. For instance, theories of learning, in contrast to theories of performance, have yet to be integrated into tutoring systems. The range of tasks for which accurate student models can be reasonably produced is relatively narrow and consists of tasks that are algorithmically tractable and that do not involve a great deal of general world knowledge. A prime example is calculus. To understand human expertise more generally will involve a great deal more empirical and simulation research.

Also, our understanding of the learning processes by which knowledge is acquired is still quite primitive. Evidence of this is the fact that no tutoring system actively uses a learning model in its computations. Any pedagogy needs to be rigorously founded in a theory of learning. Obviously, the cognitive science efforts in learning (Anderson, 1983; Holland et al., 1986; Laird, Rosenbloom, & Newell, 1986; Langley, 1985; VanLehn, 1983) are prime candidates for support. Related to issues of learning are the issues of the origins of bugs. As is illustrated in the work on BUGGY, the representation of knowledge can be closely connected to possible bugs. Currently, most tutor builders have to invest large amounts of time building up bug catalogs. It would accelerate the development of tutors if we had a theory or theories of the origin of bugs.

There seems to be little point in supporting work in artificial intelligence, which is not cognitively motivated, if we want to further the goal of developing intelligent tutoring systems. There are two domains in artificial intelligence that are exceptions, however: qualitative process models and natural language processing for tutorial dialogues. Our need for mechanisms in these fields is so great that insisting on cognitive fidelity in the artificial intelligence system would be premature.

Development of the expert module is not independent of the rest of the tutoring system in which it resides. Much of my discussion of the expert module has been concerned with its implications for other components of a tutoring system. Although there is need for research on models of human expertise in the abstract, there is also need for research on how such modules will fit into an overall tutoring architecture. We have seen that various types of modules tend to be linked to various styles of tutoring—black box models with issue-based tutoring, cognitive rule systems with model tracing, and declarative systems with Socratic tutoring. There is room for expanding our catalog of architectures and their relationships to expert modules. We also need to explore how the design of an interface can change the nature of the expert module. To take a simple example, the advent of structure-based editors has eliminated the need for programming tutors to be concerned about teaching syntax.

Finally, we need a meta-theory of the expert formalisms we are using and of how they can be taught. Right now the development of expert modules is the domain of a few cognitive scientists even more select than the builders of expert systems. We need to develop methods for teaching the use of cognitive science formalisms to curriculum developers. Not only is this an important practical goal, but in pursuing it I think we will come to a deeper understanding of the nature of a cognitive theory.

I think we are in a position to develop an authoring environment around expert system formalisms such as production systems or schema systems. We could develop a set of tools and instructional materials that would make it easy for curriculum developers to use these systems. The first steps toward tutoring systems that teach students how to program with production systems already exist (Zhang, 1986). The facilities for actually delivering the tutoring could be made a prepackaged part of the authoring environment. All the curriculum designers would have to do is develop the expert module, which, of course, is currently half the job of developing an intelligent tutoring system. However, delivery of the tutoring could at least be automated, and the expertise for developing the expert module could be more widely distributed.

NEAR-TERM GOALS

Relatively little activity is currently occurring in intelligent tutoring that does not have the status of a basic research project whose goal is to get more basic knowledge rather than to actually build useful intelligent tutoring systems. However, the point has been reached where a few applications are feasible, and it might be worthwhile to pursue some of them both for the relatively immediate benefit and for some sense of how the engineering of these projects will progress.

In my view the one area in which we might develop reasonably good cognitive models that could be made part of intelligent tutors is that of rule-based systems for algorithmically tractable domains. These domains include mathematics at the high school or junior college level, basic sciences like physics, basic electricity and electronics, some engineering and statistics, introductory programming, and use of various packages like LOTUS 1-2-3. This is not to say that development in these domains will be cheap. It will probably take hundreds of hours just to analyze and codify the expert module for each hour of instruction, let alone build a full tutor. However, such time frames are at least within the same order of magnitude as those that go into building conventional educational software.

Another area that may yield some short-term payoff is use of off-the-shelf expert modules either developed as black boxes or developed out of the knowledge-engineering tradition of artificial intelligence. This tactic circumvents the hundreds of hours that go into building the expert module. As we have seen, issue-oriented methodology shows some potential for utilizing these tutors. Basic researchers have been somewhat reluctant to follow up these issue-oriented methods because of their perceived limitations. Researchers have been moving to expert modules with greater cognitive fidelity, and even if they continue to use an issue-oriented methodology, they use a methodology appropriate for such modules. There may be a great practical payoff to seeing how to develop methods for use with the available expert systems. It would also be in the interest of the Air Force to identify and sponsor some project of particular interest to the military. Besides possibly delivering an actual system, this effort would uncover the issues specific to military applications. I can only guess where the needs of the military are, but I would think electronics and electricity instructors in service of maintenance would be a prime candidate. A fair amount of work has already been done in this field, although of a rather theoretical variety. It would be profitable to see what would happen if we made the practical compromises necessary to implement an intelligent tutorial system in an actual classroom.

REFERENCES

Anderson, J. R. (1976). *Language, memory, and thought*. Hillsdale, NJ: Lawrence Erlbaum Associates.

Anderson, J. R. (1983). *The architecture of cognition.* Cambridge, MA: Harvard University Press.

Anderson, J. R. Analysis of student performance with the LISP tutor. In N. Fredericksen, R. Glaser, A. Lesgold, & M. Shafto (Eds.), *Diagnostic monitoring of skill and knowledge acquisition.* Hillsdale, NJ: Lawrence Erlbaum Associates, in press.

Anderson, J. R. (in press). Methodologies for studying human knowledge. *Behavioral and Brain Sciences.*

Anderson, J. R., Boyle, C. F., & Yost, G. (1985). The geometry tutor. In A. Joshi (Ed.), *Proceedings of the Ninth International Joint Conference on Artificial Intelligence* (pp. 1-7). Los Altos, CA: Morgan Kaufmann.

Anderson, J. R., Corbett, A. T., & Reiser, B. J. (1986). *Essential LISP.* Reading, MA: Addison-Wesley.

Barr, A., Beard, M., & Atkinson, R. C. (1975). Information networks for CAI curriculum. In O. Lecareme & R. Lewis (Eds.), *Computers in education* (pp. 477-482). Amsterdam: North Holland.

Bobrow, D. G., & Winograd, T. (1977). An overview of KRL: A knowledge representation language. *Cognitive Science, 1,* 3-46.

Bobrow, S., & Bower, G. H. (1969). Comprehension and recall of sentences. *Journal of Experimental Psychology, 80,* 455-461.

Brackman, R. J. (1978). *A structural paradigm for representing knowledge* (Tech. Rep. 3605). Cambridge, MA: Bolt Beranek & Newman Inc.

Brown, J. S. (1983). *Process versus product: A perspective on tools for communal and informal electronic learning* (Tech. Rep.). In *Report from the learning lab: Education in the electronic age.* Educational Broadcasting Corporation.

Brown, J. S., & Burton, R. R. (1975). Multiple representation of knowledge for tutorial reasoning. In D. Bobrow & A. Collins (Eds.), *Representation and understanding: Studies in cognitive science* (pp. 311-349). New York: Academic Press.

Brown, J. S., Burton, R. R., & deKleer, J. (1982). Pedagogical, natural language and knowledge engineering techniques in SOPHIE I, II and III. In D. Sleeman & J. S. Brown (Eds.), *Intelligent tutoring systems* (pp. 227-282). New York: Academic Press.

Brown, J. S., & VanLehn, K. (1980). Repair theory: A generative theory of bugs in procedural skills. *Cognitive Science, 4,* 379-426.

Buchanan, B., & Shortliffe, E. (1984). *Rule-Based Expert Systems.* Reading, MA: Addison-Wesley.

Burton, R. R. (1982). Diagnosing bugs in a simple procedural skill. In D. Sleeman & J. S. Brown (Eds.), *Intelligent tutoring systems* (pp. 157-183). New York: Academic Press.

Burton, R. R., & Brown, J. S. (1982). An investigation of computer coaching for informal learning activities. In D. Sleeman & J. S. Brown (Eds.), *Intelligent tutoring systems* (pp. 79-98). New York: Academic Press.

Carbonell, J. R. (1970). AI in CAI: An artificial intelligence approach to computer-aided instruction. *IEEE Transactions on Man-Machine Systems, 11,* 190-202.

Clancey, W. J. (1982). Tutoring rules for guiding a case method dialogue. In D. Sleeman & J. S. Brown (Eds.), *Intelligent tutoring systems* (pp. 201-225). New York: Academic Press.

Collins, A. M. (1976). Processes in acquiring knowledge. In R. C. Anderson, R. Spiro, & W. E. Montague (Eds.), *Schooling and the acquisition of knowledge* (pp. 339-363). Hillsdale, NJ: Lawrence Erlbaum Associates.

Collins, A. M. & Quillian, M. R. (1972). Experiments on semantic memory and language comprehension. In L. Gregg (Ed.), *Cognition in learning and memory* (pp. 117-137). New York: Wiley.

Collins, A. M., Warnock, E. H., Aiello, N., & Miller, M. L. (1975). Reasoning from incomplete knowledge. In D. G. Bobrow & A. M. Collins (Eds.), *Representation and understanding* (pp. 383-415). New York: Academic Press.

Collins, A., Warnock, E., & Passafiume, J. (1975). Analysis and synthesis of tutorial dialogues. In G. Bower (Ed.), *The psychology of learning and motivation* (Vol. 9, pp. 49-87). New York: Academic Press.

deKleer, J., & Brown, J. S. (1984). A physics based on confluences. *AI Journal, 24,* 7-83.

Forbus, K. D. (1984). Qualitative process theory. *Artificial Intelligence, 24,* 85-168.

Forgy, C. L. (1982). Rete: A fast algorithm for the many pattern/many object pattern match problem. *Artificial Intelligence, 19,* 17-37.

Genesereth, M. R. (1982). The role of plans in intelligent teaching systems. In D. Sleeman & J. S. Brown (Eds.), *Intelligent tutoring systems* (pp. 137-155). New York: Academic Press.

Goldstein, I. (1982). The genetic graph: A representation for the evolution of procedural knowledge. In D. Sleeman & J. S. Brown (Eds.), *Intelligent tutoring systems* (pp. 51-77). New York: Academic Press.

Goldstein, I. P., & Roberts, R. B. (1977). NUDGE, a knowledge-based scheduling program. *Proceedings of the Fifth International Joint Conference of Artificial Intelligence* (pp. 257-263).

Hayes, J. R. (1985). Three problems in teaching general skills. In S. Chipman, J. Segal, & R. Glaser (Eds.), *Thinking and learning skills* (pp. 391-406). Hillsdale, NJ: Lawrence Erlbaum Associates.

Hayes-Roth, F., Waterman, D. A., & Lenat, D. B. (1983). *Building expert systems.* Reading, MA: Addison-Wesley.

Hollan, J. D., Hutchins, E. L., & Weitzman, L. (1984). Steamer: An interactive inspectable simulation-based training system. *AI Magazine, 5,* 15-27.

Holland, J. H., Holyoak, K., Nisbett, R. E., & Thagard, P. R. (1986). *Induction: Processes of inference, learning, and discovery.* Cambridge, MA: Massachusetts Institute of Technology Press.

Kimball, R. (1982). A self-improving tutor for symbolic integration. In D. Sleeman & J. S. Brown (Eds.), *Intelligent tutoring systems* (pp. 283-307). New York: Academic Press.

Kuipers, B. (1984). Commonsense reasoning about causality: Deriving behavior from structure. *Artificial Intelligence, 24,* 169-203.

Laird, J. E., Rosenbloom, P. S., & Newell, A. (1986). Chunking in SOAR: The anatomy of a general learning mechanism. *Machine Learning 1,* 11-46.

Langley, P. (1985). Learning to search: From weak methods to domain-specific heuristics. *Cognitive Science, 9,* 217-260.

Miller, M. L. (1982). A structured planning and debugging environment for elementary programming. In D. Sleeman & J. S. Brown (Eds.), *Intelligent tutoring systems* (pp. 119-135). New York: Academic Press.

Minsky, M. (1975). A framework for representing knowledge. In P. H. Winston (Ed.), *The psychology of computer vision* (pp. 211-277). New York: McGraw-Hill.

Nagel, L. W., & Pederson, D. O. (1973). Simulation program with integrated circuit emphasis. *Proceedings of the Sixteenth Midwest Symposium on Circuit Theory.*

Newell, A. (1973). Production systems: Models of control structures. In W. G. Chase (Ed.), *Visual information processing* (pp. 463-526). New York: Academic Press.

Newell, A., & Simon, H. (1972). *Human problem solving.* Englewood Cliffs, NJ: Prentice-Hall.

Reiser, B. J., Anderson, J. R., & Farrell, R. B. (1985). Dynamic student modeling in an intelligent tutor for LISP programming. *Proceedings of the International Joint Conference on Artificial Intelligence-85* (Vol. 1, pp. 8-14). Los Altos, CA: Morgan Kaufmann.

Rouse, W. B., & Morris, N. M. (1985). *On looking into the black box: Prospects and limits in the search for mental models* (Tech. Rep. No. 85-2). Atlanta: Georgia Institute of Technology.

Schank, R. C., & Abelson, R. P. (1977). *Scripts, plans, goals, and understanding.* Hillsdale, NJ: Lawrence Erlbaum Associates.

Shortliffe, E. H. (1976). *Computer-based medical consultations: MYCIN.* New York: American Elsevier.

Sleeman, D. (1982). Assessing aspects of competence in basic algebra. In D. Sleeman & J. S. Brown (Eds.), *Intelligent tutoring systems* (pp. 185-199). New York: Academic Press.

Stefik, M. (1980). *Planning with constraints* (Tech. Rep. No. 784). Palo Alto, CA: Stanford University.

Stevens, A., & Collins, A. M. (1977). The goal structure of a Socratic tutor. (Tech. Rep. No. 3518). Cambridge, MA: Bolt, Beranek, and Newman, Inc.

Stevens, A., Collins, A. M., & Goldin, S. E. (1982). Misconceptions in students' understanding. In D. Sleeman & J. S. Brown (Eds.), *Intelligent tutoring systems* (pp. 13-24). New York: Academic Press.

VanLehn, K. (1983). *Felicity conditions for human skill acquisition: Validating an AI-based theory* (Tech. Rep. CIS-21). Palo Alto, CA: Xerox Parc.

Wenger, E. (1987). Artificial intelligence and tutoring systems: Computational approaches to the communication of knowledge. Los Altos, CA: Morgan Kaufmann.

Westcourt, K., Beard, M., & Gould, L. (1977). Knowledge-based adaptive curriculum sequencing for CAI: Application of a network representation. *Proceedings of the Association for Computing Machinery Annual Conference.* Association for Computing Machinery (ACM-77) (pp. 234-240).

White, B. Y., & Fredericksen, J. R. (1986). Progressions of qualitative models as foundations for intelligent learning environments (BBN Report 6277). Cambridge, MA: Bolt, Beranek, and Newman, Inc.

Zhang, G. (1986). *Learning to program in OPS5.* Unpublished doctoral dissertation. Pittsburgh, PA: Carnegie-Mellon University.

Student Modeling

Kurt VanLehn
Carnegie-Mellon University

This chapter reviews the research literature concerned with the student modeling component of intelligent tutoring systems. An intelligent tutoring system, or ITS, is a computer program that instructs the student in an intelligent way. There is no accepted definition of what it means to teach intelligently. However, a characteristic shared by many ITSs is that they infer a model of the student's current understanding of the subject matter and use this individualized model to adapt the instruction to the student's needs. The component of an ITS that represents the student's current state of knowledge is called the *student model*. Inferring a student model is called *diagnosis* because it is much like the medical task of inferring a hidden physiological state (i.e., a disease) from observable signs (i.e., symptoms). An ITS diagnostic system uncovers a hidden cognitive state (the student's knowledge of the subject matter) from observable behavior.

The student model and the diagnostic module are tightly interwoven. The student model is a data structure, and diagnosis is a process that manipulates it. The two components must be designed together. This design problem is called the *student modeling problem*. This chapter reviews solutions that have been found to the student modeling problem and discusses the techniques that have been discovered.

THE STUDENT MODELING PROBLEM

Most design problems in computer science can be specified by describing the desired output of the program and the available input. The design problem here is not, unfortunately, so neatly circumscribed.

Generally speaking, the input for diagnosis is garnered through interaction with the student. The particular kinds of information available to the diagnosis module depend on the overall ITS application. The information could be answers to questions posed by the ITS, moves taken in a game, or commands issued to an editor. In some applications, the student's educational history is also available to the diagnostic component.

The output from the diagnostic module is even harder to circumscribe. In fact, it doesn't even make sense to talk about the product of diagnosis as "output" (here, the analogy to medical diagnosis breaks down). Rather, the result is a data base, the student model, which accurately reflects the student's knowledge state. The student model is drawn on by other ITS modules for many purposes. Following are listed some of the most common uses for the student model.

Advancement. Some ITSs use a structured curriculum. A student is moved to the next topic in the curriculum only when he or she has mastered the current topic. In such applications, the student model represents the student's level of mastery. Periodically, the ITS asks the student model for the level of mastery on the current topic, weighs it, and decides whether to advance the student to the next topic. This use of student models is called *advancement.* Advancement is useful not only with linearly structured curricula, where instruction dwells on one topic at a time, but also in componentially structured curricula, where a student exercises several topics or skills at the same time. For instance, in the WUSOR ITS (Goldstein, 1982), the student uses several reasoning skills at the same time to hunt a beast in a maze filled with dangerous pits and bats. The techniques for estimating the dangerousness of caves can vary independently of the techniques for determining what caves are likely to contain the beast. The ITS can advance a student through the skill levels for assessing danger independently of advancing the student through the skill of locating quarry. This illustrates how advancement is used in ITSs that do not use a linearly structured curriculum.

Offering unsolicited advice. Some ITSs are like athletic coaches in that they offer advice only when they see that the student needs it.

If the student is performing well, the coach remains silent. A good coach will also remain silent if the student makes a mistake in a situation that is too complicated for a successful pedagogical interaction to take place. In order to offer unsolicited advice at just the right moments, the ITS must know the state of the student's knowledge. For this, it reads the student model.

Problem generation. Some ITSs generate problems for the student dynamically rather than sequencing through a predefined list of problems or letting the student invent problems to solve. In many applications, a good problem is just a little beyond the student's current capabilities. To find out where the student's current capabilities lie, the problem generation module consults the student model.

Adapting explanations. When good tutors explain something to the student, they use only concepts that the student already understands. For an ITS to issue good explanations, it must determine what the student knows already. To do so, it consults the student model.

The preceding functions are some of the most common ways the ITS components use the student model. Because there are so many ways to use the student model, we cannot talk sensibly about the output of the diagnosis module, nor can we classify student modeling problems by the desired input–output relationship. What does make sense is to classify these problems according to the structural properties of the student model. For instance, the student model might represent various levels of mastery of a subskill by a single bit (mastered versus not yet mastered), by a number, or by a complicated qualitative description. Such structural properties of the student model determine how complicated the student modeling problem is and what kinds of techniques are best suited for its solution.

A THREE-DIMENSIONAL SPACE OF STUDENT MODELS

This section reviews existing student modeling systems in the context of a classification based partially on structural properties of the student model and partially on properties of the input available to the diagnosis module. At this writing, approximately 20 student modeling systems have been built, and more are under development. There are many differences among them. The classification presented here is intended to capture the differences in the student modeling problem that really make a difference in the solution techniques. If this classification is correct, it can be used to predict what kinds of student modeling techniques would be most useful for some new student modeling problem. Needless to say, such a prediction would be only the starting point in a long design process that results in a system adapted to the demands of a particular ITS. Indeed, as more ITSs are constructed, the perception of what differences really matter can be expected to change. That change is one reason why ITS construction is still in the research stage and has not yet become a mature technology. In short, the following classification is both heuristic and tentative.

The classification has three dimensions. The first one relates to the input, and the others are structural properties of the student model.

Bandwidth

The input to the diagnosis unit consists of various kinds of information about what the student is doing or saying. From this, the diagnosis unit must infer what the student is thinking and believing. Clearly, the less information the unit has, the harder its task is. The *bandwidth* dimension is a rough categorization of the amount and quality of the input.

Three levels of information suffice to capture most of the variation among existing ITSs. In order to explain them, we will assume that students are solving problems posed either by themselves (e.g., What cave shall I explore next?) or by the ITS (e.g., What is 283-119?) If the problem solving takes more than a few milliseconds, then we can safely assume that the students go through a series of mental states. The highest bandwidth an ITS could attain would be a list of the mental states that the students traverse as they solve problems. Human mental states are not directly accessible by machines, so no ITS can really achieve this "mental states" bandwidth. However, by asking enough questions or by eliciting verbal protocols, an ITS can obtain indirect information that approximates the students' mental states. So the highest bandwidth category is *approximate mental states*.

In more complicated forms of problem solving, such as solving algebraic equations or playing chess, the students make observable changes that carry the problem from its initial unsolved state to its final, solved state. This results in a series of observable intermediate states, such as the midgame board positions in chess or the equations written before the last equation during algebraic equation solving. Sometimes an ITS has access to these intermediate states, and sometimes it can see only the final state—that is, the answer. The other two categories of bandwidth are *final states* and *intermediate states*.

To summarize, the three categories, from highest to lowest bandwidth, are mental states, intermediate states, and final states. Each category is intended to include the information in the category beneath it. Mental states includes intermediate and final states. Intermediate states includes final states.

The subject domain of programming provides good examples of the bandwidth dimension because an ITS exists for each bandwidth category. Anderson's LISP Tutor (Reiser, Anderson, & Farrell, 1985) contains a detailed model of the cognitive processes that Anderson believes underlie the skill of programming. The tutor uses a menu-driven interface to offer the student choices about what goals to attack next, what strategies to use, what code fragments to write down, and so on. The model aims to offer so many choices that any problem-solving path that a student wants to take is available. The belief is that the menus do not interfere with the path of mental states but merely allow the ITS to track the student's cognitive progress. Thus, the input to the diagnosis component is an approximation to a sequence of mental states. The LISP Tutor nicely illustrates the bandwidth level of mental states.

The Spade ITS (Miller, 1982) was never completed; but if it had been, it would illustrate the second level of bandwidth. Spade acts as a coach who watches a student program. The student uses a structure editor, that is, an editor that knows about the programming language and allows only syntactically legal edits. Spade sees all the intermediate observable steps as the student creates a program. Unlike Anderson's LISP Tutor, Spade cannot see the student's decisions about programming goals and strategies. Its input bandwidth fits squarely in the category of intermediate states.

In contrast, PROUST (Johnson & Soloway, 1984a; Johnson & Soloway, 1984b) is given only the first complete program that the student submits to a PASCAL compiler. PROUST does not have access to the student's scratch work or incomplete programs.

The bandwidth dimension is perhaps the most important of the three dimensions. More so than the others, it determines the algorithm used for diagnosis. As is shown in Diagnostic Techniques, where diagnosis algorithms are discussed in detail, there are nine basic algorithms. Five are useful with final state bandwidth systems, three are appropriate for intermediate state bandwidth systems, and one is appropriate for mental states bandwidth systems.

Target Knowledge Type

Student models can actually solve the same problems that students do and can therefore be used to predict the students' answers. This is a distinguishing characteristic of the student models used in ITSs. Student models used in older systems for computer-based training cannot actually generate problem solutions, although they may be able to generate a probability of a correct solution.

Solving problems requires some kind of interpretation process that applies knowledge in the student model to the problem. There are two common types of interpretation, one for *procedural* knowledge and one for *declarative* knowledge.[1] The interpreter for procedural knowledge is simple. It does not search but makes decisions based on local knowledge. It is like a little man with a flashlight who can see only a little way from the strand of knowledge he is standing in; based on his view of the knowledge locale and the current state of the problem, he decides which strand of knowledge to turn onto and follow. A declarative interpreter constantly searches over its whole knowledge base. It is like a librarian who searches out the answer to a client's query by searching reference books, assembling the facts, and deducing the answer from them. Procedural knowledge representations have been used for skills such as algebra equation solving (Sleeman, 1982), game playing (Burton & Brown, 1982; Goldstein, 1982; Goldstein & Carr, 1977), multicolumn arithmetic (Brown & Burton, 1978; Burton, 1982; Langley & Ohlsson, 1984), and solving calculus integrals (Kimball, 1982). Declarative knowledge representations have been used for geography (Carbonell, 1970; Carbonell & Collins, 1973; Grignetti, Hausman, & Gould, 1975) and meteorology (Stevens, Collins, & Goldin, 1982).

The distinction between procedural and declarative knowledge is notorious in artificial intelligence as a fuzzy, seldom useful differentiation. Because it is based on how much work the interpreter does, and because work is an essentially continuous quality, the boundary between them is not sharp and clear. For instance, GUIDON's knowledge of medicine (Clancey, 1982) is partly declarative—because it says what symptoms indicate which diseases—and partly procedural—because it says which questions to ask the patient under what circumstances. PROUST's knowledge of programming (Johnson & Soloway, 1984a, 1984b) is even more difficult to classify. It is mostly about which PASCAL code templates to use to achieve what purposes. In this respect, it is declarative knowledge about PASCAL. However, a simple top-down programming strategy readily converts this knowledge into programmer actions.

Nonetheless, the distinction between procedural and declarative knowledge is important here because the complexity of diagnosis is directly proportional to the complexity of interpretation. In fact, diagnosis is the inverse of interpretation. Interpretation takes a

---

[1]The section on directions for future research discusses the student modeling problem for a third type of knowledge, qualitative mental models of complex systems.

knowledge base and a problem and produces a solution. Diagnosis takes a problem and a solution and produces a knowledge base. When declarative knowledge is interpreted, many items may be accessed in order to produce a solution. When declarative knowledge is diagnosed, the responsibility for a wrong answer may lie with any one of the many items that could be accessed in producing this answer. In general, the more complicated the interpretation, the more complicated the diagnosis.

These considerations underlie a second dimension in the space of student modeling problems, the *type* of knowledge in the student model. The major distinction—procedural versus declarative—has been mentioned already. It is useful to divide procedural knowledge into two subcategories: *flat* and *hierarchical*. Hierarchical representations allow subgoaling; flat ones do not. For instance, the ACM diagnosis system (Langley & Ohlsson, 1984) uses a flat representation for a subtraction procedure. Operations such as taking a column difference or adding 10 to a minuend digit are selected solely on the basis of the current state of the problem. In the BUGGY diagnosis system (Brown & Burton, 1978), subtraction procedures are represented as goal hierarchies with goals like "Borrow" or "Borrow across zero." Operators are selected on the basis of the problem state *and* the currently active subgoals.

The distinction between flat and hierarchical representations affects the diagnosis. A diagnostic system for flat representation needs to infer what problem-state conditions trigger each operator. This is easy because the system can see both the problem states and the operator applications. A diagnostic system for hierarchical representations needs to infer conditions and both the problem states and the subgoals. But it cannot see the currently active subgoals, so its inference problem is much harder.

In summary, there are three types of knowledge representation: flat procedural, which makes the student modeling problem the easiest; hierarchical procedural, which increases the difficulty of the student modeling problem; and declarative, which makes the student modeling problem most difficult.

Differences Between Student and Expert

ITSs usually employ an expert model as well as a student model.[2] The expert model is used for many purposes, such as providing

---

[2]In this chapter, "expert" is intended to mean a master of the ITS's subject matter. The subject matter is usually only a fraction of the knowledge possessed by a true expert in that area.

explanations of the correct way to solve a problem. Because students will (one hopes) move gradually from their initial state of knowledge toward mastery, student models must be able to change gracefully from representing novices to representing experts. Consequently, most ITSs use the same knowledge representation language for both the expert model and the student model. Conceptually, the ITS has one knowledge base to represent the expert and a different knowledge base to represent the student.

However, economy and other implementation considerations frequently dictate a merger of the two models. The student model is represented as the expert model plus a collection of differences. There are basically two kinds of differences: missing conceptions and misconceptions. A missing conception is an item of knowledge that the expert has and the student does not. A misconception is an item that the student has and the expert does not.

Some student modeling systems can represent only missing conceptions. Conceptually, the student model is a proper subset of the expert model. Such student models are called *overlay models* because the student model can be visualized as a piece of paper with holes punched in it that is laid over the expert model, permitting only some knowledge to be accessible. A student model, therefore, consists of the expert model plus a list of items that are missing. A variant of overlay modeling puts weights on each element in the expert knowledge base; for example, 1 indicates mastery, -1 indicates ignorance, and 0.5 indicates partial mastery. Overlay models are the most common type of student model.

Other systems represent both misconceptions and missing conceptions. The most common type of student model in this class employs a library of predefined misconceptions and missing conceptions. The members of this library are called *bugs*. A student model consists of an expert model plus a list of bugs. This *bug library* technique is the second most common type of student modeling system. This system diagnoses a student by finding bugs from the library that, when added to the expert model, yield a student model that fits the student's performance.

Assembling the library is the biggest hurdle in the bug library approach. The library should be nearly complete. If a student has a bug that is not in the library, then the student model will try to fit the behavior with some combination of other bugs. It may totally misdiagnose the student's misconceptions.

There are only a few techniques for obtaining a bug library:

1. Bugs can be gleaned from literature, particularly from the older works in the educational literature. For instance, Buswell (1926) listed numerous "bad habits of thought" for arithmetic.

2. Bugs can be found by careful hand analysis of students' behaviors. Hand analysis of several thousand subtraction tests yielded a bug library of 104 bugs for Burton and Brown's DEBUGGY program (Burton, 1982; VanLehn, 1982).

3. If there is a learning theory for the subject domain, it may be able to predict the bugs that students have. For instance, Repair Theory (Brown & VanLehn, 1980; VanLehn, 1982) predicts subtraction bugs. When its predictions were added to DEBUGGY's library and students, tests were reanalyzed, some of the students' answers were fit much better by the new bugs (VanLehn, 1983). So, theory can be a valuable contributor of bugs to a bug library.

An alternative to the bug library approach is to construct bugs from a library of bug parts. Bugs are constructed during diagnosis rather than being predefined. For instance, each bug constructed by the ACM system (Langley & Ohlsson, 1984) is a production rule consisting of a condition, which is a conjunction of predicates, and a single action. The predicates and the action are drawn from predefined libraries. If the predicate library has P predicates, and the action library has A actions, then ACM can represent approximately $A * 2^P$/distinct bugs. As in the bug library approach, a student model may have more than one bug. So ACM can represent a very large number of student models using only two small libraries of bug parts. Of course, the libraries of bug parts must be assembled by the creators of the ITS. The problems of filling these libraries are exactly analogous to the problem of filling a bug library. However, because libraries of bug parts are smaller, the problems may be easier to solve. This approach to representing differences between the student and the expert is the newest and least common. Its properties are largely unknown.

To summarize, the three major techniques for representing differences between the student ahd the expert are overlays, bug libraries, and bug part libraries.

A Chart of the Space

The preceding section defined three dimensions of student models, each with three distinguished values. Figure 3.1 summarizes them. Under each dimension, the order of the categories corresponds to the difficulty of the diagnostic problem, easiest first. There are 3^3 possible student models. The student models that make diagnosis easiest are overlay models on flat procedural knowledge, where the student's mental states are available to the diagnostic program. The hardest problem is a bug-parts-library student model over declarative knowledge when only the final result of the student's reasoning is available to the diagnostic program.

Not all of the 27 possible types of student models have been implemented. Figure 3.2 shows some of the existing student modeling systems and their location in the space of the student models. The bandwidth dimension is the Y-axis and the knowledge type dimension is the X-axis. The student–expert differences dimension is indicated by asterisks: ** means a bug parts library, * means a bug library, and no asterisks means an overlay. The ITSs referenced in the figure are all quite complex, and there is ample room for disagreement over how they should be classified.

DIAGNOSTIC TECHNIQUES

Nine diagnostic techniques have appeared so far in the ITS literature. This section reviews them one by one. Most techniques have been used in just a few kinds of student models. As a framework for further discussions, Figure 3.3 shows how the diagnostic techniques align with the student models. The space of student models is shown in the same format as Figure 3.2; but the cells are filled with the names of the diagnostic techniques that have been employed in the corresponding student modeling systems. It is important to note that this chart is based on actual systems and the diagnostic techniques they use. It is likely that some of the techniques can be used with other types of student models.

Model Training

The model-tracing technique (Anderson, Boyle, & Yost, 1985) is probably the easiest technique to implement because it assumes that all of the student's significant mental states are available to the diagnostic program. The basic idea is to use an underdetermined interpreter for modeling problem solving. At each step in problem solving, the underdetermined interpreter may suggest a whole set of rules to be applied next, whereas a deterministic interpreter can suggest only a single rule. The diagnostic algorithm fires all these suggested rules, obtaining a set of possible next states. One of these states should correspond to the state generated by the student. If so, then it is

1. Bandwidth -- How much of the student's activity is available to the diagnostic program?

   a. Mental states -- All the activity, both physical and mental, is available.

   b. Intermediate states -- All the observable, physical activity is available.

   c. Final states -- Only the final state -- the answer -- is available.

2. Knowledge Type -- What is the type of the subject matter knowledge?

   a. Flat procedural -- Procedural knowledge without subgoaling.

   b. Hierarchical procedural -- Procedural knowledge with subgoals.

   c. Declarative.

3. Student-Expert Difference -- How does the student model differ from the expert model?

   a. Overlay -- Some items in the expert model are missing.

   b. Bug library -- In addition to missing knowledge, the student model may have incorrect "buggy" knowledge. The bugs come from a predefined library.

   c. Bug part library -- Bugs are assembled dynamically to fit the student's behavior.

FIGURE 3.1   The three dimensions of student models.

Knowledge type / Bandwidth	Procedural-flat	Procedural-Hierarchical	Declarative
Mental States		**Kimball's calculus tutor **Anderson's LISP tutor **Anderson's Geometry tutor	GUIDON
Intermediate States	WEST WUSOR	**The MACSYMA Avisor **Spade **Image	*SCHOLAR *WHY *GUIDON
Final States	**LMS **Pixie **ACM	*BUGGY *DEBUGGY *IDEBUGGY	*MENO *PROUST

FIGURE 3.2   The space of student models.

Knowledge type / Bandwidth	Procedural-flat	Procedural-Hierarchical	Declarative
Mental States		Model tracing	
Intermediate States	Issue tracing	Plan recognition	Expert system
Final States	Path finding Condition Induction	Decision tree Generate and test Interactive	Generate and test

FIGURE 3.3 Diagnostic techniques.

reasonably certain that the student used the corresponding rule to generate the next mental state and so must know that rule. The student model is updated accordingly. The name *model tracing* comes from the fact that the diagnostic program merely traces the (under-determined) execution of the model and compares it to the student's activity.

Obviously, the model of problem solving must be highly plausible psychologically for this technique to be applicable. Even if such a model is available, practical deployment of this technique requires solving several tricky technical issues. Here are just three: (a) What should the system do if the student's state does not match any of the states produced by the rules in the model? (b) Suppose the student generates a next state by guessing or by mistake; the system will erroneously assume that the student knows the corresponding rule; (c) When should the system change its mind about its student model?

Path Finding

If the bandwidth is not high enough to warrant the assumption that the student has applied just one mental rule, then model tracing is inapplicable. However, it is feasible to put a path-finding algorithm in front of the model-tracing algorithm. Given two consecutive states, it finds a path, or chain of rule applications, that takes the first state into the second state. The path is then given to a model-tracing algorithm, which treats it as a faithful rendition of the student's mental state sequence.

The main technical problem with path finding is that there are usually many paths between the two given states. Should the path finder send all the paths to the model tracer and let it deal with the ambiguity? Should it use heuristics to reject unlikely paths? (Ohlsson's DPF system [Ohlsson & Langley, 1985] takes this approach.) Should it ask the students what they did? These issues deserve further research.

Condition Induction

Model tracing assumes that any two consecutive states in the student's problem solving can be connected by a rule in its model. This puts strong demands on the completeness of the model. Overlay models often will not work. Bug library models must contain a large number of bugs. Bug part libraries are therefore used as the basis for student modeling. Given two consecutive sates, the system *constructs* a rule that converts one state to the other. Although there are potentially many ways to construct such buggy rules, the only technique that has been tried so far is *condition induction* (Langley & Ohlsson, 1984).

This technique requires two libraries. One is a library of operators that convert one state to another. The other is a library of predicates. The technique assumes that the operator library is rich enough that any two consecutive mental states can be matched by applying some operator. That operator becomes the action side of the production rule that will be generated. The hard job is determining what logical combination of predicates should constitute the condition side of the production. The condition should be true of states in which the rule was applied and false otherwise. The system currently has one state for which it is true; that is, the first state in the state pair. In order to reliably induce a condition, it needs to examine more states. These states can come from a record of the student's past problem solving. The system can also delay construction of the rule until more states are examined in later problem solving. This technique seems to require much more data on the student's problem solving than diagnostic techniques for overlay models or bug library models do. This is just what one would expect from information theory. The bug part library can represent many more hypotheses than the other kinds of models can, so more data is needed to discriminate among them.

Plan Recognition

In principle, path finding followed by model tracing, with or without rule induction, can diagnose anything, However, when the paths between observable states get long, diagnosis may become infeasible or unreliable. Plan recognition is a diagnostic technique that is smiliar to path finding in that it is a front end to model tracing. However, it is more effective than path finding for the special circumstances in which it applies.

Plan recognition requires that the knowledge in the student model be procedural and hierarchical and that all or nearly all of the physical, observable states in the student's problem solving be made available to the diagnostic program. These two requirements together dictate that an episode of problem solving can be analyzed as a tree. The leaves of the tree are primitive actions, such as moving a chess piece or writing an equation down. The nonleaf nodes in the tree are subgoals, such as trying to take the opponent's queen or factoring $x^2 + 3x - 1$. The root node of the tree is the overall goal (e.g., Win this chess game, or solve $x[x + 4] -x = 1$). Links between nodes in the tree represent goal–subgoal relationships. Such a tree is often called a *plan*—a misnomer from its early development in robotics. Plan recognition is the process of inferring a plan tree when only its leaves are given. Computationally, plan recognition is similar to parsing a string with a context-free grammar—a parse tree is constructed whose leaves are the elements of the string. The CIRRUS system, (VanLehn and Garlick, 1987) uses parsing for plan recognition.

When plan recognition is used for diagnosis, it serves as a front end to model tracing. Assuming that plan recognition can find a unique plan tree that spans the student's actions, then the student's mental path is assumed to be a depth-first, left-to-right traversal of the tree. This path can be input to a model-tracing algorithm, which updates the student model accordingly.

There are two technical issues to confront: What if the plan recognizer finds more than one tree that is consistent with the student's actions? What if it doesn't find any? To avoid the second situation, plan recognition systems often use bug library models rather than overlay models. Bug part library models could also be used by taking advantage of a machine-learning technique called *learning* by *completing explanations* (VanLehn, 1987). The diagnosis programs that have used plan recognition (Genesereth, 1982; London & Clancey, 1982; Miller, 1982) have been more concerned with the first problem, that is, determining which plan tree among several trees consistent with the student's actions is most plausibly the student's mental plan. These programs use a variety of heuristics.

Issue Tracing

The model-tracing technique assumes that the rules in the student model are a fairly accurate psychological model of the units of knowledge employed by a student. In some cases, such a detailed model of student cognition is infeasible or unnecessary. In particular, a fine-grained student model is probably more work than it's worth if the tutoring cannot be adapted to the intricacies of a particular student's misconceptions. For instance, a perfect model of a student's subtraction bug is necessary if the tutor's remedy is merely to teach the procedure over again. In general, the level of diagnosis and tutoring should be the same.

If a coarse-grained student model is desired, then a variant of model tracing called *issue tracing* is appropriate. It is based on analyzing a short episode of problem solving into a set of microskills or issues that are employed during that episode. The analysis does not explicate *how* the issues interacted or what role they played in the problem solving. It claims only that the issues were used.

The WEST system (Burton & Brown, 1982) pioneered this diagnostic technique. Its task is to teach a simple board game. A turn consists of choosing an arithmetic combination of three randomly chosen numbers in such a way that the value of the expression, when added to the current position of the player's token, results in a new position that is closer to the goal position. Expressions may contain any arithmetic operation or parentheses. There are several tricks involving "bumping" an opponent or taking a shortcut. WEST analyzes a student's move into several issues, including *plus, minus, times, divide, parentheses, bump,* and *shortcut.* If a student forms the expression 5*2 - 1, then the move is analyzed as involving the issues *times* and *minus,* and not involving the others. The student's actual problem solving probably involved trying several expressions, seeing where they moved the token, and selecting the expression that maximized progress toward the goal. A model-tracing technique would have to model this trial-and-error search in gory detail. The issue-tracing technique ignores the details. Its analysis claims only that the student apparently understands these two issues because the student's move embodied them.

The first step in issue tracing is to analyze the student's move and the expert's move into issues. Each issue has two counters, used and missed. Used counters are incremented for all the issues in the student's move. Missed counters are incremented for all the issues in the expert's move that are not in the student's move. If the used counter is high and the missed counter is low, the student probably understands the issue. If the missed counter is high and the used counter is low, then the student probably does not understand the issue. If both counters are zero, the issue has not come up yet.[3]

This simple diagnostic procedure has a hidden problem. Ignorance of any one of the issues involved in an expert's move is sufficient to cause the student to overlook that move; yet issue tracing blames all the issues evenly by incrementing all their missed counters. This introduces some inaccuracy into the student model. WEST's solution is to require that the ratio missed/used be fairly high before it assumes that the student needs tutoring on that issue. WUSOR (Goldstein, 1982; Goldstein & Carr, 1977) has a more complicated scheme. It has a system of expectations about what issues are likely to be learned first and what issues typically follow later.

These prior probabilities are folded into the evaluation of whether a student knows an issue or not. Evaluations based on statistical functions have been used in Kimball's calculus tutor (Kimball, 1982) and other systems for similar purposes.

Expert Systems

Clancey's GUIDON system (Clancey, 1982) uses a large-grained student model just as WEST and WUSOR do. Instead of issues, GUIDON uses inference rules. The rules concern medical diagnosis and model moderately large chunks of knowledge that summarize a variety of cognitive operations. A typical rule is:

Rule 545
    if 1. the infection was acquired while the patient was hospitalized, and
         2. the white blood cell count is less than 2.5 thousand,
    then
         a. there is strong evidence that the organism is E. coli, and
         b. there is suggestive evidence that the organism is Klebsiella pneumonia, and
         c. there is suggestive evidence that the organism is Pseudomonas.

Because such rules are more complicated than issues, the diagnosis

---

[3]If both counters are high, the model is inadequate in some way. This situation is called *tear* (Burton & Brown, 1982). In WEST, it occurred when the student's objective in the game was not what it was assumed to be (i.e., some students did not care about winning but just wanted to bump their opponent as often as possible). WEST is equipped to handle this. It searches for the student's objective by generate and test. It has lists of possible student objectives from which it can choose, and it then reanalyzes the entire game using that objective. If the tear is reduced, then WEST has found the student's objective.

problem is harder. For instance, if a student is given a case that matches the antecedent clauses in Rule 545, and yet the student hypothesizes only one of the conclusions (e.g., conclusion (a), that the organism is E. coli) but not the other two, then it is not clear whether the student has used the rule or not. Another rule, triggered by some other feature of the case, may have led the student to conclude that the organism was E. coli.

There are many possible ways for rules to interact. To handle the myriad of combinations, GUIDON uses an expert systems approach. It has dozens of diagnostic rules such as this one:

> if 1. the student's hypotheses include ones that can be concluded by this rule, and
>   2. the student's hypotheses do not include all the conclusions of this rule,
>
> then
>   a. decrease the degree of belief that the student knows this rule by 70%.

This particular diagnostic rule applies in the situation just described. GUIDON, which uses an overlay model with continuous weights, accordingly downgrades the weight in the student model for Rule 545.

The basic idea of the expert systems approach to diagnosis is to provide diagnostic rules for all the situations that arise. Some technical issues are: If two diagnostic rules match the current situation, how are their conclusions combined? What if no diagnostic rule matches? How much will diagnostic rules have to change if the rules in the knowledge base for the task domain change?

Decision Trees

All diagnostic techniques must deal with the fact that students rarely have just one knowledge deficit. They usually have several. Some of the techniques described earlier—notably model tracing, path finding, and plan recognition—assume that at most one rule fires between consecutive mental states, so each deficit will show up in isolation as a buggy rule application. Because bugs appear in isolation, each bug can be accurately diagnosed even when there are several of them. Systems like WEST and GUIDON, which have less bandwidth, use a less accurate description of knowledge deficits (e.g., weakness on issues), which allows them to model combinations of deficits simply.

The next three techniques aim for highly accurate diagnoses with low bandwidths. They all work with final states, which constitutes

Problems:	50	712
	−28	− 56
Answers:		
0 − N = 0	30	656
N − M = |N − M|	38	744
Both	30	744

FIGURE 3.4 Two bugs, in isolation and co-occurring.

the lowest bandwidth in the student model space. The student models are based on bug libraries. The bugs are highly accurate: When installed, they predict the sequence of intermediate states and perhaps even the sequence of mental states.

Diagnosis of multiple bugs would be simple if systems could generate the symptoms of co-occurring bugs by taking the union of the symptoms they display in isolation. This is not always possible. To illustrate, Figure 3.4 shows two subtraction bugs, in isolation and co-occurring. On the first problem, 50 − 38, the answer of the co-occurring bugs, 30 equals the answer of the first bug in isolation. On the second problem, 712 − 56, the answer matches the answer of the second bug in isolation, even though the first bug also gets this problem wrong when it occurs in isolation. When the second bug occurs in isolation on 712 − 56, the borrow in the units column changes the tens column to 0 − 5, which triggers the bug. When the second bug occurs together with the first, it suppresses the borrow, so the tens column remains 1 − 5, and the first bug is not triggered. In this simple case, there is a causal interaction between the two bugs that makes them manifest differently. In general, bugs can interact in even more complex ways.

The decision-tree technique is a brute force approach to bug compounding. It was employed by the BUGGY diagnostic system (Brown & Burton, 1978). BUGGY enlarged the library of bugs by forming all possible pairs. Because there were 55 bugs, this expansion generated about $55^2 (= 3025)$ bug pairs. In order to efficiently diagnose this many bugs, BUGGY preanalyzed the subtraction test that students were given and formed a decision tree that indexed the bugs by their answers to the problems. The top node of the tree corresponds to the first problem. Answers from all possible diagnoses (a diagnosis is a bug or a bug pair) are collected. Most answers will be generated by several diagnoses. For each answer, a daughter node is attached to the root node, labeled by the answer. Associated with each node are the diagnoses that gave that answer. The tree-building operation recurses, once for each new node, using the second test problem. When BUGGY is finished, a huge tree has been built. Each diagnosis corresponds to a path from the root to some leaf. If the test items are well chosen, then every such path is unique—each leaf corresponds to exactly one diagnosis. In general, it is very difficult to find a short test with such high diagnostic capabilities. Burton (1982) discusses this important issue further.

All this tree building occurs before any students are seen. It is the most expensive part of the computation. Diagnosis of a student's answers is simple, at least in principle. If a student makes no careless errors, then his or her answers are used to steer BUGGY on a path from the root to the diagnosis that is appropriate. Of course, most students do make unintentional errors (often called *slips*, to distinguish them from bug-generated errors), such as subtracting 9 – 5 and getting 3. Slips mean that a simple tree-walk will not always lead to a leaf, so BUGGY performs a tree search to find a diagnosis while allowing a minimal number of slips.

The advantage of the decision-tree approach is that the tree search is simple enough to be implemented on a microcomputer. A larger computer can be used for the computationally intensive tree-building process. The disadvantage of this technique is that it does not really handle multiple co-occurring bugs. Instead, it computes in advance all possible combinations (pairs, in BUGGY's case) and treats the bug combinations just like primitive bugs. This is usually too expensive if more than two bugs can occur together. Burton's hand analysis of the data uncovered students with four co-occurring bugs. For BUGGY to diagnose these students would require approximately $55^4 (= 9$ million) bug tuples, which means a diagnostic tree with trillions of nodes.

Generate and Test

DEBUGGY (Burton, 1982) was designed to diagnose up to four or five multiple co-occurring bugs. Unlike BUGGY, it does not calculate the answers of co-occurring bugs in advance. Rather, it generates bug combinations dynamically. It begins by finding a small set of bugs that match some, but not necessarily all, of the student's answers. There might be 10 bugs in this set. It then forms all these bugs (about 100 bug pairs). It also makes pairs using a stored list of bugs that are known to be difficult to spot because they are often covered by other bugs. From this set of perhaps 200 bugs, DEBUGGY selects the ones that best match the student's answers. Using these favorites, the bug-compounding process occurs again and again until no further improvement in the match is found. The resulting tuple of bugs is output as DEBUGGY's diagnosis of the student.

DEBUGGY's algorithm is a species of a very general technique for diagnosis, called *generate and test*. The diagnostic algorithm generates a set of diagnoses, finds the answers that each predicts, tests those answers against the student's answers, and keeps the ones that match best. In general, generate and test is rather inefficient. Domain-specific heuristics are often needed in order to speed it up.

Interactive Diagnosis

DEBUGGY and BUGGY work with a predefined subtraction test and the student's answers to it. Thus, they can be used as off-line diagnostic systems: The teacher administers the test, mails the answers to DEBUGGY, gets the diagnosis a few days later, and administers the appropriate remedial instruction. VanLehn (1982) reported the results of such a use of DEBUGGY.

Within a tutoring system, there is no need to stick with a fixed list of test items. The system can choose a problem whose answer will help diagnosis the most. IDEBUGGY (Burton, 1982) is such a system. Given a set of diagnoses consistent with the students' answers so far, it tries to construct a subtraction problem that will cause each diagnosis to generate a different answer. Thus, the problem splits the hypothesis space, so to speak. It is not always possible to find such a problem, so IDEBUGGY puts only a fixed amount of effort into this strategy, then presents the best problem it has found so far to the student. Still, the student can sometimes wait too long for IDEBUGGY to present the next problem. Interactive diagnosis, where the diagnosis algorithm drives the tutorial interaction, puts heavy demands on the speed of the diagnostic algorithm. Nonetheless, it can yield highly accurate diagnoses with many fewer test items than a fixed-item test would require in order to achieve the same accuracy. Reducing the length of the diagnostic session may reduce students' fatigue and increase their willingness to cooperate.

RESEARCH ISSUES

Cognitive diagnosis is a new field, and there are vast numbers of questions for research to address. There are many questions of the form "Does technique X work well with student models of form Y on subject domain Z?" From an engineering and educational standpoint, these are the most important questions to address, for they turn a miscellaneous collection of techniques, each of which has been used once or twice, into a well-understood technology. To this collection of issues, I would nominate a few more that are not of the XYZ form.

Most research has gone into finding diagnostic techniques that can produce very detailed descriptions of the students' knowledge. Simpler techniques such as issue tracing produce less detailed descriptions. There is a tacit assumption that tutoring based on fine-grained student models will be more effective than tutoring based on coarse-grained models. No one has attempted to check this assumption. We need to know when fine-grained modeling is worth the effort. This is not really a question of how to do student modeling but, rather, when to do what kinds of student modeling. In order to address this question, one could situate two or more student modeling systems inside the same ITS and see which one tutors more effectively.

Research oriented toward improving student modeling could go in several directions. One is to employ explicit models of learning. This topic was touched on in the WUSOR ITS (Goldstein & Carr, 1977; Goldstein, 1982). Incorporating models of learning into diagnosis has much potential power because it can radically reduce the space that the diagnostic algorithm must search.

Interactive diagnosis, where the diagnostic program selects problems to pose to the student, is another technique that has great potential power. It has been briefly explored with the IDEBUGGY student modeling program (Burton, 1982), the GUIDON ITS (Clancey, 1982), and the WHY project (Stevens, Collins, & Goldin, 1982). This topic—the skill of posing problems—seems almost as rich as diagnosis, which is the skill of interpreting the student's answers to problems.

As user interfaces improve and powerful personal computers become cheaper, we are likely to see more ITS designers choosing the high bandwidth option, where the student's behavior is very closely monitored by the system. The amount of time between the student's actions is one type of information that is available for free but that so far has been ignored by every ITS I know of. Chronometric data has been used in psychology for years as a basis for deciding between potential models of human cognition. It would be interesting to see whether chronometric data would favor fine-grained student modeling.

Much of the early ITS research concerned students learning about physical systems. The SOPHIE project (Brown, Burton, & deKleer, 1982) studied students learning about electronic circuits. The WHY project (Stevens, Collins, & Goldin, 1982) studied rainfall. The Steamer project (Hollan, Hutchins, & Weitzman, 1984) studied naval steam plants. These projects gradually evolved into long-term, basic research on the mental models that people seem to employ for mentally stimulating physical systems (Gentner & Stevens, 1984). Research on mental models has progressed to the point that it might be worth reopening the investigation into ITSs for physical systems. The student modeling problem will be very difficult. The students' responses depends on mentally running a model constructed from their understanding of the device. If the response is wrong, it could be because of a bug in how they ran their mental model, or in how they constructed it, or in both. Relative to the three-dimensional space of student models, mental models are a brand-new knowledge type— a new column in the chart of Figure 3.2—with unique new technical issues to conquer.

REFERENCES

Anderson, J. R., Boyle, C., & Yost, G. (1985). The geometry tutor. *Proceedings of Ninth International Joint Conference on Artificial Intelligence* (pp. 1–7). Los Altos, CA: Morgan Kaufmann.

Brown, J. S., & VanLehn, K. (1980). Repair Theory: A generative theory of bugs in procedural skills. *Cognitive Science, 4,* 379–426.

Brown, J. S., & Burton, R. B. (1978). Diagnostic models for procedural bugs in basic mathematical skills. *Cognitive Science, 2,* 155–192.

Brown, J. S., Burton, R. B., & deKleer, J. (1982). Pedagogical, natural language and knowledge engineering techniques in SOPHIE I, II and III. In D. Sleeman & J. S. Brown (Eds.), *Intelligent tutoring systems* (pp. 227–282). New York: Academic Press.

Burton, R. B. (1982). DEBUGGY: Diagnosis of errors in basic mathematical skills. In D. H. Sleeman & J. S. Brown (Eds.), *Intelligent tutoring systems* (pp. 157–183). New York: Academic Press.

Burton, R. B., & Brown, J. S. (1982). An investigation of computer coaching for informal learning activities. In D. Sleeman & J. S. Brown (Eds.), *Intelligent tutoring systems* (pp. 79–98). New York: Academic Press.

Buswell, G. T. (1926). *Diagnostic studies in arithmetic.* Chicago, IL: University of Chicago Press.

Carbonell, R. (1970). AI in CAI: An artificial intelligence approach to computer aided instruction. *IEEE Transactions on Man-Machine Systems, 11,* 190–202.

Carbonell, J. R., & Collins, A. (1973). Natural semantics in artificial intelligence. *Proceedings of the Third International Joint Conference on Artificial Intelligence* (pp. 344–351). Los Altos, CA: Morgan Kaufmann.

Clancey, W. J. (1982). Tutoring rules for guiding a case method dialogue. In D. Sleeman & J. S. Brown (Eds.), *Intelligent tutoring systems* (pp. 201–225). London: Academic Press.

Genesereth, M. R. (1982). The role of plans in intelligent teaching systems. In D. Sleeman & J. S. Brown (Eds.), *Intelligent tutoring systems* (pp. 137-155). New York: Academic Press.

Gentner, D., & Stevens, A. (1984). *Mental models.* Hillsdale, NJ: Lawrence Erlbaum Associates.

Goldstein, I. (1982). The genetic graph: A representation for the evolution of procedural knowledge. In D. Sleeman & J. S. Brown (Eds.), *Intelligent tutoring systems* (pp. 51-77). New York: Academic Press.

Goldstein, I., & Carr, B. (1977). The computer as coach: An athletic paradigm for intellectual education. *Proceedings of ACM77* (pp. 227-233).

Grignetti, M., Hausman, C., & Gould, L. (1975). An intelligent on-line assistant and tutor: NLS-Scholar. *Proceedings of the National Computer Conference* (pp. 775-781).

Hollan, J. D., Hutchins, E. L., & Weitzman, L. (1984). Steamer: An interactive inspectable simulation-based training system. *The AI Magazine, 5*(2), 15-27.

Johnson, L., & Soloway, E. (1984a). Intention-based diagnosis of programming errors. *Proceedings of American Association of Artificial Intelligence Conference* (pp. 162-168). Los Altos, CA: Morgan Kaufmann.

Johnson, L., & Soloway, E. (1984b). PROUST: Knowledge-based program debugging. *Proceedings of the Seventh International Software Engineering Conference* (pp. 369-380).

Kimball, R. (1982). A self-improving tutor for symbolic integration. In D. Sleeman & J. S. Brown (Eds.), *Intelligent tutoring systems* (pp. 283-308). New York: Academic Press.

Langley, P., & Ohlsson, S. (1984). Automated cognitive modeling. *Proceedings of American Association of Artificial Intelligence* (pp. 193-197). Los Altos, CA: Morgan Kaufman.

London, B., & Clancey, W. J. (1982). Plan recognition strategies in student modeling: Prediction and description. *Proceedings of the American Association of Artificial Intelligence Conference* (pp. 193-197). Los Altos, CA: Morgan Kaufmann.

Miller, M. L. (1982). A structured planning and debugging environment for elementary programming. In D. Sleeman & J. S. Brown (Eds.), *Intelligent tutoring systems* (pp. 119-135). New York: Academic Press.

Ohlsson, S., & Langley, P. (1985). *Identifying solution paths in cognitive diagnosis* (Tech. Rep. CMU-RI-TR-84-7). Pittsburgh, PA: Carnegie-Mellon University, Robotic Institute.

Reiser, B. V., Anderson, J. R., & Farrell, R. G. (1985). Dynamic student modeling in an intelligent tutor for lisp programming. *Proceedings of Ninth International Joint Conference on Artificial Intelligence* (pp. 8-14). Los Altos, CA: Morgan Kaufman.

Sleeman, D. H. (1982). Assessing competence in basic algebra. In D. Sleeman & J. S. Brown (Eds.), *Intelligent tutoring systems* (pp. 186-199). New York: Academic Press.

Stevens, A., Collins, A., & Goldin, S. E. (1982). Misconceptions in students' understanding. In D. Sleeman & J. S. Brown (Eds.), *Intelligent tutoring systems* (pp. 13-24). New York: Academic Press.

VanLehn, K. (1982). Bugs are not enough: Empirical studies of bugs, impasses and repairs in procedural skills. *The Journal of Mathematical Behavior, 3*(2), 3-71.

VanLehn, K. (1983). *Felicity conditions for human skill acquisition: Validating an AI-based theory* (Tech. Rep. CIS-21). Palo Alto, CA: Xerox Palo Alto Research Center.

VanLehn, K. (1987). Learning one subprocedure per lesson. *Artificial Intelligence, 31*(1), 1-40.

VanLehn, K., & Garlick, S. (1987). Cirrus: An automated protocol analysis tool. In P. Langley (Ed.), *Proceedings of the Fourth Machine Learning Workshop*. Los Altos, CA: Morgan Kaufmann.

Curriculum and Instruction in Automated Tutors

Henry M. Halff
Halff Resources, Inc.

People learn many things without benefit of instruction, but we are distinguished as a species by our ability to pass knowledge from the competent to the less competent. To endow machines with this same instructional ability is, to a large extent, to cast the principles of instruction in precise information processing terms. This chapter assesses the progress that has been made on one important aspect of this task, namely that of codifying the principles of tutoring.

Intelligent Tutoring Systems

This chapter is concerned with only one genre of instruction, tutoring,[1] and with only one design approach to this instruction, that based on artificial intelligence technologies. It is necessary therefore to say a bit more about what constitutes an intelligent tutor from an instructional point of view.

Tutoring. Tutors can use many different instructional techniques, but tutorial interactions, however they are conducted, must exhibit three characteristics:

1. A tutor must exercise some control over curriculum, that is, the selection and sequencing of material to be presented.

---

[1]This is not to say that tutoring per se is the only way that automated tutors can function. Team or group instruction could be and has been (Brown, Burton, & deKleer, 1982) implemented to considerable advantage with automated tutors.

2. A tutor must be able to respond to students' questions about the subject matter.

3. A tutor must be able to determine when students need help in the course of practicing a skill and what sort of help is needed.

Some tutors, automated and human, have very weak models for one or two of these functions, but the design of any tutorial system must include some approach to each.

Curriculum and instruction. By *curriculum* I mean the selection of and sequencing of material to be presented to students. By *instruction* I mean the actual presentation of that material to students.

For teaching methods such as lectures, which are less dynamic than tutoring, both curriculum and instruction can be developed prior to delivery, with as much or as little accountability to instructional principles as the developers feel is needed. Tutorial systems afford no such luxury because a tutor, human or machine, is bound to tailor the selection, sequencing, and methods of delivering instruction to meet the ever-changing needs of individual students. The problem of developing curricula and instruction for tutoring, therefore, is the problem of developing methods for selecting and sequencing material, and methods for presenting that material.

The organization of this chapter is straightforward. After a brief discussion of some issues central to intelligent tutoring, the major approaches to curriculum and instruction in automated tutors are considered. The chapter concludes with a discussion of major research issues and some tentative guidelines for implementing automated tutors.

Three Central Issues

Throughout the chapter, several major issues or distinctions recur. They deserve some mention at the outset. The common view of learning and teaching tends to obscure these distinctions, but they are all too evident in the context of intelligent tutoring systems.

The nature of learning. Most approaches to instruction are based on an unspoken "blank slate" assumption. Entering students who cannot perform a particular task or recall a particular fact are viewed as lacking the skill or missing the fact. Although this assumption may hold in a number of situations, there may well be others in which students possess all the wrong skills or all too much knowledge. Since the time of Socrates, scholars have recognized this possibility, but it has certainly not received widespread recognition in current educational practices. There is little in advice to teachers or instructional designers that directs them to weed out inappropriate knowledge at the same time that they sow useful knowledge.

The nature of teaching. The view of learning that dominates current instruction is derived from studies of how individual organisms manage to learn on their own in a variety of environments. The unwritten assumption behind this approach is that instruction should be designed to take best advantage of the mechanisms of individual learning. However, much learning, and indeed the learning that distinguishes us as human, is a cooperative venture that depends crucially on certain conventions (primarily linguistic) for communication among students and teachers. Because communication is a particularly salient aspect of tutoring, we need to understand instruction not only from the point of view of conventional learning theory but also as a process of communication.

The nature of the subject matter. The short history of automated tutoring exhibits a curious split in the choice of instructional objectives, a split that has implications for all aspects of the field including curriculum and instruction. Some tutors, which are called *expository tutors,* are primarily concerned with factual knowledge and inferential skills. They teach students a body of factual knowledge and the skills needed to draw first-order inferences from that knowledge. They rely on declarative knowledge in the sense discussed by Anderson (chapter 2). Dialogue is the primary instructional tool used by these tutors. Carbonell's tutor (1970), for example, engaged students in systematic discussions of South American geometry. Collins and Stevens (1982) described a tutor that uses dialogue to teach certain principles of meterology.

Other tutors, which are called *procedure tutors,* teach skills and procedures that have application outside of the tutorial situation. Although memory for facts is important in learning such skills, tutors of this genre are much more concerned with the procedures that operate on memory. As a consequence, procedure tutors function much more like coaches. They present examples to exhibit problem-solving skills, and they pose exercises for purposes of testing and practice.

CURRICULUM

The problem of curriculum can be broken into two problems: formulating a representation of the material, and selecting and sequencing particular concepts from that representation. In automated tutors, representing knowledge for instruction involves, at the least, an adequate expert module of the type discussed by Anderson (chapter 2). Only one topic need be added to his discussion, and that is *propaedeutics,* the knowledge needed for learning but not for proficient performance. A brief treatment of propaedeutics precedes the major topic of this section, namely selection and sequencing of material.

Propaedeutics:
Representing Knowledge for Instruction

The most common strategy among those few who design automated tutors is to adopt an expert model as the representation of material to be taught. The rationale for this strategy is that learning involves progressive acquisition of the cognitive structures that support expert performance. Under many circumstances, this strategy may be the most appropriate, but there also may be cases in which a tutor should use a knowledge representation that is suited to instruction but not to skilled performance. One example of such a representation is NEOMYCIN (Clancey, 1984; Clancey & Letsinger, 1984), described in chapter 2. Another example is the work of Heller and Reif (Heller & Reif, 1984; Reif & Heller, 1982) on verbal representation of some procedures for solving physics problems (see Table 4.1 for an example).

These intermediate or propaedeutic representations serve to support performance while more efficient procedures are acquired through practice. Propaedeutic representations have two character- istics. First, they make explicit the functional basis of the procedures used in exercising the skill. Second, they are manageable with the limited cognitive resources available to students. Thus they serve (a) to relate theory to practice; (b) to justify, explain, and test possible problem solutions; (c) as a stepping-stone to more efficient problem- solving strategies; and (d) as strategies for management of working memory during intermediate stages of learning.

Anderson, Boyle, Corbett, and Lewis (1986) provide some insight into the use of these intermediate representations in instruction. They suggest that declarative knowledge is encoded in special schemata called *PUPS*[2] *structures,* which indicate, among other things, the form and function of the declarative knowledge that they encode. These schemata are interpreted in the course of working exercises, and the trace of that interpretation is the procedural knowledge underlying

---

[2]"PUPS" stands for the Penultimate Production System, a rule-based system that Anderson uses to formalize his cognitive theory.

TABLE 4.1
Procedure for Generating a Theoretical
Problem Description in Mechanics

Relevant times and systems: At each relevant time (previously identified in the basic description of the problem) identify those systems relevant in the problem because information about them is wanted or because they interact with such systems directly or indirectly.

Description of relevant systems: At each relevant time, describe in the following way each relevant system (if simple enough to be considered a single particle), introducing convenient symbols and expressing simply related quantities in terms of the same symbol:

Description of motion: Draw a "motion diagram" indicating available information about the position, velocity, and acceleration of the system.

Description of forces: Draw a "force diagram" indicating available information about all external forces on the system. Identify these forces as follows:

   Short-range forces: Identify each object which touches the given system and thus interacts with it by short-range interaction. For each such interaction, indicate on the diagram the corresponding force and all available information about it.

   Long-range forces: Identify all objects interacting with the given system by long-range interactions. (Ordinarily this is just the earth interacting with it by gravitational interaction.) For each such interaction, indicate on the diagram the corresponding force and all available information about it.

Checks of description: Check that the descriptions of motion and interaction are qualitatively consistent with known motion principles (e.g., that the acceleration of each particle has the same direction as the total force on it, as required by Newton's motion principle m**a** = **F**).

Note. From "Prescribing Effective Human Problem-Solving Processes: Problem Description in Physics" by J. I. Heller and F. Reif, 1984, *Cognition and Instruction, 1,* 177–216.

the skill to be learned. Although a declarative representation plays no role in the exercise of an established skill, it is crucial to the acquisition of that skill.

Selection and Sequencing

The differences between expository tutors and procedure tutors are evident in the problems associated with selecting and sequencing material. For expository tutors, the problems are those of maintaining focus and coherence and of covering the subject matter in an order that supports later retrieval of the concepts being taught. Procedure tutors have the additional problem of properly ordering the subskills of the target skill and selecting exercises and examples to reflect that order.

Topic selection in expository tutors. Curricula in expository tutors must deal with two sources of constraints. One set of constraints arises from the subject matter. Topics must be selected to maintain coherence and to convey the structure of the material being taught. A second set of constraints comes from the tutoring context. Selection of some topic or fact for discussion must reflect the student's reaction to previous tutoring events.

The methods used to construct curricula that reflect the structure of the material have been the subject of much research, both in the context of automated tutors and in the larger educational community itself. Work at Bolt Beranek and Newman, starting with SCHOLAR (Carbonell, 1970) and continuing with research by Collins, Stevens, and others (Collins & Stevens, 1982; Collins, Warnock, & Passafiume, 1975; Stevens & Collins, 1977, 1980), has systematically examined how both human and automated tutors plan curricula. Influential work of the same sort can be found in other educational literature (Ausubel, 1968; Reigeluth & Stein, 1983).

The general conclusion of this work is that curricula should conform to an approach called *web teaching* by Norman (1973). Two principles guide the selection of materials in web teaching:

1. Relatedness: Give priority to concepts that are closely related to existing knowledge.
2. Generality: Discuss generalities before specifics.

Web teaching can be justified by reference to a complementary notion called *web learning*. According to this notion, students develop cognitive structures that reflect the curriculum. The structure provided by web teaching is a framework of general concepts that is anchored in existing knowledge and that serves to support more detailed knowledge.

Web teaching and related approaches provide a static framework for curricula. They do not address the powerful mechanisms that tutors can use to formulate and reformulate curricula within the dynamic context of the tutoring situation. They do not tell us, for example, whether the curriculum should be redirected as the result of some unanticipated question from the student.

Woolf and McDonald (1985) have developed a sophisticated methodology for studying dynamic formulation and reformulation of curricula. This methodology, implemented in a program called Meno-tutor, has two distinct mechanisms for directing the tutorial dialogue. One mechanism implements planning mechanisms like web theory for maintaining coherence and focus in the dialogue. These mechanisms are represented in an ATN grammar,[3] called a *Discourse Management Network* (DMN).

Meno-tutor has a second curricular mechanism that allows it to respond to a student's particular situation. This mechanism is a set of *meta-rules* that examine the overall context of instruction for conditions that dictate a change from the normal path of instruction represented in the DMN. The meta-rules consist of conditions on the overall state of the DMN and actions that can effect transitions not allowed by DMN's syntax. For example, when the tutor finishes the discussion of one topic, a meta-rule assesses the tutor's overall knowledge of the student's competence. If it turns out that the tutor knows little about the student, the meta-rule will drive the tutor to a strategy calling for exploration of student knowledge.

Exercise and example selection in procedure tutors.   Procedural skills are nearly always taught by exercise and example. In these cases the major curricular issue is that of choosing the correct sequence of exercises and examples. Ideally, the choice of exercises and examples should be dictated by a model of learning, but, as Anderson (chapter 2) points out, there is no theory of learning that is precise and powerful enough to support an interactive tutoring system. Research on the selection and sequencing of exercises has suggested several standards.

1. *Manageability.* Every exercise should be solvable and every example should be comprehensible to students who have completed previous parts of the curriculum.

Recommendations for meeting the manageability criterion are well known by researchers concerned with Instructional Systems Design (ISD). Gagné and Briggs (1979) recommend analyzing the skills to be taught into a prerequisite hierarchy of instructional objectives. The highest level of the hierarchy consists of primary objectives. The descendants of each objective in the hierarchy consist of that objective's immediate prerequisites, called *enabling objectives.* Gagné and Briggs recommend a curriculum that devotes a single lesson to each instructional objective, that imposes a mastery criterion on the learning of each lesson, and that presents the lesson for each objective after the lessons for its enabling objectives.

---

[3]Augmented Transition Network (ATN) grammars are general and powerful mechanisms for representing procedures. Their principle use is for natural-language understanding, but they can serve, as in Meno-tutor, to represent complex procedures for other tasks. See Winston (1984, pp. 304–309) for a technical discussion of these grammars.

ISD also makes some recommendations concerning the fine-grain structure of curricula within lessons. These recommendations rely on a taxonomy for the cognitive features of instructional objectives and rules that construct lessons based on the classification of each objective in the taxonomy. For example, component display theory (Merrill, 1983) recommends two principles for the selection of examples and exercises in classification learning. The *divergence principle* calls for broadly representative sampling of instances, and the *matching principle* calls for presentation of both positive and negative instances of the concept, procedure, or principle being taught.

In summary, manageability can be achieved by isolating each objective to be taught, by providing enough material to allow students to master each objective, and by teaching prerequisites first.

2. *Structural transparency.* The sequence of exercises and examples should reflect the structure of the procedure being taught and should thereby help the student induce the target procedure.

This principle proposes that curriculum is a form of communication with the student in that the sequence of exercises and examples tells the student something about the subject matter. Theories of this kind of communication must therefore have two components. They must specify how to derive a sequence of exercises and examples from the structure and content of the procedure being taught, and they must explain how a student can interpret the sequence in order to learn something about the procedure.

To date, only two efforts have addressed both components of the structural transparency issue. Smith, Walker, and Spool (1982) proposed certain structuring principles for an existing course in symbolic logic that consisted largely of exercises and examples of proof problems. Smith and colleagues also constructed a learning model that used these principles to induce the strategies supporting skilled problem solving in the course. This learning model is schema-driven. It matches each unit of the course (e.g., a sequence of examples) to a template that specifies an induction principle. The induction principle can be used to infer some problem-solving strategy from the unit. Smith and colleagues argue that the templates constitute communicative conventions shared by instructional designer and student for the purpose of conveying procedural knowledge through curriculum structure.

A similar but more thorough line of work can be found in VanLehn (1983, 1985, 1987). His concern was with curricula in which students induce a procedure solely from the exercises and examples presented to them. Most of his work focused on curricula for multicolumn subtraction problems and student performance in those curricula. In a theory of these curricula called *step theory,* he proposed that learning is possible in such cases only if certain conventions, called *felicity conditions,* govern the construction of the curricula. The felicity condition that relates to selection and sequencing requires that the curriculum be divided into discrete lessons, each of which adds a single decision point or step in the procedure to be learned (hence the name *step theory*). The examples and exercises in each lesson can use only the step to be learned or steps previously addressed in the curriculum. Although VanLehn did not present a particular learning model in his theory, he did demonstrate that no learning procedure could possibly induce the correct procedure unless the curriculum conforms to step theory and the procedure takes advantage of this fact.

3. *Individualization.* Exercises and examples should be chosen to fit the pattern of skills and weaknesses that characterize the student at the time the exercise or example is chosen.

The approaches to manageability and structural transparency previously described are static in that they do not take advantage of a tutor's ability to dynamically formulate a curriculum to conform to the ongoing instructional context and, in particular, to the student's changing state of mastery. Each exercise or example should be chosen so that it is (a) manageable with skills already possessed by the individual student; and (b) easily related to skills already possessed by the individual student.

BIP-II (Wescourt, Beard, & Gould, 1977) is the only example of a procedural tutor that addresses these desiderata. BIP-II teaches the BASIC programming language by offering students exercises that can be solved in a powerful but nonintelligent programming environment. Of interest here are BIP-II's methods for selecting each exercise.

The three components of BIP-II are illustrated in Figure 4.1. A semantic *skills network* represents some 93 skills needed for competent BASIC programming and the salient pedagogical relations among them. A *student profile*[4] maintains an assessment of the student's mastery of each skill in terms of five states of learning. This profile is updated after every exercise, based on student performance. An *exercise library* contains a large number of exercises and the skills required for each.

---

[4]I hesitate to call this a student model in the sense in which VanLehn (chapter 3) uses the term because it is not an information-processing account of how students solve problems in the course.

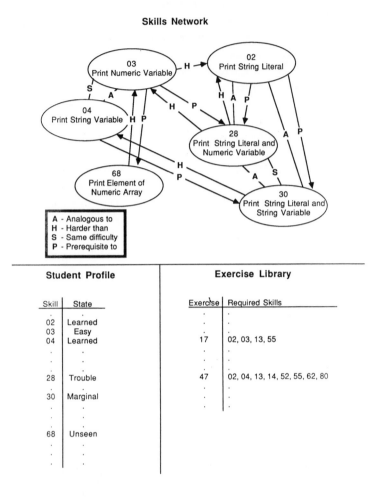

FIGURE 4.1 Components of BIP-II.

These components allow **BIP-II** to dynamically address manageability and structural transparency in its selection of exercises. That is, its selection algorithm chooses exercises that have some optimal combination of learned and unlearned skills and contain unlearned skills that are conceptually related to learned skills.

Selection and sequencing criteria. What lessons do the foregoing examples and suggestions have for curricula in automated tutoring systems? The primary lesson is that one should look more to the overall goals of curriculum construction than to principles for design in particular situations. Curricula for tutoring situations serve several functions:

1. A curriculum should divide the material to be learned into manageable units. These units should address at most a small number of instructional goals and should present material that will allow students to master them.
2. A curriculum should sequence the material in a way that conveys its structure to students.
3. A curriculum should ensure that the instructional goals presented in each unit are achievable.
4. Tutors should have mechanisms for evaluating the student reaction to instruction on a moment-to-monent basis and for reformulating the curriculum.

INSTRUCTION

This section concerns the instructional methods that an automated tutor might use to deliver a curriculum. These methods must cover initial presentation of the material, ways of responding to students' questions, and the conditions and content of tutorial intervention.

Presentation Methods

The methods used to present material depend on the subject matter and the instructional objectives. Expository tutoring uses dialogue as the chief method of conveying material. Tutors oriented toward procedural skills use examples and coached exercises to develop those skills.

Dialogue. The issues involved in formulating dialogue for expository tutors are similar to those involved in formulating curricula for these tutors. In particular, dialogues need to be planned to address the instructional objectives at issue, and dialogues must be sensitive to the evolving tutorial context.

Collins and Stevens (1982) and Collins and colleagues (1975) have derived some general guidelines for conducting tutorial dialogues once the instructional objective of the dialogue has been established. They treat three types of objectives: the teaching of facts and concepts, the teaching of rules and functional relations, and the teaching of skills for deriving these rules. Note that this classification corresponds to

TABLE 4.2
Tutorial dialogue Strategies for Different Instructional Objectives

Instructional Objective	Strategies
Teach facts and concepts	Elicit fact or concept
Explain fact or concept	Teach rules and relations Case selection strategies Entrapment
Teach induction skills	Exercises and examples oriented to subskills

that used in recommendations from ISD (Gagné and Briggs, 1979; Merrill, 1983).

Table 4.2 summarizes Collins and Stevens' guidelines for dialogues addressing each objective. Teaching of facts and concepts is accomplished by asking for or explaining the material. The decision to ask or tell is made on the basis of the importance of the material and the student's knowledge thereof. Teaching of rules in tutorial sessions usually involves inducing the student to consider the relevant data and to formulate the rule. This can be done by presenting case data that makes the rule clear or by entrapment strategies that enable the student to eliminate incorrect versions of the rule. Skills for deriving rules are taught as procedures. These procedures are broken down into their components (e.g., listing factors, generating cases to specification), and exercises and examples are provided that address each subskill.

The dialogue plans suggested by Collins and Stevens are interactive in the sense that particular tutorial utterances are conditioned by the student's responses, but these dialogues do conform to rigid plans that cannot be reformulated in the middle of an interaction. By contrast, Woolf and McDonald's Meno-tutor (1985), which has been described previously, offers the same dynamic flexibility at the instructional level as it does at the curricular level. Meno-tutor's DMN has some 27 instructional (as opposed to curricular) states, each representing a different method of presenting tutorial materials. The DMN, for example, makes a distinction between feedback used to dismiss a topic (a simple "no" or "well . . .") and that used to maintain the topic at the center of attention.

More to the point, meta-rules allow for dynamic reformulation of the tutorial at the instructional level as well as the curricular level. The method of presentation can therefore be determined by default assumptions in the DMN, or, if circumstances dictate, by needs that arise in the particular instructional context. Normal circumstances might, for example, dictate active correction of a student error, but Meno-tutor possesses a rule that allows it to give a less emphatic correction if it decides that the student is confused at that point in the dialogue.

Instructional modeling. Instructional modeling, the use of worked examples or guided practice, is a prime vehicle for introducing students to procedures that they must learn. Essential to the success of modeling in intelligent tutoring systems is the formulation and presentation of procedures for working the examples. These procedures must be based on the representations (including propaedeutic representations) that students need to acquire the target skills, and they must be presented to the student in a manner that shows how each step applies to the case being modeled.

SOPHIE II (Brown, Burton, & deKleer, 1982) is one early example of a training system that faced these issues. It demonstrated procedures for troubleshooting arbitrary faults in a simple electronic device. The significance of the work of Brown and colleagues is in the discipline they used to formulate and present SOPHIE II's troubleshooting procedure. In particular, they restricted SOPHIE II to general (device-independent) procedures that were cognitively faithful to human troubleshooters, and they gave SOPHIE the facility to verbally account for its troubleshooting decisions as it demonstrated these procedures.

Language is not the only vehicle that can be used to explain procedures during instructional modeling. Hutchins and his colleagues (Hutchins & McCandless, 1982; Hutchins, McCandless, Woodworth, & Dutton, 1984) developed MANBOARD, a system to aid in the training of relative-motion problems in naval surface operations. This system is able to demonstrate procedures and illustrate these demonstrations with displays (like the one in Figure 4.2) of ships in both relative and geographic coordinates. These displays make clear the geometric basis of the procedures being taught.

VanLehn (1983) found another important application of visual explanation, not in a tutoring situation, but in his examination of multicolumn subtraction procedures. He found that the indications of crossing out and borrowing in worked examples (see Figure 4.3) were crucial to learning in that they made explicit the intermediate steps of procedures. Without these indications, students are, in principle, unable to induce the procedure from the examples given them in typical curricula. The import of this show-work felicity condition is obvious for instructional modeling; a tutor should provide whatever description is necessary to ensure that the student can grasp the intermediate mental steps of the procedure.

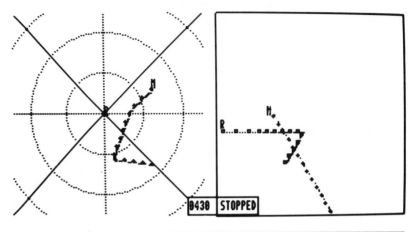

Have computer generate a new set of values

FIGURE 4.2 Display of Hutchins et al.'s training system for relative motion problems. The left panel provides a relative-motion plot, and the right panel provides the corresponding geographic plot. *Note.* From Cognitive Science and Military Training by H. M. Halff, J. D. Hollan, and E. L. Hutchins, *American Psychologist, 41,* 1131–1139.

Answering Questions

Responding to questions is an essential function of human tutors, and one might expect to find the same function in automated tutors. In fact, however, question answering has not been the focus of many of the automated tutors that have been developed. The major stumbling block to effective question answering, as Anderson (chapter 2) mentions, is the difficulty of natural language comprehension and generation. One attempt to work around the problem can be found in SCHOLAR's use of a template-matching strategy to deal with students' questions (Carbonell, 1970).

SOPHIE (Brown, Burton, & deKleer, 1982) was a more sophisticated attempt to deal with both epistemological and linguistic aspects of answering students' questions. SOPHIE I (Brown, Burton, & Bell, 1974) answered the questions of students learning to troubleshoot the device also used in SOPHIE II. Many of these questions, such as hypotheticals, might have required considerable search, but SOPHIE I determined the answers by systematically running a mathematical model of the device under various conditons. Because no reasoning was involved in these runs, SOPHIE I had no way to explain and justify the methods used in the search and could therefore not produce the reasoning needed to answer such questions. This problem and later observations of both novice and expert troubleshooters led Brown and colleagues to the conclusion that causal explanations of device function were necessary for understanding that device. Investigations associated with and subsequent to SOPHIE III have provided some deep insights in the field of qualitative mental models (deKleer, 1984; deKleer & Brown, 1983). These investigations are treated more fully by Anderson (chapter 2).

Tutorial Intervention

One of the prime benefits of tutoring is the opportunity that a tutor has to break into a student's ongoing learning activities with whatever intervention is needed to speed the course of instruction. Tutorial intervention is needed to maintain control of the tutorial situation, to protect the student from inappropriate or incorrect learning, and to keep the student from exploring paths that are not instructionally useful.[5] Automating the process of tutorial intervention involves devising rules for deciding when (or when not) to intervene, and formulating the content of the intervention.

Conditions for intervention. There are two major approaches to decisions about tutorial intervention. *Model tracing* calls for intervention whenever the student strays from a known solution path. *Issue-based tutoring* calls for tutorial intervention only when the tutor can make a positive identification of a particular occasion for intervention.

Both Anderson (chapter 2) and VanLehn (chapter 3) have explained the essentials of model tracing. A tutor using this technique maintains a model of the student's cognitive processing as the student works through an instructional unit. This model reflects the cognitive processes of a competent performer in the instructional setting. As the student progresses, the model traces that behavior, attempting to match it to one of the paths that could be taken by the ideal student. When the matching process fails, the tutor intervenes with advice that will return the student to a successful path.

---

[5]What constitutes an instructionally useful path depends on instructional objectives. If these objectives include teaching error-recovery skills, then allowing the student to make errors is an importnat part of instruction.

Trading Hundreds First

There are 304 birds at the Lincoln Zoo.
126 birds are from North America.
How many birds are from other places?

$304 - 126 = \blacksquare$

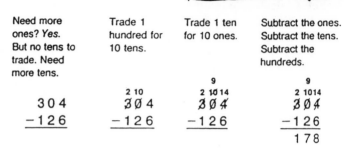

Need more ones? *Yes.* But no tens to trade. Need more tens.	Trade 1 hundred for 10 tens.	Trade 1 ten for 10 ones.	Subtract the ones. Subtract the tens. Subtract the hundreds.
3 0 4 −1 2 6	2 10 3̸ 0̸ 4 −1 2 6	9 2 10 14 3̸ 0̸ 4̸ −1 2 6	9 2 10 14 3̸ 0̸ 4̸ −1 2 6 1 7 8

$304 - 126 = 178$ 178 birds are from other places.

Subtract.

1. 401 − 182	**2.** 205 − 77	**3.** 300 − 151	**4.** 102 − 4	**5.** 406 − 28

| **6.** 700
− 513 | **7.** 608
− 39 | **8.** 503
− 304 | **9.** 900
− 28 | **10.** 802
− 9 |

| **11.** 806
− 747 | **12.** 500
− 439 | **13.** 407
− 8 | **14.** 904
− 676 | **15.** 600
− 89 |

| **16.** 100
− 56 | **17.** 306
− 197 | **18.** 204
− 7 | **19.** 600
− 29 | **20.** 508
− 429 |

21. 402 − 16   **22.** 700 − 8   **23.** 900 − 101

FIGURE 4.3 A page from a third-grade mathematics book illustrating the show-work principle. *Note.* From *Third-Grade Mathematics*, by G. G. Bitter, C. E. Greenes, M. A. Sobel, et al., 1981, New York: McGraw Hill. Reprinted with permission of McGraw-Hill. Copyright 1981.

Whereas model tracing suggests intervention whenever the tutor cannot positively identify the student's response, issue-based tutoring suggests intervention only when the tutor can make some sense of the student's response. Issue-based tutoring has certain advantages over model tracing. For one thing, it need not restrict its intervention to remedial instruction. Identifiably good performance may be an occasion for intervention along with identifiably bad performance.

In addition, issue-based tutors can be more informative in the content of their intervention because they can speak to the issue that caused the intervention. Issue-based tutors can also function with less than perfect expert modules. Model-tracing tutors will intervene even when the student finds a better approach than the expert module, but issue-based tutors will remain silent in these circumstances.

These and other benefits of issue-based tutors are well illustrated in the tutor called WEST, developed by Burton and Brown (1982) and described by Anderson (chapter 2). WEST offers advice to the player of a computerized arithmetic game. It characterizes the game in terms of a number of issues or strategies that may be of use to a player on certain moves, and it tutors in these issues by reminding the student of them on carefully chosen occasions throughout the game. The primary criteria for these occasions are the student's failure to use the issue when appropriate and evidence that the student's knowledge of the issue is weak.

Systems like WEST offer the opportunity to try a variety of different principles for deciding on intervention. These principles can address cognitive concerns. For example, WEST never intervenes on the first few moves, so that students can concentrate on the mechanics of the game. Other principles are motivational. WEST, for example, does not offer advice if a player is doomed to lose no matter what, and it congratulates players on exceptionally good moves.

There is no reason why model-tracing and issue-based techniques cannot exist in the same tutor. Anderson's tutors (Anderson, Boyle, & Reiser, 1985; Anderson, Boyle, & Yost, 1985) incorporate some aspects of issue-based tutoring within a model-tracing framework. In particular, they rely on a *bug catalog* (discussed by VanLehn in chapter 3), a set of inappropriate or incorrect rules that are commonly observed at intermediate stages of learning. When the model trace matches one of these buggy rules, the tutor can direct its advice to the bug.

Gentner (1979) and Gentner and Norman (1977) used another combined approach in Coach, a tutor that monitors students learning a very simple programming language called FLOW. Coach was designed to monitor their every keypress in real time[6] and to intervene under particular circumstances.

Coach's tutoring methods are based on a schema model that encodes the structure of the course as well as the structure of the language FLOW. The model is hierarchical in nature, with high-level schemata representing, say, chapters in the manual or entire

---

[6]It is important to understand, however, that Coach was never implemented in real time. Instead, it was evaluated in terms of its ability to deal with replays of untutored students' protocols.

exercises, and low-level schemata representing individual keypresses. Coach implements student modeling in both a top-down (model-tracing) and bottom-up (issue-based) fashion. It also has context-independent buggy schemata (e.g., a schema for improperly ordered steps), an activation-driven mechanism for dealing with unfulfilled expectations, and a mechanism for separating bugs from the slips on the basis of past performance. Coach is an outstanding example of the leverage that sophisticated student and expert modules can contribute to tutoring.

The content of intervention. When a tutor decides to intervene it must also formulate the content of the intervention. There is no uniform approach to the content of intervention among the few computer coaches in the literature. The most obvious technique, directly correcting the problem that caused the intervention, is not used in any of them, and with good reason. Simply informing a student of the low-level actions needed to recover from a bad situation would waste the opportunity for the tutor to teach students about the situation. Thus, some tutors, such as WEST and those of Anderson (Anderson, Boyle, & Reiser, 1985; Anderson, Boyle, & Yost, 1985), provide advice at the next higher level of abstraction, requiring students to apply this advice to their own concrete situation. Coach attempts to locate the particular schema where the problem arose and to offer advice addressing that schema.

Perhaps the most sophisticated approach to formulating the content of tutorial advice is described by Goldstein (1982). He suggested that as students acquire skill, they can be characterized in terms of increasingly sophisticated information-processing models. Tutorial advice should be responsive not only to the student's particular difficulty but also to the student's level of sophistication in the task. A neophyte making an error should receive suggestions of a relatively coarse nature. A more sophisticated student making the same error should receive advice of a more detailed nature.

RESEARCH AND PRACTICE IN AUTOMATED TUTORS

From the foregoing description of where research in automated tutors has been over the past 15 or 20 years, we can look forward in several directions. This section begins with some suggestions for the direction of research in the field. It does not present a laundry list of potential research projects but, instead, concentrates on three fundamental research issues. Brief suggestions for the kinds of projects that might illuminate those issues are included. Also mentioned in this section are some lines of research that, although interesting, are not appropriate for investigation at this time. Finally, for those interested in immediate applications, a brief discussion of currently feasible implementations is presented.

Research Issues

A broad view of current research in intelligent tutoring systems and in education in general reveals a few crucial issues that deserve serious consideration in any planned research and development effort:

1. An important concern in both research and development is the scope of the efforts, that is, the range and combination of different situations which those efforts address. Researchers in intelligent tutoring systems should look to ISD as a field that is particularly concerned with the broad range of instructional applications.

2. Equally important from a scientific point of view is the necessity of being specific about mechanisms. It is not sufficient to simply build automated tutors that work. An effort must be made to characterize the principles of learning and instruction that account for the effectiveness of these tutors.

3. In addition, attention should be paid to the structure of the discipline. A major aim of the research discussed here is the codification of instructional principles. Future researchers need to seriously question the extent to which these principles can be codified independently of the material that they teach and the extent to which they are an integral part of that material.

Automated tutors and instructional design. One of the major tasks facing researchers in automated tutors is that of relating their work to other research in training and education. Other instructional research has not been discussed prior to this section, because the relationship of research on automated tutors to other instructional research is an important issue in its own right and because the discussion would have been difficult to understand without the context set by the foregoing description of research in automated tutoring.

Most instructional research is tangentially relevant, if it is relevant at all, to automated tutoring systems, either because it addresses other forms of instruction or is simply not sufficiently oriented to design to be of direct help. But one branch of instructional research, namely ISD, seeks to provide methods that can be used to design instructional systems. Moreover, the ISD community is in general agreement about the methodology that should be used to design instructional systems.

ISD is a mixed blessing for automated tutors. On the one hand, it offers the kind of systematic decomposition of the instructional problem and the comprehensive coverage of instructional applications that is sorely needed in the intelligent tutoring field at this point. On the other hand, ISD strives for a level of specificity that is appropriate for instructional designers but nowhere near appropriate for computer tutors. In addition, because it has not been particularly concerned with tutoring methods, it makes no recommendations for the kind of student–tutor interaction that makes these methods so effective. To see the research implications of these statements it is necessary to take a more detailed look at each one.

Starting with the benefits of an ISD view of automated tutors, note that ISD proposes a decomposition of the design process that is consistent with the one discussed in this volume and in this chapter in particular. ISD makes a distinction between analysis of instructional needs (the subject of chapter 2) and development of curriculum and instruction (the subject of this chapter). Also, ISD distinguishes between curriculum and instruction. Reigeluth and Merrill (1978) refer to these aspects of instruction as *macro-* and *micro-strategies,* respectively. ISD also holds that decisions about curriculum and instruction can be based on a cognitive classification of the instructional objectives. Specific recommendations in this regard can be found for curriculum in Reigeluth and Stein (1983) and for instruction in Merrill (1983). In the automated tutoring literature, many of these recommendations (e.g., teach procedures with exercises and examples) are implicit and far from complete.

A second potential benefit of ISD is the fact that it aims for a comprehensive treatment of instructional design. Even a casual reader of the literature in automated tutoring would have to be struck by the narrow, piecemeal nature of the offerings. The chances of finding an intelligent tutor that meets the needs of a randomly chosen application are quite small indeed. By contrast, ISD offers a top-down approach that covers a large area of the instructional waterfront. This means, for one thing, that researchers or designers need not tailor their application to ISD methodology; rather, the methodology will tailor itself to the application. In addition, ISD can deal with complex combinations of different kinds of instructional objectives and find the corresponding combination of instructional methods. Most skills require a combination of declarative and procedural knowledge. Whereas most automated tutors are specialized to teach one or the other, ISD offers as part of the design process methods for teaching both where they are needed.

However, ISD is not without features that make it difficult to apply to intelligent tutoring systems. One of the most evident of these problems is the fact that ISD is meant to be used by intelligent designers, and it takes full advantage of their powers of intellect. Although the prescriptions of ISD are precise enough to be understood by people (and are often seen as annoying in their precision), they come nowhere near the specificity necessary for formalization and programing on a computer. Designers can fill in many of the details in, say, Merrill's divergence principle (discussed previously); but the task of writing a single computer program that could apply that principle to concepts as diverse as well-formed Russian sentences and identifier names in Pascal is well beyond the state of the art.

The state of the art in intelligent tutoring systems is quite different. Well-specified solutions exist, but only for a small number of problems. Of course, it is possible to create, by hand, additional solutions by writing programs that apply ISD principles in particular cases; but this strategy will not significantly advance the task of formalizing those principles themselves. If ISD has any power that is independent of the intellect of its users, then expressing its principles in formal mechanistic terms is a most appropriate venture.

Another feature of ISD that limits its current applicability to automated tutors is its lack of emphasis on tutorial situations. Tutoring, after all, is an expensive and uncommon instructional method, and for this reason alone may have failed to capture the attention of the ISD community. Woolf and McDonald's (1985) research suggests a parallel that helps make the shortcomings of ISD apparent in tutorial situations. Recall that they proposed two levels of tutorial interaction. One, governed by the DMN, corresponds to the kinds of instructional plans that can be developed using ISD. The other, governed by meta-rules, allows for global evaluation of the instructional context and dynamic modification of the instructional plan. The principles for effecting the former, planned level of interaction are consistent with the principles of ISD and in fact are given an extensive treatment in Gagné and Briggs (1979). However, I see no way that the second, more global level of interaction can be accommodated under ISD as it currently stands. Extending ISD to allow for ongoing global evaluation of the instructional context would make it more applicable to automated tutoring and would be a significant advance in ISD itself.

Research suggestions for instructional design. As a first step toward a design approach to automated tutors, laboratories for the systematic manipulation of alternative tutoring methods are needed. Meno-tutor and WEST are good examples of these laboratories because they provide a tutorial shell that can host a variety of instructional methods. Design knowledge can also come from observation. Of interest in this regard are *Wizard-of-Oz* systems,[7] semiautomated tutors in which a human tutor (like the Wizard of Oz) replaces some or all of the instructional functions of an automated tutor (like the machine that the Wizard used to project a wizardly presence to visitors). Studies of these systems might range from systematic observations of tutors' case-selection strategies to development of a sophisticated tutor's assistant, designed to support real tutoring activities as well as collect data on tutors' behaviors.

Theories of learning and instruction. Many of the problems that afflict ISD and other approaches to instruction occur because they lack a foundation in a precise theory of learning. That is, there are no models of the mechanisms that govern a student's interpretation of particular instructional presentations. An obvious solution to these problems is to discover laws of learning that specify these mechanisms, and in fact much work over the past century has been devoted to the discovery of such laws. A question posed earlier by Anderson (chapter 2) again arises: Why are there no automated tutors that can work with a model of a learning student?

The answer lies in the complexity of the instructional enterprise, a complexity manifest on several levels. The first level is that of cognition. Laws of learning apply not to overt stimuli and responses but, rather, to internal symbolic representations of the type described by Anderson and VanLehn (chapters 2 and 3). A second level of complexity stems from the communicative nature of the instructional enterprise. Laws of learning are incomplete descriptions of what goes on in instructional situations. Needed is a joint theory of how instruction is formulated by the tutor and how it is interpreted by the student; neither aspect makes sense without the other. Even greater complexity is introduced by the possibility that students do not already know the instructional conventions when they come to the tutorial but, rather, must learn them during the course of instruction. Do children come to second grade fully prepared to take advantage of VanLehn's felicity conditions, and if not, what laws govern their learning about these conditions? Does a tutor based on laws of instruction have to arrange to teach those laws to students? There is also the possibility that the principles that govern teaching and learning are not immutable but rather are selected, modified, or generated through negotiation between tutor and student. A tutor who fails in using one form of communication may change the rules in hopes that another form will succeed.

---

[7]I would like to thank Jim Miller for suggesting this concept and the term *Wizard of Oz.*

The abbreviated argument presented here takes us from a simple stimulus–response theory of learning to a complex theory of instruction that makes little reference to basic laws of learning. I do not mean to suggest that simple laws have no use in instructional design. Indeed, Schneider (1985) has gotten considerable instructional mileage from a few simple stimulus–response principles. I do, however, want to make clear that there is much to the tutoring enterprise that does not follow from simple laws of learning and that demands a theory of instruction in its own right. A research program in automated tutoring must have a special concern for the particular nature of instruction as a cooperative enterprise involving instructional designer, teacher, and student.

Suggested research on learning and instruction. In summary, the field of automated tutoring needs an account of the mechanism whereby automated tutors achieve (or fail to achieve) their effectiveness. Such an account may rest on fundamental laws of learning or it may appeal to complex theories of communication between tutor and student. Research on this question is therefore needed at several levels. Theories of human learning and machine models of those theories (notably Anderson, 1983) have provided and will continue to provide singular benefits to the field of automated tutoring. Observations of natural tutorial interactions, and particularly of procedure tutoring, are also needed. In addition, new theoretical stances need to be applied to research and development in tutoring. Mehan's analysis of communicative mechanisms in a classroom (1979) might well be extended to tutorial situations in a way that supports the development of automated tutors.

Modularity: The independence of instructional and domain knowledge. One of the most important working hypotheses in research on automated tutors is that diagnostic and instructional methods can be formulated in a domain-independent fashion and that, conversely, the domain knowledge (i.e., the expert module) can be formulated without reference to particular instructional methods. This hypothesis, which I call the *modularity hypothesis,* suggests that diagnostic and instructional modules can be used across a broad range of domains. It also suggests the less common converse, namely, the use of several different instructional methods for the same material; see Crawford and Hollan (1983) for an example of this kind of experiment.

Because it lies at the foundation of the work on automated tutors, the modularity hypothesis deserves serious examination in its own right. Parts of the foregoing discussion call this hypothesis into question. For one thing, it is known that different diagnostic and instructional methods apply to different kinds of instructional objectives. In view of this, rules of correspondence of the sort detailed in Merrill (1983) might be used to preserve modularity. These rules allow for the systematic tailoring of diagnostic and instructional modules to different kinds of domains. Conceivably, there could be a tutor maker that would use these rules of correspondence to generate an automated tutor for a particular application.

A more serious retreat from modularity might be needed in the light of the foregoing discussion of propaedeutic representations. Recall that these representations are models of the subject matter that are needed for instruction but not for skilled performance. Because these representations are derived from a combination of first principles about the domain and the cognitive capacities of students, there is little hope of generating them from any expert model. Propaedeutic representations are therefore a form of instructional knowledge that is specific to a particular domain.

Research on modularity. A number of research approaches could illuminate our understanding of the modularity problem. Studies on tutoring shells or tutor generators are certainly appropriate. Such studies should develop the rules that govern the design of automated tutors and attempt to implement these rules in programs that generate or configure automated tutors for particular applications. Also needed are broader studies of propaedeutic representations. NEOMYCIN and Reif and Heller's work (Heller & Reif, 1984; Reif & Heller, 1982) are the most systematic efforts in this area to date. Needed are more examples, and particularly needed are instructional studies that examine how these representations function in learning. The development of techniques that tutors could use to tailor their materials to particular specifications could also illuminate the structure of the material to be taught. Domain-independent tutors may start with domain-independent methods for generating instructional materials from the expert module.

Research Pitfalls

Research in intelligent tutoring systems is somewhat like a mine field, so it is fitting to point out a few of the issues that researchers do not know how to approach but that could easily sink a development effort.

Tutors that must learn the material. The common working

assumption for intelligent tutoring systems is that the expert model is fully competent in what it is trying to teach or at least possesses much more competence than the student does. Two common situations for which this assumption holds are illustrated in Figure 4.4, panels a and b. Panel a illustrates a blank-slate situation in which the student knows little or nothing about the domain, and the tutor knows just about all that there is to know. Panel b illustrates a situation appropriate for Socratic teaching. The student has little useful knowledge but a good deal of misconceptual knowledge. The tutor, as in Panel a, is a master of the subject matter.

Panels c and d of Figure 4.4 illustrate two situations that may often occur in real tutoring situations. Panel c illustrates a peer-tutoring situation in which the tutor has only a small advantage over the student. Communication between tutor and student is dramatically altered in this situation because the tutor must effectively convey his or her own shortcomings to the student. Also, both tutor and student in these situations are often involved in a cooperative learning enterprise in which each grows in competence. Meeting either one of these demands is well beyond the state of the art at this time, and the combination is even further from the grasp of current methods.

Panel d of Figure 4.4 presents an even more difficult case, one in which the student is actually more competent than the tutor. Automated tutors that can function well in this kind of situation have a tremendous advantage over those limited to the situations illustrated in panels a and b because they can be of use even with a less than complete expert module.

Tutors that must learn to teach.   The underlying goal of most research in intelligent tutoring systems is the successful representation of teaching knowledge and its implementation in a machine. However, at least two efforts in the field have inquired into the possibility that automated tutors could, themselves, learn to teach. Both of these efforts missed the mark, in my opinion. One tutor (Kimball, 1982) improved its technique through successive refinement not of teaching strategies but of its student model. The other (O'Shea, 1982) used a complex generate-and-test procedure to try out various commonsensical notions about teaching techniques. Little is known about good teaching and less about how it is learned. Our own ignorance aside, it is doubtful that any intelligent system, human or machine, could learn to teach on the basis of experience alone. Hence, automated tutors that can really improve their technique on the basis of interactions with students are probably not going to appear in the foreseeable future.

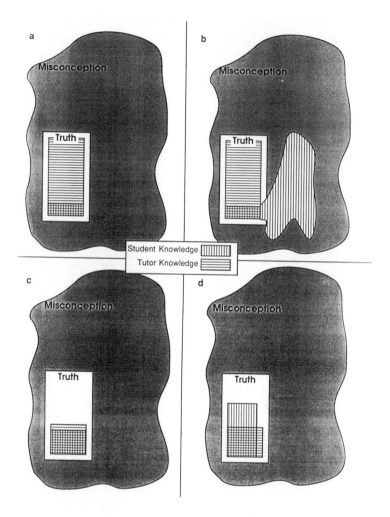

FIGURE 4.4 Possible configurations of student and tutor knowledge: (a) blank-slate model, (b) Socratic model, (c) inexpert tutor, inexpert student, (d) inexpert tutor, expert student.

Building Automated Tutors with Today's Technology

Finding one's way to a feasible application of automated tutors is a difficult job at best. Nonetheless, I offer the following guidelines for deciding when and how to implement automated tutors. The reader should be aware that the shelf life of lists such as these is vanishingly small.

Considerations in
Choosing an Application

1. Work with a domain that can be formalized. Choose an application that can be formalized, one for which, in particular, it is feasible to build an expert module, a propaedeutic representation, or both. Formal problem-solving situations such as troubleshooting or programming are highly suitable. In domains such as tactical planning, which have a more subjective content, select subtasks that can be formalized. Domains such as literary criticism or foreign policy analysis are not within the reach of today's automated tutors.

2. Stay away from natural language. Anderson (chapter 2) has pointed out that natural language understanding is the Achilles' heel of many potential tutors and of expository tutors in particular. If an application calls for an expository tutor, look for techniques such as those described in Crawford and Hollan (1983) that do not require natural language understanding.

Instructional Design Considerations

3. Use known principles of sound instruction. Although a good many of the principles of ISD are difficult to automate, many can be used in the design of an automated tutor. At the least, tutors can be designed to conform to the curricular constraints that make for manageability, coherence, and structural trnsparency. In addition, the show-work principle from step theory deserves serious consideration in any procedure tutor.

4. Use both model-tracing and issue-based tutoring. Both of these instructional techniques are known to work in selected cases. They can be combined in the same system, and they will compensate for each other's failures. Hence the design of an automated tutor, starting with the student and expert modules, should provide for both of these techniques.

A General Design Consideration

5. Design for modularity and robustness. Implementing automated tutors is a risky business. They should therefore be designed to function even if one or more of the parts is ineffective or inoperable. With respect to curriculum and instruction, for example, the tutor should be designed to function with a fixed default curriculum, and it should provide a useful instructional environment even if the tutor is completely silent. The Wizard-of-Oz systems previously mentioned, which use human tutors instead of machine tutors, may also be a possibility in some cases.

CONCLUSION

What then is the current state of the task of codifying the principles of effective tutoring? There are a number of instructional guidelines (e.g., step theory) that can support the design of automated tutors, and there are some technological tools (e.g., model tracing) that can be used to build effective automated tutors for certain applications.

The existence of these guidelines and the tools for implementing them represent real progress in the field of intelligent tutoring systems. However, the major issues associated with curriculum and instruction in intelligent tutoring systems are still unresolved. The design principles needed to specify the range of automated tutoring applications and the structure of that range do not exist. Precise mechanistic theories that can account for the effectiveness of particular instructional techniques have not been formulated. Clear notions of what constitutes an instructional principle and what constitutes an instructionally useful aspect of some particular domain are also not available.

The very fact that these issues are recognized is a sign of real progress. Fifteen years ago, when the field was in its infancy, there was little to say about the representation of knowledge for teaching purposes and even less to say about the instructional process. Until very recently, a representation of expert knowledge was deemed sufficient for teaching purposes, and theories of learning in uninstructed situations were deemed sufficient for describing instructed learning. Awareness of these issues and the technology for exploring them will make the next few years of research in intelligent tutoring systems at least as exciting and profitable as the past 15 years.

REFERENCES

Anderson, J. R. (1983). *The architecture of cognition.* Cambridge, MA: Harvard University Press.

Anderson, J. R., Boyle, C. F., Corbett, A., & Lewis, M. (1986). *Cognitive modeling and intelligent tutoring* (Tech. Rep. No. ONR-86-1). Pittsburgh, PA: Carnegie-Mellon University, Psychology Department.

Anderson, J. R., Boyle, C. F., & Reiser, B. J. (1985). Intelligent tutoring systems. *Science, 228,* 456–462.

Anderson, J. R., Boyle, C. F., & Yost, G. (1985). The geometry tutor. In A. Joshi (Ed.), *Proceedings of the Ninth International Joint Conference on Artificial Intelligence* (Vol. 1, pp. 1–7). Los Altos, CA: Morgan Kaufmann.

Ausubel, D. P. (1968). *Educational psychology: A cognitive view.* New York: Holt, Rinehart & Winston.

Bitter, G. G., Greenes, C. W., Sobel, M. A., et al. (1981). *Third-grade mathematics.* New York: McGraw-Hill.

Brown, J. S., Burton, R. R., & Bell, A. G. (1974). SOPHIE: A step towards a reactive learning environment. *International Journal of Man–Machine Studies, 7,* 675–696.

Brown, J. S., Burton, R. R., & deKleer, J. (1982). Pedagogical, natural language, and knowledge engineering techniques in SOPHIE I, II, and III. In D. Sleeman & J. S. Brown (Eds.), *Intelligent tutoring systems* (pp. 227–282). New York: Academic Press.

Burton, R. R., & Brown, J. S. (1982). An investigation of computer coaching for informal learning activities. In D. Sleeman & J. S. Brown (Eds.), *Intelligent tutoring systems* (pp. 79-98). New York: Academic Press.

Carbonell, J. R. (1970). AI in CAI: An artificial intelligence approach to computer-aided instruction. *IEEE Transactions on Man-Machine Systems. MMS-11,* 190-202.

Clancey, W. J. (1984). Methodology for building an intelligent tutoring system. In W. Kintsch, J. R. Miller, & P. G. Polson (Eds.), *Method and tactics in cognitive science* (pp. 51-83). Hillsdale, NJ: Lawrence Erlbaum Associates.

Clancey, W. J., & Letsinger, R. (1984). NEOMYCIN: Reconfiguring a rule-based expert system for application to teaching. In W. J. Clancey & E. H. Shortliffe (Eds.), *Readings in Medical Artificial Intelligence: The First Decade* (pp. 361-381). Reading, MA: Addison-Wesley.

Collins, A., & Stevens, A. L. (1982). Goals and strategies of inquiry teachers. In R. Glaser (Ed.), *Advances in instructional psychology* (Vol. 2, pp. 65-119). Hillsdale, NJ: Lawrence Erlbaum Associates.

Collins, A., Warnock, E. H., & Passafiume, J. J. (1975). Analysis and synthesis of tutorial dialogues. In G. Bower (Ed.), *The psychology of learning and motivation* (Vol. 9, pp. 49-87). New York: Academic Press.

Crawford, A. M., & Hollan, J. D. (1983). *Development of a computer-based tactical training system* (Spec. Rep. NPRDC-SR-83-13). San Diego, CA: Navy Personnel Research and Development Center.

deKleer, J. (1984). How circuits work. In D. G. Bobrow (Ed.), *Qualitative reasoning about physical systems* (pp. 205-280). Cambridge, MA: MIT Press.

deKleer, J., & Brown, J. S. (1983). Assumptions and ambiguities in mechanistic mental models. In D. Gentner & A. L. Stevens (Eds.), *Mental models* (pp. 155-190). Hillsdale, NJ: Lawrence Erlbaum Associates.

Gagné, R. M., & Briggs, L. J. (1979). *Principles of instructional design.* New York: Holt, Rinehart & Winston.

Gentner, D. R. (1979). *Coach: A schema-based tutor* (Rep. No. 7903). La Jolla: University of California, San Diego, Center for Human Information Processing.

Gentner, D. R., & Norman, D. A. (1977). *The FLOW tutor: Schemas for tutoring* (Rep. No. 7702). La Jolla: University of California, San Diego, Center for Human Information Processing.

Goldstein, I. P. (1982). The genetic graph: A representation for the evolution of procedural knowledge. In D. Sleeman & J. S. Brown (Eds.), *Intelligent tutoring systems* (pp. 51-77). New York: Academic Press.

Halff, H. M., Hollan, J. D., & Hutchins, E. L. (1986). Cognitive science and military training. *American Psychologist, 41,* 1131-1139.

Heller, J. I, & Reif, F. (1984). Prescribing effective human problem-solving processes: Problem description in physics. *Cognition and Instruction, 1,* 177-216.

Hutchins, E., & McCandless, T. P. (1982). *MANBOARD: A graphic display program for training relative motion concepts* (NPRDC Tech. Note 82-10). San Diego, CA: Navy Personnel Research and Development Center.

Hutchins, E., McCandless, T. P., Woodworth, G., & Dutton, B. (1984). *Maneuvering board training system: Analysis and redesign* (NPRDC Tech. Rep. 84-19). San Diego, CA: Navy Personnel Research and Development Center.

Kimball, R. (1982). A self-improving tutor for symbolic integration. In D. Sleeman & J. S. Brown (Eds.), *Intelligent tutoring systems* (pp. 283-307). New York: Academic Press.

Mehan, H. (1979). *Learning lessons: Social organization in the classroom.* Cambridge, MA: Harvard University Press.

Merrill, D. M. (1983). Component display theory. In C. M. Reigeluth (Ed.), *Instructional design theories and models: An overview of their current status* (pp. 279–332). Hillsdale, NJ: Lawrence Erlbaum Associates.

Norman, D. A. (1973). Memory, knowledge, and the answering of questions. In R. L. Solso (Ed.), *Contemporary issues in cognitive psychology: The Loyola Symposium* (pp. 135–165). Washington, DC: V. H. Winston & Sons.

O'Shea, T. (1982). A self-improving quadratic tutor. In D. Sleeman & J. S. Brown (Eds.), *Intelligent tutoring systems* (pp. 309–336). New York: Academic Press.

Reif, F., & Heller, J. I. (1982). Knowledge structure and problem solving in physics. *Educational Psychologist, 17*, 102–127.

Reigeluth, C. M., & Merrill, D. M. (1978). A knowledge base for improving our methods of instruction. *Educational Psychologist, 13*, 57–70.

Reigeluth, C. M., & Stein, F. S. (1983). The elaboration theory of instruction. In C. M. Reigeluth (Ed.), *Instructional design theories and models: An overview of their current status* (pp. 335–381). Hillsdale, NJ: Lawrence Erlbaum Associates.

Schneider, W. (1985). Training high-performance skills: Fallacies and guidelines. *Human Factors, 27*, 285–300.

Smith, R. L., Walker, P., & Spool, P. (1982). *The recognition of instructional strategies in the modeling of student acquisition of problem-solving skills* (Final Rep. 1). New Brunswick, NJ: Rutgers-The State University, Laboratory for Computer Science Research.

Stevens, A., & Collins, A. (1977, October). The goal structure of a Socratic tutor. In *Proceedings of the 1977 Annual Conference, Association for Computing Machinery* (pp. 256–263). New York: Association for Computing Machinery.

Stevens, A. L., & Collins, A. (1980). Multiple conceptual models of a complex system. In R. Snow, P. A. Federico, & W. Montague (Eds.), *Aptitude, learning, and instruction: Vol. 2. Cognitive process analyses of learning and problem solving* (pp. 177–197). Hillsdale, NJ: Lawrence Erlbaum Associates.

VanLehn, K. (1983). *Felicity conditions for human skill acquisition: Validating an AI theory* (Report No. CSL-21). Palo Alto, CA: Xerox Palo Alto Research Center.

VanLehn, K. (1985). *Acquiring procedural skills from lesson sequences* (Rep. No. ISL-9). Palo Alto, CA: Xerox Palo Alto Research Center.

VanLehn, K. (1987). Learning one subprocedure per lesson. *AI Journal, 32*, 1–40.

Wescourt, K., Beard, M., & Gould, L. (1977). Knowledge-based adaptive curriculum sequencing for CAI: Application of a network representation. In *Proceedings of the 1977 Annual Conference, Association for Computing Machinery* (pp. 234–240). New York: Association for Computing Machinery.

Winston, P. H. (1984). *Artificial intelligence* (2nd ed.). Reading, MA: Addison-Wesley.

Woolf, B., & McDonald, D. D. (1985). Building a computer tutor: Design issues. *AEDS Monitor, 23*(9-10), 10–18.

5

The Environment Module of Intelligent Tutoring Systems

Richard R. Burton
Intelligent Systems Laboratory
Xerox Palo Alto Research Center

INTRODUCTION
TO THE ENVIRONMENT MODULE

This chapter describes the environment part of intelligent tutoring systems (ITSs). The term *environment* is used to refer to that part of the system specifying or supporting the activities that the student does and the methods available to the student to do those activities. That is, the environment defines the kinds of problems the student is to solve and the tools available for solving them. For example, in the SOPHIE I electronic troubleshooting environment (Brown & Burton, 1975, 1987; Brown, Burton, & deKleer, 1982), the activity is finding a fault in a broken piece of equipment, and the primary tool available to solve the problem is the ability to ask in English for the values of measurements made on the equipment. The environment part of SOPHIE supports these activities by providing a circuit simulation, a program to understand a subset of natural language, and the routines to set up contexts, keep history lists, and so forth. Our definition of environment includes some aspects of help that the system provides to the student while he or she is solving problems but does not include those forms of help that one would classify as requiring intelligence; these will be left to the chapter on tutoring, curriculum, and instruction (chapter 4). This chapter is of necessity brief and selective in its coverage of instructional environments. Wenger

109

(1987) provided a more detailed overview of many of the systems mentioned here, and more.

A Pedagogical Philosophy

The combination of highly reactive and individualized dialogues in ITSs enabled by research in cognitive science about the nature of understanding has allowed a revisiting and a revising of pedagogical philosophy. Some of these ideas are new, some are old. The important point here is that their realization in actual educational practice is made more feasible by the combination of technology and psychology. The following precepts, adapted from Nickerson (1986), provide a worthwhile perspective on the view of education that underlies much of the research in intelligent instructional environments:

> *Constructivism.* Learning is the construction of knowledge, not the absorption of it. The learner is not an empty vessel into which knowledge is poured. The learner must be active and must be relating new knowledge to existing knowledge.
>
> *Importance of conceptual understanding.* It is inappropriate to have students learn procedures by rote. The rationalizations for procedural knowledge must be taught or discovered if students are to extend learned procedures to situations beyond those taught. In most cases, students will have to construct their own rationalization of a collection of procedures just to remember them (Brown, Moran, & Williams, 1982).
>
> *Preconceptions.* Given that learning is constructive, the role of preconceptions that even introductory students bring to a subject is critical. Some of the preconceptions are likely to be wrong. These misconceptions may need to be identified and corrected for correct learning to occur.
>
> *Connecting in-school and out-of-school learning.* A major impediment to learning is the failure to connect classroom learning to experiences in everyday life. A similar problem is the failure to connect knowledge learned in different subjects. In other words, learning is not normally integrated. The structure of the instructional environment must be made real to avoid the schooling phenomenon, that is, the tendency of students to learn to solve the problem by using the structure of the instructional environment rather than the knowledge it is trying to teach. For example, math students quickly learn that the first problem at the end of a chapter is simple and requires only the techniques presented in that chapter, whereas the last problems often require techniques from earlier chapters and have more complex solutions (Schoenfeld, 1985).
>
> *Self-monitoring and self-management techniques.* Effective learners take responsibility for managing and monitoring their own thinking and

learning activities. Some of the skills they need for these activities are planning, directing attention, assessing comprehension, and controlling anxiety. Instructional environments are increasingly being designed to foster the development of meta-skills.

Lifelong learning. Education is not something acquired in school and used throughout life. Increasingly, job skills are prone to obsolescence. Education must be an ongoing process.

Examples of Instructional Environment Tools and Activities

Learning is greatly enhanced by a proper facilitating environment. This section presents examples of effective instructional environments that have been developed by cleverly formulating problems and constructing tools to solve them. Some of these environments are considered intelligent, others are not. They are presented here to point out the range of tools and activities that have been developed.

The Lego Logo environment (Papert, 1986) is a good example of creating tools and activities to produce an effective instructional environment. This environment consists of a collection of Lego construction blocks (some of which are computer monitored and controlled) motors, switches, and sensors. An early activity for students is to build soapbox racers and to race them to see whose goes farthest. Students quickly develop ideas about why some go farther than others, such as weight, distribution of weight, and aerodynamic shape. Eventually, they discover that the most important thing about making a long-running car is to reduce friction. Of course, they may not know the name of this principle, but they are very much aware of the concept. Such experiences form a good basis for later formalization in physics.

Problem selection plays a major role in instructional environments. The Historian's Microworld (Copeland, 1984) illustrates how clever problem selection greatly enhances an education activity. This system gives students a chance to discover what a historian does. It is used in a classroom by several teams of students, each of which is trying to find the answer to a perplexing historical situation. For example, paraphrased from Copeland (1984):

> From 1565 until 1769, the "Manilla Galleon," laden with rich cargo, sailed from Manilla to Acapulco. Prevailing winds forced the ship to sail north, contact the California coast north of San Francisco, and then sail down the coast to Acapulco. Because of the great distance traveled and the poor weather conditions, this nine-month voyage was very difficult. For more than 200 years, with passengers and crew weak

or dying from starvation and vitamin deficiency, the galleons on this route did not stop but sailed past what is today one of the most fertile and inviting coastlines in the world. Why?

The teams brainstorm about possible causes, such as fog, hostile natives, or a rocky coast, and arrive at a hypothesis the group supports. They then gather data to support the hypothesis by asking the system for information (it uses keywords to analyze their queries), and reject, refine, or expand their hypothesis. Finally, each team publishes its results and compares its analysis and conclusions to those of other teams. All of this pedagogically valuable activity depends crucially on the selection of a suitably captivating problem.

One powerful way that an environment can aid learning is by making explicit or manifest a previously implicit or hidden property of the content. The environment portion of Anderson's Geometry Tutor (Anderson, Boyle, Corbett, & Lewis, 1986; Anderson, Boyle, & Yost, 1985) is a good example of an environment that brings out implicit properties in the task, making it easier to learn. In the standard way of doing geometry proofs, a proof is seen as a sequence of statements that starts with premises and uses theorems and applications of modus ponens to previous statements to build a logical chain from the premises to the conclusion. This view masks two important properties of geometry proofs. One is that they are really tree-structured, not linear. The other is that they can be developed by working both forward from the premises and backward from the conclusion. The representation provided by the Geometry Tutor (see Figure 5.1) brings out both of these properties. Thus, the environment of the Geometry Tutor, even if it did not contain the tutor, would be a valuable aid to learning. It is noteworthy that research into the cognitive nature of the task preceded and guided the design of the environment (Anderson, 1981).

The BUGGY game (Brown & Burton, 1978) is another example of an environment that makes students aware of hidden processes; in this case, their own thinking. From studying student error patterns in arithmetic, Brown and Burton developed a computational model that was able to duplicate students' behavior. The BUGGY game arose from using the computational model to simulate "buggy" students so that students or student teachers could experience diagnosing realistic erroneous behavior. The object of the game is to discover a computer-simulated student's bug by giving it problems to solve. This forces the players to consider as an object study the subtraction algorithm that they have heretofore been following by rote. To play the game, they must trace through their own procedure, checking at each step to see whether the simulated student's answer agrees with

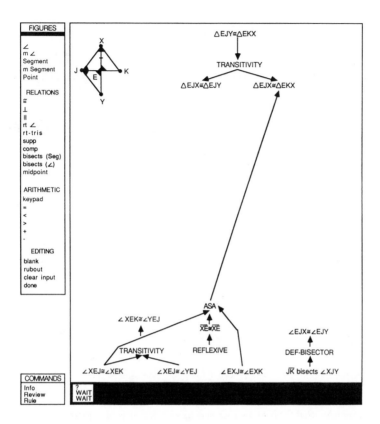

FIGURE 5.1 View of the workspace from the Geometry Tutor (Anderson & Skwarecki, 1986). The large window on the right contains a diagram of the theorem in the upper left corner, the proposition to be proven at the top, and the assumptions at the bottom. The nodes between the top and bottom are statements derived by rules of inference. The proof can be grown from either the bottom upward, using forward inferencing, or top downward, using backward reasoning.

theirs and, when it disagrees, considering what alternatives to their own procedure would cause the observed behavior. The game introduces the players, who are students or teachers themselves, to the idea of debugging and gives them a concrete example of thinking about their own thinking.

One theme that repeatedly appears in ITSs is the presentation of processes and information from multiple perspectives to get students to appreciate the power of different ways of conceptualizing a problem. The Envisioning Machine in Figure 5.2, a physics world being developed by Roschelle (in press), provides parallel displays of physical motion. In one display, students throw objects around and observe their motion. In the other display, students create and observe motions

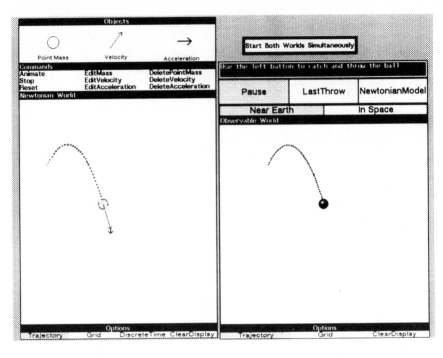

FIGURE 5.2 Example of the Envisioning Machine. The window on the right, "Observable World," contains a simulation of objects moving in real space. In this window, the user can grab the ball and drop or throw it and watch its trajectory. The window on the left, "Newtonian World" contains a force diagrammatic view of objects in motion. In this window, the user sets vectors that give velocity and acceleration to point masses. The activity shown here is to duplicate the trajectory of a thrown ball with velocity and acceleration vectors. *Note.* From "The Envisioning Machine: Facilitating Student's Reconceptualization of Physics" by J. Roschelle, 1986, ISL working paper. Copyright 1986 by the Xerox Corporation. Reprinted by permission.

using force diagrams. ARK (Smith, 1986) is another environment that allows students to play with the motion of objects from different perspectives. In ARK, students activate and watch objects that obey different laws of motion. Thus, for example, students can compare motion in worlds that have gravity to motion in those that do not.

Using multiple perspective is a powerful pedagogical technique that other systems use as well. The MANBOARD system (Hutchins & McCandless, 1982), described in the curriculum and instruction chapter (see chapter 4, Figure 4.2) seeks to develop the student's concept of relative motion by displaying the paths of ships in both geographic and relative (egocentric) coordinates and by pointing out how certain problems become easier to solve in one coordinate system than in the other. Steamer, which will be discussed later, allows the student to view the operation of a steam plant from external, internal, or mechanistic points of view. Arithmekit (Brown, 1983) provides parallel worlds, one symbolic and one semantic, based on Dienes Blocks, in which arithmetic algorithms can be displayed. The student constructs a procedure in the symbolic world and watches its execution simultaneously in both the symbolic and the semantic worlds.

ISSUES OF INSTRUCTIONAL ENVIRONMENTS

This section lays out several dimensions along which instructional environments differ. Examples are given of systems at different positions along the dimensions.

Knowledge: What Is Being Learned?

One important dimension of instructional environments is the question of what is being taught. Loosely speaking, the knowledge a person has about a domain consists of facts about the domain, skills or knowledge of procedures in the domain, and concepts that organize the facts and procedures in the domain. In addition, the person has meta-skills that aid in the learning of new skills. Different instructional environments focus on teaching different aspects of the knowledge by changing the activities and tools in the environment. However, most of the intelligent instructional environments have concentrated on the learning of domain-specific skills.

Even in the same domain there can be many different kinds of activities teaching different skills. This can be seen in a number of systems that have all been built around the domain of plane geometry.

The Geometry Tutor mentioned earlier provides an environment in which students can prove geometry theorems. The system monitors their performance and corrects them when they make a mistake. The skill this system teaches is how to prove geometry theorems that someone else has provided.

The Geometry Supposer (Schwartz & Yerushalmy, in press) allows students to construct geometric figures and perform measurements on them. Important, it keeps track of their construction and can redo the operations under varying conditions. This facility allows the students to invent conjectures and see whether they are true for different examples. This system is used to develop students' skills in forming and testing hypotheses, a central activity in the art of mathematics. It also instills an understanding of the need for proof as the basis for settling disagreements about the validity of conjectures. Note that this instructional environment does not provide the problem. The problem must come from the teacher, the student, or a fellow student. Thus the social environment in which the Geometry Supposer is used is important to its success.

Papert (1980) developed Turtle Geometry to take advantage of children's physical experience in space to provide entry into a world in which mathematics is useful. Papert uses the domain of geometry but in a sense does not care whether students learn geometry per se. By exploring the Turtle Geometry microworld, students develop skills in and an appreciation of the power of mathematical thinking. In an extension of Papert's work, Abelson and diSessa (1980) present a path that uses Turtle Geometry to explore a particular set of mathematical ideas.

As can be seen from these examples, all of which teach different parts of the same subject, it is important to consider what an instructional environment is trying to teach. It is also important to identify what the student is (or can be) learning. The two may be very different. An anecdote about the potential for mismatch concerns a student discovered by Erlwanger (1973). The student had taken several years of a computerized arithmetic curriculum that had been structured into small units. Each unit taught a simple subskill, such as how to borrow from the next column, and was followed by a test to ensure mastery. The criterion for moving to the next unit was to get 80% right on a test. The student was one of the better students in the program at the time Erlwanger interviewed him. What Erlwanger discovered was that, far from having a coherent notion of the arithmetic operations, the student knew a large collection of ad hoc rules, each of which worked on a particular subset of the problems. Furthermore, the student's concept of mathematics included a belief that the correct arithmetic algorithm is something that produces the right answer 80% of the time!

The design of an instructional environment needs to be informed by careful observations and perhaps in-depth clinical interviews about what is actually being learned. This is one important role for formative evaluations, as discussed in chapter 8.

Level of Abstraction

Another issue in the design of the environment is the level of abstraction at which knowledge is presented, i.e., what features of the real world to represent and why. This issue can be illustrated by considering a range of instructional environments that could be used to teach

FIGURE 5.3 Instructional environments vary in the level of abstraction with which they represent the subject matter.

steam plant procedures. Figure 5.3 lays out five examples along a level of abstraction dimension. For the purposes of this example, assume that the activity, diagnosing a problem in the steam plant, is the same for every environment. Although FAULT and TASK have not been applied to this domain, they could be in a straightforward way.

The most realistic experience is to train in the actual steam plant. The students' tools in this environment are the actual gauges, visual inspection of the pipes, and so forth. An alternative to incurring the expense and risk of allowing a trainee to experiment with a real steam plant and its attached ship is to use a mock-up. This is typically a full-size duplicate of the components of the steam plant, with the gauges being driven by a mathematical simulation model rather than by the actual flow of fluid in the pipes.

Steamer. Steamer (Hollan, Hutchins, & Weitzman, 1984; Hollan, Hutchins, McCandless, Rosenstein, & Weitzman, in press) provides graphical display and control of a simulation of a steam plant. The steam plant can be viewed at different levels of detail, and the processes involved in the functioning of the plant can be seen in different ways. For example, one of the approximately 100 displays shows, using animation, the flow of fluid through the plant (see Figure 5.4). Another display shows dials that give the pressure at various points in the plant. A third display shows a graph of pressure as it changes through time or indicates the rate of change (see Figure 5.5). The different displays are used to demonstrate different properties of the plant's operation. The flow animation may be used to indicate causal connections between different parts of the plant, whereas processes that depend on the rate of change in pressure are best demonstrated by the graph. The displays allow the student to view abstractions of the processes involved in steam plant operation in a manner not possible in a real steam plant, and to observe in one place information that may be spread out over an entire ship.

FAULT. The FAULT system (Johnson, 1987) works on a functional representation of the equipment, a level that does not include any

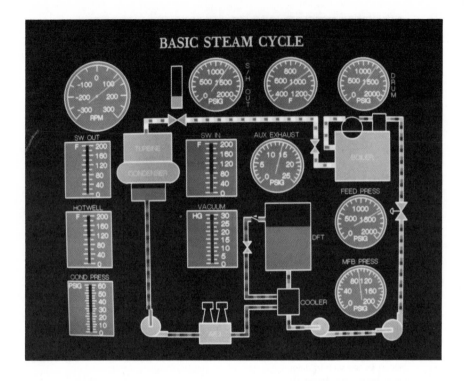

FIGURE 5.4 The basic steam cycle from Steamer, giving a high level view of the whole steam plant. When the simulation is running, motion in the pipes is animated to show the causal connections. Steamer can depict the steam plant at many different levels. *Note.* From "Steamer: An Interactive Inspectable Simulation-Based Training System" by J. D. Hollan, E. L. Hutchins, & L. Weitzman, 1984, *AI Magazine, 5*(2), pp. 15-28. Copyright 1984 by the Center for Applied Artificial Intelligence. Reprinted by permission.

mechanisms across the connections. Figure 5.6 shows an example of the representation of one device, a car engine. The student gains information in the troubleshooting task by asking for the status between two components and is told whether the status is normal or not. During troubleshooting, the student is charged according to the costs of performing tests in a real piece of equipment.

TASK. The TASK system, Troubleshooting by the Application of Structural Knowledge, is actually a precursor to FAULT (Johnson, 1987; Johnson, Maddox, Rouse, & Kiel, 1985; Rouse, 1979; Rouse & Hunt, 1984). It eliminates all domain knowledge and represents only the information needed to develop generic troubleshooting skills, such

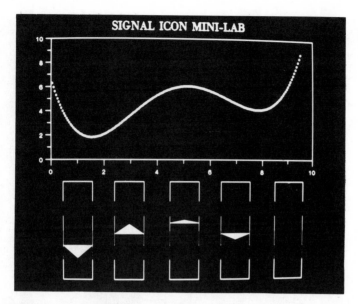

FIGURE 5.5 A signal icon from Steamer. The graph at the top of the figure shows the value of a variable across time; the icons at the bottom depict the rate of change of that variable. Displays such as this one are used to make visible some aspects of automatic control systems that are difficult to see with traditional gauges. *Note.* From "Steamer: An Interactive Inspectable Simulation-Based Training System" by J. D. Hollan, E. L. Hutchins, & L. Weitzman, 1984, *AI Magazine, 5*(2), pp. 15–28. Copyright 1984 by the Center for Applied Artificial Intelligence. Reprinted by permission.

as the half-split method. It views the troubleshooting task at the level of abstract components connected to other components, as shown in Figure 5.7. The connection between any two components is either acceptable or unacceptable. The student queries the connections and looks for the one component that has all acceptable inputs but unacceptable outputs.

Fidelity of Environments

In the training literature, the concept of how closely the simulated environment matches the real world is referred to as *fidelity*. A high-fidelity simulation is one that is nearly indistinguishable from the real thing. Researchers have identified several different kinds of fidelity that serve in different situations. There are at least four kinds: *physical fidelity* (feels the same), *display fidelity* (looks the same), *mechanistic*

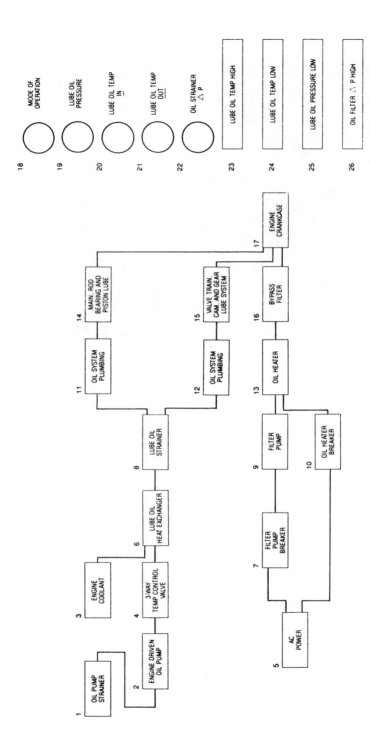

FIGURE 5.6 A diagram showing the representation level of a diesel engine lubrication system in the FAULT system.

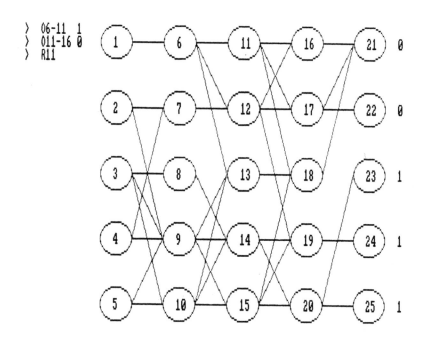

```
> 06-11  1
> 011-16 0
> R11
```

TASK

FIGURE 5.7 A diagram of a system as shown to a student using TASK. The system focuses on domain-independent troubleshooting skills; the student is not told what the numbered components are.

fidelity (behaves in the same way), and *conceptual fidelity* (is thought of as the same).[1]

Researchers are beginning to understand that the importance of each kind of fidelity depends on the conceptual framework of the learner. By studying the difference between experts and novices in different domains, cognitive psychologists have discovered that students go through different conceptual stages in learning a subject (Brown & Burton, 1987; Chi, Feltovich, & Glaser, 1981; diSessa, 1983; Larkin, 1983; Wiser & Carey, 1983). Related work has shown that students can learn advanced theories well enough to pass tests but still act in the real world in ways that contradict the theories (Clement, 1983; diSessa, 1982). This finding lends new support to the view of learning not as the pouring of knowledge into an empty vessel but

---

[1]For ITSs, there is an additional kind of fidelity, *expert fidelity*. This characterizes how the methods used by the student and the computer expert to solve the problem correspond. A computer expert that corresponds in a useful way is referred to as an *articulate expert* (see chapter 2).

as a process of reconceptualization, of getting students to construct the appropriate knowledge out of the knowledge that they already have. It is important to take students through a progression and not merely to teach them the expert's notion, because it is through this progression that new knowledge connects to students' experience of the real world. (See Brown & Burton, 1987 for further discussion.)

From experiences using TASK and FAULT, Johnson (1987) reported that for beginning students, a high level of display fidelity is important. That is, the displays in which information is given must resemble the real equipment: Beginning students have no domain concepts and hence rely on the appearance of the equipment to organize their knowledge. As the students learn more, this reliance decreases, and they will use a display with more digested information about the internal state of the equipment in preference to a color, visually realistic display of the external state. As their concept of the domain becomes more abstract, they can recognize and work with the more digested information if it corresponds to their way of breaking down information. For experienced students, even the abstract view of troubleshooting presented in TASK is valuable because their knowledge has advanced to this level. Interestingly, this finding implies that more realistic (i.e., more physically accurate) simulations are more important for beginning students, and, therefore, the multimillion-dollar steam plant mock-up, or real equipment, ought to be used with beginning students, who, after their first experiences, can be moved to much cheaper computer systems. Fortunately, this is not the case, as Johnson (1987) reports that visually accurate simulations seem to be as effective as the real equipment for training.

In their attempts to evaluate human–computer interfaces, Hutchins, Hollan, and Norman (1985) defined the term *semantic distance* as the distance between the concepts that the system uses and the ones the user has. Combining the idea of semantic distance with the movement in conceptual structures that takes place in the development from novice to expert leads to the conclusion that the environment that is cognitively accurate for the novice will not necessarily be so for the expert, and vice versa. The conception of the domain in the environment may need to change to create intermediate stages to move the student to a final state.

For example, students just learning to program in LISP look at a function such as

```
(DEFUN fact (n)
    (COND ( ( = n 0) 1)
          (T (* n (fact n-1)) ) ) ) )
```

and see text. For them, a text editor is the appropriate tool for changing programs. If they want to add an additional conditional clause to check whether n is less than zero, they would think of it as inserting the characters "(< n 0) 0)" after the string "COND." As they learn to recognize the program structure that the text represents, they will begin to conceive of this edit as adding a new conditional clause; and it is then appropriate for the editor to provide them with commands that operate on structure as well.[2] Thus, proper environment, or instructional environment, may change as students' conceptualization of the domain changes.

Sequences of Environments

Fischer, Brown, and Burton propose a framework for learning complex skills that arose from studying downhill skiing as a successful example of teaching (Burton, Brown, & Fischer, 1984; Fischer, Brown, & Burton, 1978). The framework views the student as being exposed to a sequence of increasingly complex microworlds that provide intermediate experiences such that within each microworld the student can see a challenging but attainable goal. An important aspect of the instruction is the instructor's choice of the proper microworld. The factors that a ski instructor manipulates to create different microworlds are the equipment (e.g., the length of the skis), the physical setting (e.g., the steepness of the slope and the kind of snow), and the task (e.g., do many turns as opposed to ski fast).

The framework of increasingly complex microworlds has been extended into the domain of learning computer environments by Fischer and his colleagues at the University of Colorado (Fischer, in press). They have identified a number of microworlds that the student must learn, such as the manipulation of multiple windows or the difference between destructive and nondestructive functions. They are also developing a variety of tools that provide different kinds of help within and across the microworlds.

VanLehn and Brown (1980) developed a formal representation for the structure of tasks and have used it to model various addition algorithms represented in both symbolic form and base-10 blocks. They were able to evolve a sequence of addition algorithms for base-10 blocks

---

[2]One could insist that beginners use a structural editor as a way of forcing them to deal with programs as structure. This will give them experiences while editing that encourage them to take a structural view of their code and may result in their arriving at the expert's conception earlier. It will certainly slow down the speed at which beginners can make changes to their code.

that begins with an algorithm that simply pushes two groups of blocks together and ends with an algorithm that is representationally equivalent to the standard symbolic addition algorithm. The sequence is such that at each step, one more constraint on the way the algorithm can be performed is included. An example of a constraint is that any final pile of blocks can have at most nine of any size of block. This constraint is needed to make canonical the representation of a number in blocks and thereby facilitate comparison of two numbers. Thus, each transition from one algorithm in the sequence to the next manifests and motivates one constraint; and the complexity of the final symbolic procedure is justified by the collection of constraints. This work demonstrates a theoretical basis for choosing a sequence of microworlds.

White and Frederiksen's (1986a, 1986b) work at Bolt Beranek and Newman provides another good example of increasingly complex microworlds. They developed a system for teaching simple electronic theory by using microworlds based on a series of qualitative models. They argue that students need to know "zero-order" electronic concepts (those employing no derivatives) and how to use connectivity to propagate the existence of voltage differences before they can learn more complicated concepts. They have identified three levels of conceptual models so their system has three corresponding levels of qualitative simulation through which students must progress. At each level, the simulation serves as the basis not only for the generation of the circuit behavior but also for the student model and for the explanations generated by an articulate expert. By knowing a student's level, the system can also know on what examples the student's models will fail and hence can push the student into the next level when he or she has mastered the current one.

Help Provided by the Environment

In addition to providing problem situations and tools, some instructional environments also provide help to further their instructional purposes. The systems differ in the degree and manner of help they provide. Each of the following different ways of offering help is appropriate for some of the difficulties students are likely to encounter.

1. Help: System has help available upon request or during errors.
2. Assistance: System does part of the task, sometimes the whole task.
3. Empowering tools: Perform bookkeeping tasks that aid learning.
4. Reactive: Reacts to student's ideas.

5. Modeling: System performs the task while the student watches.
6. Coach: Breaks in and makes suggestions.
7. Tutor: System maintains control over the interaction.

(Tutoring is discussed in the chapter on tutoring and curriculum [chapter 4] and will not be discussed further here.)

Help systems. Almost all instructional environments provide some kind of help system. Help systems are useful when students recognize that they need help or when they make an explicit mistake. Help systems can be complex. The UNIX Consultant (Wilensky, Arens, & Chin, 1984) provides help by answering the user's questions in English based on a knowledge base of UNIX commands. The MACSYMA Advisor (Genesereth, 1982) builds a plausible plan that explains the user's actions leading up to an error, proposes a misconception that might have caused the user to make the error, and advises the user with a natural language explanation tailored to repair the misconception. Johnson (1987) found that on-line documentation and operating instructions are an important kind of help that makes a significant difference in the acceptance of the instructional environment. The learning-by-doing style of learning that ITSs support applies to the system as well as the domain.

Assistance. Some systems can take over parts of the problem-solving task, freeing students to concentrate on the remaining parts. In general, such systems enable students to see beyond the details that can overwhelm them during the early stages of learning and to grasp the larger structural properties of the domain. Properly designed, such an environment can facilitate the development of sound conceptual understanding and encourage the higher-order thinking skills involved in solving problems strategically.

In AlgebraLand (Brown, 1985; Foss, 1987) (see Figure 5.8) and in the Algebra Tutor (Anderson et al., 1986), students are freed from having to perform manually all the calculations associated with different algebraic operations. Instead, when solving a problem, students select operations and observe as the computer performs them. With the system performing the time-consuming mechanical tasks of symbol manipulation, students are free to see the range of applications for an operation, to learn to recognize situations in which an operation will be effective, and to understand the limits of its use.

Empowering tools. One important form of assistance an instructional environment can provide is tools that encourage students to reflect on their problem-solving activities. Such tools capture a

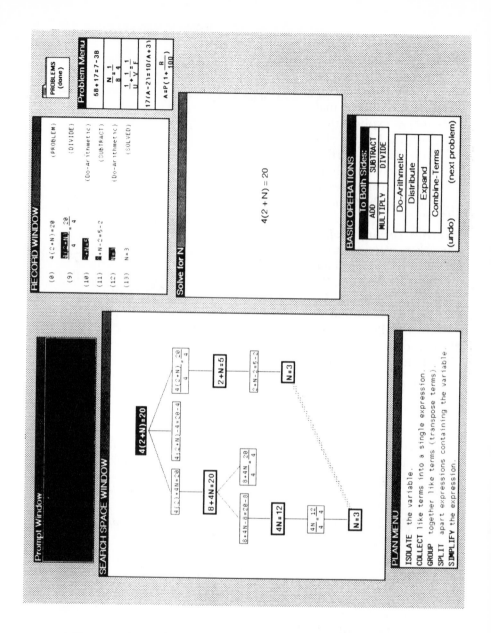

FIGURE 5.8 Screen image of AlgebraLand. The window titled "solve for N" shows the current state of the student's work. The window titled "search space window" presents a visual representation of all the previous problem states, preserving their temporal order. In the search space window, duplicate nodes are linked together with gray lines. The window titled "basic operations menu" contains the operations that the student can apply to the current state. *Note.* We thank Carolyn Foss for providing the screen image of AlgebraLand.

student's actions and decisions, structure them in an appropriate manner, and allow the student to browse through them. AlgebraLand (Figure 5.8) provides a good example of empowering tools. Each decision the student makes is captured and displayed in a tree form that makes explicit the structure of the search space. AlgebraLand also keeps a history of previous solution spaces so that the student can look back to earlier work. The role played by these tools is to reify the problem-solving process so that the student is made aware of it and can more easily study it. The two-dimensional proof tree supported by the Geometry Tutor (Figure 5.1) plays a similar role.

Reactive learning environments. In a reactive learning environment, the system responds to the student's actions in a manner that extends the student's understanding of his or her action in the context of the specific situation. This kind of environment is useful for getting students to "break set" because they are forced to state the ramifications of their beliefs so that the system can challenge them. SOPHIE I (J. S. Brown & Burton, 1975, 1987; A. Brown, Burton, & deKleer, 1982) is a good example of a reactive learning environment. While troubleshooting a simulated piece of equipment, the student can, at any time, offer a hypothesis about what might be wrong. SOPHIE I reacts to this request by evaluating the hypothesis relative to the measurements the student has thus far made. That is, the system tells the student not whether the hypothesis is a correct identification of the fault but whether it is logically consistent with the information the student should have learned about the device from the measurements. Thus, when the hypothesis is inconsistent, the student is confronted with examples that his or her current knowledge does not adequately explain. A key property of reactive learning environments is to get students to articulate their hypotheses as opposed to just acting them out.

Modeling systems. A form of help that some systems provide is to model for the student the way an expert does the activity. It is important that this model articulate the decisions it is faced with and the strategies it is using to make these decisions. The "articulate expert" in SOPHIE II is a good example of a modeling system. It allows the student to insert a fault into the circuit and then troubleshoot it by making measurements just as the student would. Before each measurement, the expert explains why it is making that measurement in terms of various debugging strategies and based on a qualitative analysis of the circuit. Similarly, after each measurement, it explains what it can now conclude. This form of modeling is one important aspect of apprenticeship-style learning (Collins, Brown, & Newman, in press), which has been used successfully by cognitive science researchers (who were not using computers, however) to teach reading (Brown & Palincsar, in press), writing (Scardamalia, Bereiter, & Steinbach, 1984), and calculus (Schoenfeld, 1985). The role played by the modeling is to make explicit the strategies an expert uses, thereby giving the student an example to follow.

Coaching systems. In a coaching system, the system tracks the student's activities, recognizes suboptimal behavior, and breaks in to give advice. Two good examples of coaching systems are WEST (Burton & Brown, 1978) and WUSOR (Goldstein, 1978; Stansfield, Carr, & Goldstein, 1976). In both systems, a model of the student is formed by comparing the student's behavior with that of an expert. When the student makes a bad move, the coach interrupts, giving advice designed to overcome the weaknesses observed in the student model. WUSOR uses an articulate expert, and the advice derives from a trace of the expert. WEST employs an expert that cannot articulate its reasoning in psychologically relevant terms. Its advice comes from local knowledge associated with particular weaknesses. WEST demonstrates the idea that even when the system cannot track everything the student does, it can recognize patterns of suboptimal behavior and provide coaching about the things it does know. Fischer (in press) has implemented a coach for a practical application, the editor for a programming language.

Structure Provided
by the Instructional Environment

Instructional environments can be distinguished according to the amount of structure they impose on the activity. Some systems, such as Lego Logo, are very unstructured. The environment is carefully designed to embody a set of ideas and concepts, and students are allowed to explore it. Unstructured systems are based on the belief that by providing a rich environment, worthwhile learning will emerge if students are encouraged to explore whatever interests them.

One of the early goals of ITS research was to make unstructured environments more productive by augmenting them with intelligent tutors. Thus, the system could help the student see and appreciate the ideas and concepts the environment had to offer. Unfortunately, the system's ability to recognize interesting situations occurring in the student's activity is limited by how well the computer can understand what the student is doing. If the student is allowed to do a wide variety of things, this problem is more difficult.

Some systems, such as Anderson's LISP Tutor (Anderson & Skwarecki, 1986), solve this problem by imposing structure on what the student is allowed to do. The LISP Tutor walks the student through the creation of a LISP function, correcting the student whenever he or she deviates from a correct path. In this way, the system can know what the student is doing at any time and can respond appropriately.

A problem with the structured approach arises when the designer of the ITS has an incomplete characterization of the knowledge learned from it. Then the system may work against the students' learning those things that have been left out, and the students may fail to learn everything they need. Having a computerized expert that performs a task does not guarantee that all of the requisite knowledge has been identified. Examples of additional kinds of knowledge include self-monitoring skills that might be necessary in a less structured environment, context-recognition skills to determine when the learned procedure applies and when it does .not, and ways of structuring knowledge that differ from that of computerized experts but are more amenable to human consumption. A good example of the inadequacy of a computer expert's knowledge for teaching can be seen in the progression from MYCIN to GUIDON to NEOMYCIN (Clancey, 1982, 1986; Richer & Clancey, 1985), where at each stage some knowledge was found to be missing. The GUIDON experience is also an example of a good research methodology: It uses each system to improve our knowledge of what needs to be learned.

TOOLS FOR BUILDING INSTRUCTIONAL ENVIRONMENTS

A variety of existing tools makes the creation of instructional environments easier. Different tools are designed to address different aspects of the problem, and examining some of them gives another perspective on the range of issues that come up in the development of an ITS.

Successful instructional environments have been built in many different programming languages and run on many different sizes of machines. As we have seen, it is possible to invent systems that require little computation or to reimplement existing systems on smaller computers. However, the bulk of the research on ITSs has been done in exploratory programming environments (Sheil, 1983a, 1983b) originally developed for artificial intelligence work. These programming environments seek to minimize the time and effort required to go from an idea to its implementation and to minimize the difficulty of modifying the implementation as the idea changes. As a result, the designer is encouraged to do formative evaluations, to actually get and use feedback by trying out early systems to improve later ones. This seems like an eminently reasonable idea. Currently, the best environments are Interlisp and Zetalisp. Within several years, it is likely that the CommonLisp community will have developed comparable environments. It can be expected that the transition from either Interlisp or Zetalisp will not be difficult. It would be premature to trade the ability to make rapid, large-scale changes that these programming systems provide for the cost savings currently available through recoding in other languages, such as C. During the coming period, it will be critical to be able to modify the systems quickly to respond to shortcomings discovered by their being placed in the field.

Much work is being done in the commercial market for artificial intelligence by companies such as Intellicorp, Inference Corporation, and Teknowledge to develop tools to make building expert systems easier. Any computing strategy for developing ITSs should be able to incorporate the good ideas that come out of these efforts.

Tools for Building
Educational Simulation Kits

Aside from programming environments, tools have been developed to attack particular areas within the ITS. One common kind of system is built around a simulator of a certain piece of equipment. Typically, these environments teach the procedures to operate, maintain, and troubleshoot the equipment. The use of simulators in the training community has a long history, and some of the earliest work in intelligent computer-assisted instruction involved augmenting a simulator with intelligent agents that facilitated exploration by students and tutoring (Brown & Burton, 1975).

Tools in Steamer. As part of the Steamer project, many tools were constructed to facilitate building complex graphical interfaces to simulations and using them in educational ways (Hollan et al., in press). The Graphics Editor was designed to allow instructors who were knowledgeable about the domain but naive about computers to create graphical interfaces and to customize displays to show exactly the features or mechanism relevant to a particular point. For example, as part of a classroom lecture, an instructor might put together a display that contained dials from two separate parts of the plant and graphs of their pressures to show the relationship between them. The

Graphics Editor allows the user to interactively place graphic objects, or icons, from a large predefined library. The icons can then be tapped into the simulation to display and, in some cases, change the values when the simulation is running.

The Icon Editor allows a more knowledgeable user to create new icons. The library of icons is organized in a multiple hierarchical manner using the Zetalisp Flavors system (Weinreb & Moon, 1981), which allows properties and behaviors to be inherited. This feature makes it very easy to customize new icons or combine existing icons into new ones. Icons "behave" in the sense that their display can change in response to either a change in the simulation or the passage of time. This latter capability makes possible the animation that is used to show fluid flowing in pipes or flames flickering under heating vessels.

The Steamer group is exploring knowledge-based editors to extend the application of the graphical-simulation technology. One is the Lesson Editor, which provides a means for specifying instructional sequences that are tied to particular behaviors of the simulation. This editor can be used to present remedial or informative text or other displays when the student's actions cause the steam plant to attain certain states.

Another knowledge-based editor is the Behavior Editor, which extends icons to include activity behavior as well as display behavior in order to remove the requirement for the mathematical model of the domain. Each icon in the library is given program code that determines its state based on the states of the icons to which it is connected. When the icons are placed on the display, their connections are inferred, and the result is not just a display but also a simulation of the process depicted. This is similar to the work of Towne's group, which will be described next. This approach to building simulation models definitely restricts the kind of behaviors that are produced because there is no mechanism to handle simultaneous constraints that are required, such as obtaining feedback. For example, this technique would not produce the complete model of the steam plant underlying Steamer. However, its exact limits are not known, and it seems clear that much useful instruction can be done within its boundaries.

The Intelligent Maintenance Training System. Towne's (in press) Intelligent Maintenance Training System (IMTS) is an interactive system for building graphical simulations for use with a variety of equipment. It performs three major functions:

   1. It provides a simulation of equipment at the functional and front-panel

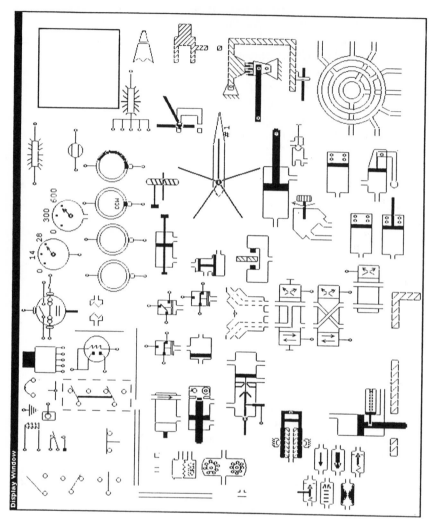

FIGURE 5.9 A portion of the generic object library of IMTS. The objects shown here can be wired together by an editor to create a simulation model of a piece of machinery.

132

levels and simulates associated test equipment while a student practices fault diagnosis.

2. It evaluates the student's diagnostic approaches, assists the student where necessary, and models preferred diagnostic techniques on problems.

3. It selects appropriate problems for the student to solve and evaluates the student's progress during troubleshooting practice.

To specify the simulation knowledge base for IMTS, an editor was developed that borrows many of the graphical and behavior editing ideas in Steamer. An author can build equipment-specific simulations by interactively assembling graphical objects that also specify behavior (see Figure 5.9). The simulation is determined automatically from the graphical connections between the objects. The author can also construct new generic objects and specify their behavior with a menu-based interface that avoids the need to program. IMTS then provides tutorial training functions on the created equipment. As mentioned in the discussion of Steamer, the complexity of simulations that can be constructed using this local technique is limited, but it is unclear how far this level of simulation can go. The system has been successfully used to construct a simulation of the blade-folding mechanism of the SH-3 helicopter, which is a moderately complex, electrically controlled hydraulic system.

The intelligent tutoring components, the automatic expert troubleshooter, the tutor, and the problem selection specialist all work from information given locally for the components. This includes information about the replacement time, the cost of spares, and mean time between failures. In addition, the problem selection is driven from a subjective level of difficulty assigned to each component by the author.

Tools for Building Tutors

PUPS Tutoring Architecture. Anderson's PUPS Tutoring Architecture (PTA) (Anderson & Skwarecki, 1986) is designed to make it easier to produce tutoring systems that follow the model-tracing methodology discussed in detail by VanLehn (chapter 3). The system strives to separate the knowledge about features specific to one domain from the general-purpose tutoring apparatus. A domain expert is written in PUPS, a production rule system that allows flexible control. The trace of the expert running on the problems the students will get is then produced. The solution trace is given to a monitoring program that can run on a MacIntosh computer and performs the model-tracing tutorial interaction with a student. Based on PTA, tutors are currently being developed for programming in Ada, LISP, and

PROLOG. PTA provides an interesting example of reducing the cost of deploying intelligent computer-aided instruction by using intelligence on one computer to produce code that actually interacts with the student on a smaller computer.

Bite-Sized Tutor. Bonar, Lesgold, and their colleagues at the Learning Research and Development Center (Bonar, 1985; Bonar, Cunningham, & Schultz, 1986) are working toward the goal of an authoring language for intelligent tutors. Their approach, called the *Bite-Sized Tutor,* is organized around the curriculum to be presented. The knowledge needed by a student is broken into "bite-sized" chunks that are represented in a formalism specialized to the task of tutoring. For example, the formalism contains links to represent relationships, such as *general-specific* or *prerequisite,* and slots for procedures, such as modeling the student's knowledge, tutoring on the content, or assessing blame for errors. The hope is that by building on an object-oriented system (LOOPS), the bite-sized tutor can accumulate generally useful routines so that the amount of specialized information needed for a new domain will be small. Tutors currently exist for several different domains; subtraction, electronics, and economics. It is still too early in the research to evaluate how well this approach will generalize.

Tools to Merge ITSs
with Existing Techniques

IDE. A group at Xerox Palo Alto Research Center is working on an authoring aid for the course development process, called the Instructional Design Environment (IDE) (Russell, Moran, & Jordan, in press). One noteworthy feature of the Xerox environment is that during all stages of the process, the author has access to a powerful computing environment, NoteCards (Xerox Special Information Systems, 1985). This environment is built on top of Interlisp-D and includes the ability to link together "cards" containing animations, simulations, ICAI activities, video disk, and speech. This feature makes it easier to design a complete course around an instructional environment.

IDE provides a collection of tools to aid the design of instructional material (see Figure 5.10). Some of these tools support knowledge acquisition and structuring, cognitive task analysis, storyboarding and course layout. One tool IDE provides, called the *rationale tool,* allows the user to annotate the design of a course, collecting the many decisions, rationales, constraints, principles, and assumptions that

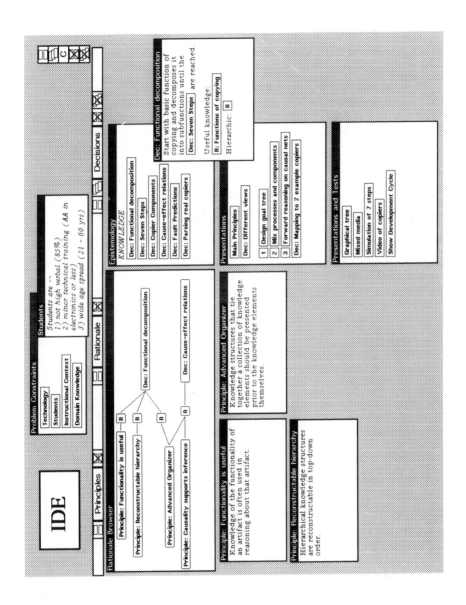

FIGURE 5.10 Screen image of the Xerox Instructional Design Environment (IDE). At the top of the screen are the course goals. The windows on the left contain instructional principles. The windows on the right contain the decisions made in structuring the course. In the middle are "rationales" that link the course decisions to the goals and principles that support it. The end result of the design process is a linked collection of descriptions of instructional units. *Note.* From "Instructional Design Environment References" by D. M. Russell, T. P. Moran, & D. S. Jordan, ISL Research Report (in press). Copyright by the Xerox Corporation. Reprinted by permission. Figure courtesy of D. M. Russell.

underlie its development. This collection of annotations captures the information needed by someone who later wants to change something about the course. It also serves as an effective communication medium for designers cooperating on the design of a course.

IDE makes it easier to incorporate an activity from an ITS into a complete course. Xerox is also working on an experimental course development and intelligent delivery system, the IDE Interpreter, that automates the sequencing of instructional material, thus allowing more flexible and personalized instruction. Instructors create instruction units that present information or determine what a student knows and provide rules that represent instructional strategies. During instruction delivery, the IDE Interpreter presents students with different sequences of instruction and units determined by the rules of the instructional strategy and based on a model of their behavior. The system was modeled after O'Shea's five-ring model for CAI authoring systems (O'Shea, Bornat, Du Boulay, Eisenstadt, & Page, 1983).

KA/IAA. Perceptronics, Control Data, and Harris started a large contract to produce knowledge acquisition and intelligent authoring aids (KA/IAA) to support the development and production of intelligent instructional environments. They proposed to follow an evolutionary approach from CAI to ICAI and stress the importance of reviewing existing authoring systems and military courses to determine which are appropriate for ICAI.

FUTURE TECHNOLOGY
AND INSTRUCTIONAL ENVIRONMENTS

There will continue to be major development in both hardware and software. Computation will continue to get cheaper. The price/performance ratio of personal workstation computers will halve each year through 1992, independent of advances in parallel processing. Read/write optical disk technology will arrive, making it possible to store massive amounts of information locally. Speech, input and output, will come along. Graphic chips incorporated into machines will provide rapid color graphics.

The research efforts in instructional environments should track these developments and be ready to exploit them when they arrive. Development systems for artificial intelligence programs will be improved, driven by market pressures. Similarly, developments will occur in graphics, natural language processing, and knowledge representation languages. The research strategy for developing ITSs should allow whatever new developments arise to be incorporated as they appear in the marketplace.

Massively parallel machines such as the Connection Machine promise tremendous increases in speed for particular applications such as simulations; and questions arise as to what we should do about this innovation. Our approach should be based on a view of ourselves as users of the developing technology for education. We should equip researchers with the best available system development environments that are cheap enough to permit testing in real classrooms of 10 to 20 students. When applications of parallel processing are demonstrated, we should incorporate these applications into our systems. In general, the program for ITS research and development should focus on problems unique to ITS.

RESEARCH OPPORTUNITIES
IN INSTRUCTIONAL ENVIRONMENTS

New technology and research ideas from cognitive science are opening up many opportunities for instructional environments. Faster, cheaper computers that have color, sound, video, and so forth, and that have access to massive amounts of data through devices such as compact disks open up a wide spectrum of new environments. One can easily imagine Steamer-like systems sitting on everyone's desk and versions of the Historian's Microworld that have access to major parts of the original source material for significant portions of history. It is important that these new systems be built on effective environments, that is, ones that present relevant problems and provide pedagogically appropriate tools. As we mentioned earlier, the environment in many ways defines the way the student looks at the subject matter. One of the significant contributions of research in intelligent instructional environments is the cognitive perspective it brings to defining the content of instruction. We have seen benefits in the Geometry Tutor environment, in AlgebraLand, and in BUGGY, where developing the system actually helped clarify what needed to be learned. Another good example is the work of Haertel (1987), which lays out a qualitative model of electricity that will provide an excellent base for a computerized curriculum on electronics.

Near-Term Opportunities

Following are several specific near-term research opportunities in ITS environment research:

Simulation kits are a promising form of instructional environment. Applications for tools like those that Steamer and IMTS provide should be found, and systems should be developed for them. Applications will improve these tools and provide examples of their use. More research is needed on how to use the tools and the environments they produce. This research is best done in a context in which many examples exist.

Medium-scale experimental testing of ITSs should be planned. The next generation of low-cost, personal LISP machines will be as fast as current research machines and will make testing more feasible. Also, the increasing availability of LISP on the 32-bit PCs makes the testing easier.

The incorporation of ITSs into standard courses and the use of knowledge-based authoring environments such as IDE should be explored.

Empowering environments that make explicit the process the student has to do should be developed and their use explored. For example, the process of troubleshooting may have a structure analogous to the geometry proof tree or the algebra search-space tree that could be made explicit to students, thereby improving their troubleshooting skills.

Technological developments such as compact disks, speech, and parallel machines should be tracked and their potential for ITS application should be determined.

Long-Term Opportunities

The stages of conceptualizations and common incorrect conceptualizations (i.e., misconcepts) that incoming trainees have should be identified. The role of misconceptions in blocking learning from instructional environments should be studied. Instructional environments should be developed to support the transition from incorrect concepts to correct ones. Research must determine when to do this by confronting the student's misconceptions and when to ignore them and just teach the student a better concept in a different way.

The other side of understanding the student's conceptualization is to understand the cognitive ramifications of changes to the instructional environment. We need to know more precisely when different kinds of fidelity are appropriate and when we should use similar environments with slightly different kinds of fidelity to remedy misconceptions.

We also do not know the extent to which the structure of the environment should impose on the student's learning. What skills are better learned with more structured rather than less structured environments? Which domains? In what situations, if any, can and should meta-skills be taught?

In the final analysis, the largest contribution of research into intelligent instructional environments may arise from redefining what skills we teach. Recent research (Orr, 1986) watching technicians at work indicates that an important part of building individual and community knowledge among copier repair technicians involves structured narratives about the machine's operation. Basically, what technicians do to organize and communicate their understanding of machines is to tell stories. Yet nowhere in any curriculum is the student taught about stories, how to tell them, or how to understand them. Similarly, collaboration, working productively together with others, is an important part of many tasks but not included in most curricula. Research in instructional environments needs to include ways of representing and teaching not only the intellectual skills but also the social skills students will need on the job.

REFERENCES

Abelson, A., & diSessa, A. A. (1980). *Turtle geometry*. Cambridge, MA: MIT Press.

Anderson, J. R. (1981). Tuning of search of the problem space for geometry proofs. In A. Drinan (Ed.), *Proceedings of the International Joint Conference on Artificial Intelligence-81* (Vol. 1, pp. 165-170). Los Altos, CA: Morgan Kaufmann.

Anderson, J. R., Boyle, C. F., Corbett, A., & Lewis, M. (1986). *Cognitive modeling and intelligent tutoring* (CMU Tech. Rep.). Pittsburgh, PA: Carnegie-Mellon University, Psychology Department.

Anderson, J. R., Boyle, C. F., & Yost, G. (1985). The geometry tutor. In A. Joshi (Ed.), *Proceedings of the Ninth International Joint Conference on Artificial Intelligence* (pp. 1-7). Los Altos, CA: Morgan Kaufmann.

Anderson, J. R., & Skwarecki, E. (1986). The automated tutoring of introductory computer programming. *Communications of the ACM, 29,* 842-849.

Bonar, J. (1985, June). Bite-sized intelligent tutoring: *Newsletter 85-3,* 1-11. Pittsburgh, PA. University of Pittsburgh, Learning Research and Development Center, Intelligent Tutoring Systems Group.

Bonar, J., Cunningham, R., & Schultz, J. (1986). An object-oriented architecture for intelligent tutoring systems. In N. Meyrowitz (Ed.), *Proceedings of the First Conference on Object Oriented Programming, Systems, Languages and Applications* (pp. 269-276). New York: ACM.

Brown, A. L., & Palincsar, A. S. (in press). Reciprocal teaching of comprehension strategies: A natural history of one program for enhancing learning. In J. B. Borkowski & J. D. Day (Eds.), *Intelligence and cognition in special children: Comparative studies of giftedness, mental retardation, and learning disabilities.* Norwood, NJ: Ablex.

Brown, J. S. (1983). Learning by doing revisited for electronic learning environments. In M. A. White (Ed.), *The future of electronic learning* (pp. 13-32). Hillsdale, NJ: Lawrence Erlbaum Associates.

Brown, J. S. (1985). Idea amplifiers: New kinds of electronic learning environments. *Educational Horizons, 63,* 108-112.

Brown, J. S., & Burton, R. R. (1975). Multiple representations of knowledge for tutorial reasoning. In D. G. Bobrow & A. Collins (Eds.), *Representation and understanding* (pp. 311-349). New York: Academic Press.

Brown, J. S., & Burton, R. R. (1978). Diagnostic models for procedural bugs in basic mathematical skills. *Cognitive Science, 2,* 155-192.

Brown, J. S., & Burton, R. R. (1987). Reactive learning environments for teaching electronic troubleshooting. In W. B. Rouse (Ed.), *Advances in man-machine systems research (Vol. 3)*. Greenwich, CT: JAI Press.

Brown, J. S., Burton, R. R., & deKleer, J. (1982). Pedagogical, natural language and knowledge engineering techniques in SOPHIE I, II and III. In D. Sleeman & J. S. Brown (Eds.), *Intelligent tutoring systems* (pp. 227-282). London: Academic Press.

Brown, J. S., Moran, T. P., & Williams, M. D. (1982). *The semantics of procedures: A cognitive basis for training procedural skills for complex system maintenance* (CIS working paper). Palo Alto, CA: Xerox Palo Alto Research Center, Intelligent Systems Laboratory.

Burton, R. R., & Brown, J. S. (1982). An investigation of computer coaching for informal learning activities. In D. Sleeman & J. S. Brown (Eds.), *Intelligent tutoring systems* (pp. 79-98). London: Academic Press.

Burton, R. R., Brown, J. S., & Fischer, G. (1984). Skiing as a model of instruction. In B. Rogoff & J. Lave (Eds.), *Everyday cognition: Its development in social context* (pp. 139-150). Cambridge, MA: Harvard University Press.

Chi, M. T. H., Feltovich, P. J., & Glaser, R. (1981). Categorization and representation of physics problems by experts and novices. *Cognitive Science, 5*, 121-152.

Clancey, W. J. (1982). Tutoring rules for guiding a case method dialogue. In D. Sleeman & J. S. Brown (Eds.), *Intelligent tutoring systems* (pp. 201-226). London: Academic Press.

Clancey, W. J. (1986). From GUIDON to NEOMYCIN and HERACLES in twenty short lessons: ONR final report 1979-1985. *AI Magazine, 7*, 40-60.

Clement, J. (1983). A conceptual model discussed by Galileo and used intuitively by physics students. In D. Gentner & A. L. Stevens (Eds.), *Mental models* (pp. 325-340). Hillsdale, NJ: Lawrence Erlbaum Associates.

Collins, A., Brown, J. S., & Newman, S. E. (in press). The new apprenticeship: Teaching students the craft of reading, writing, and mathematics. In L. B. Resnick (Ed.), *Cognition and instruction: Issues and agendas*. Hillsdale, NJ: Lawerence Erlbaum Associates.

Copeland, W. D. (1984). Creating a historian's microworld. *Classroom Computer Learning, 5*, 48-53.

diSessa, A. (1982). Unlearning Aristotelian physics: A study of knowledge-based learning. *Cognitive Science, 6*, 37-75.

diSessa, A. (1983). Phenomenology and the evolution of intuition. In D. Gentner & A. L. Stevens (Eds.), *Mental models* (pp. 15-34). Hillsdale, NJ: Lawrence Erlbaum Associates.

Erlwanger, S. H. (1973). Benny's conception of rules and answers in IPI mathematics. *Journal of Children's Mathematical Behavior, 1*, 7-26.

Fischer, G. (in press). Enhancing incremental learning processes with knowledge-based systems. In H. Mandl & A. Lesgold (Eds.), *Learning issues for intelligent tutoring systems*. New York: Springer Verlag.

Fischer, G., Brown, J. S., & Burton, R. (1978). Aspects of a theory of simplification: Debugging and coaching. *Proceedings of the Second National Conference of Canadian Society for Studies of Intelligence* (pp. 139-145).

Foss, C. L. (1987). *Learning from errors in AlbegraLand* (IRL Tech. Rep. 3). Palo Alto, CA: Xerox Palo Alto Research Center, Institute for Research on Learning.

Geneserreth, M. (1982). The role of plans in intelligent teaching systems. In D. Sleeman & J. S. Brown (Eds.), *Intelligent tutoring systems* (pp. 137-156). London: Academic Press.

Goldstein, I. P. (1982). The genetic graph: A representation for the evolution of procedural knowledge. In D. Sleeman & J. S. Brown (Eds.), *Intelligent tutoring systems* (pp. 51–78). London: Academic Press.

Haertel, H. (1987). *A qualitative approach to electricity* (IRL Tech. Rep.). Palo Alto, CA: Xerox Palo Alto Research Center, Institute for Research on Learning.

Hollan, J. D., Hutchins, E. L., McCandless, T. P., Rosenstein, M., & Weitzman, L. (in press). Graphical interfaces for simulation. In W. B. Rouse (Ed.), *Advances in man-machine systems research* (Vol. 3). Greenwich, CT: JAI Press.

Hollan, J. D., Hutchins, E. L., & Weitzman, L. (1984). Steamer: An interactive inspectable simulation-based training system. *AI Magazine, 5*, 15–28.

Hutchins, E. L., Hollan, J. D., & Norman, D. A. (1985). Direct manipulation interfaces. *Human-Computer Interaction, 1*, 311–338. Hillsdale, NJ: Lawrence Erlbaum Associates.

Hutchins, E., & McCandless, T. P. (1982). *MANBOARD: A graphic display program for training relative motion concepts* (NPRDC Tech. Note 82-10). San Diego: Navy Personnel Research and Development Center.

Johnson, W. B. (1987). Development and evaluation of simulation-oriented computer-based instruction for diagnostic training. In W. B. Rouse (Ed.), *Advances in man-machine systems research (Vol. 3)*. Greenwich, CT: JAI Press.

Johnson, W. B., Maddox, M. E., Rouse, W. B., & Kiel, G. C. (1985). *Diagnostic training for nuclear plant personnel: Volume I. Courseware development* (EPRI NP-3829). Palo Alto, CA: Electric Power Research Institute.

Larkin, J. H. (1983). The role of problem representation in physics. In D. Gentner & A. L. Stevens (Eds.), *Mental models* (pp. 75–98). Hillsdale, NJ: Lawrence Erlbaum Associates.

Nickerson, R. (1986). *Technology in education in 2020: Thinking about the not-distant future.* Background paper for Harvard Center for School Technology Conference. Cambridge, MA: Bolt, Beranek, and Newman, Inc.

Orr, J. E. (1986). Narratives at work: Story telling as cooperative diagnostic activity. *Proceedings of the Conference on Computer-Supported Cooperative Work* (pp. 62–72).

O'Shea, T., Bornat, R., Du Boulay, B., Eisenstadt, M., & Page, I. (1983). Tools for designing intelligent computer tutors. In A. Elithorn & R. Banerjii (Eds.), *Human and artificial intelligence* (pp. 181–199). London: North-Holland.

Papert, S. (1980). *Mindstorms.* New York: Basic Books.

Papert, S. (1986, May 2). *Rethinking mathematics learnability in a computer culture.* The Karl de Leeuw Memorial Lecture. Stanford, CA: Stanford University.

Richer, M., & Clancey, W. J. (1985). GUIDON-WATCH: A graphical interface for viewing a knowledge-based system. *IEEE Computer Graphics and Applications, 11*, 51–64.

Roschelle, J. (1986). *The envisioning machine: Facilitating students' re-conceptualization of physics* (ISL working paper). Palo Alto, CA: Xerox Palo Alto Research Center, Intelligent Systems Laboratory.

Rouse, W. B. (1979). Problem solving performance of maintenance trainees in a fault diagnosis task. *Human Factors, 21*, 195–203.

Rouse, W. B., & Hunt, R. M. (1984). Human problem solving in fault diagnosis tasks. In W. B. Rouse (Ed.), *Advances in man-machine systems research* (Vol. 1). Greenwich, CT: JAI Press.

Russell, D. M., Moran, T. P., & Jordan, D. S. (in press). Instructional design environment. In J. Psotka, L. D. Massey, & S. A. Mutter (Eds.), *Intelligent tutoring systems: Lessons learned.* Hillsdale, NJ: Lawrence Erlbaum Associates.

Scardamalia, M., Bereiter, C., & Steinbach, R. (1984). Teachability of reflective processes in written composition. *Cognitive Science, 8,* 173–190.

Schoenfeld, A. H. (1985). *Mathematical problem solving.* New York: Academic Press.

Schwartz, J. L., & Yerushalmy, M. (in press). The geometry supposer: Using microcomputers to restore invention to the learning of mathematics. In D. N. Perkins, J. Lochhead, & J. Butler (Eds.), *Thinking: The second international conference.* Hillsdale, NJ: Lawrence Erlbaum Associates.

Sheil, B. (1983a). The artificial intelligence tool box. In W. Reitman (Ed.), *Proceeding of the NYE Symposium on Artificial Intelligence and Business* (pp. 287–295). Norwood, NJ: Ablex.

Sheil, B. (1983b). Power tools for programmers. *Datamation, 29,* 131–144.

Smith, R. B. (1986). The alternate reality kit: An animated environment for creating interactive simulations. *Proceedings of the IEEE Computer Society Workshop on Visual Languages* (pp. 99–106). Washington, DC: IEEE Computer Society Press.

Stansfield, J., Carr, B., & Goldstein, I. P. (1976). *Wumpus Advisor I: A first implementation of a program that tutors logical and probabilistic reasoning skills* (MIT AI Laboratory Memo No. 381). Cambridge, MA: Massachusetts Institute of Technology.

Towne, D. M. (in press). The generalized maintenance trainer: Evolution and revolution. In W. B. Rouse (Ed.), *Advances in man-machine systems research* (Vol. 3). Greenwich, CT: JAI Press.

VanLehn, K., & Brown, J. S. (1980). Planning nets: A representation for formalizing analogies and semantic models for procedural skills. In R. W. Snow, P. A. Fredico, & W. E. Montague (Eds.), *Aptitude learning and instruction: Vol. 2. Cognitive process analyses of learning and problem-solving* (pp. 95–137). Hillsdale, NJ: Lawrence Erlbaum Associates.

Weinreb, D., & Moon, D. (1981). *Lisp Machine manual.* Cambridge, MA: MIT Artificial Intelligence Laboratory.

Wenger, E. (1987). *Artificial intelligence and tutoring systems: Computational approaches to the communication of knowledge.* Los Altos, CA: Morgan Kaufmann.

White, B. Y., & Frederiksen, J. R. (1986a). Intelligent tutoring systems based upon qualitative model evolutions. *Proceeding of AAAI-86* (pp. 313–319). Los Altos, CA: Morgan Kaufmann.

White, B. Y., & Frederiksen, J. R. (1986b). *Progressions of qualitative models as foundations for intelligent learning environments* (BBN Report 6277). Cambridge, MA: Bolt, Beranek and Newman, Inc.

Wilensky, R., Arens, Y., & Chin, D. (1984). Talking to UNIX in English: An overview of UC. *Communications of the ACM, 27,* 574–593.

Wiser, M., & Carey, S. (1983). When heat and temperature were one. In D. Gentner & A. L. Stevens (Eds.), *Mental models* (pp. 267–298). Hillsdale, NJ: Lawrence Erlbaum Associates.

Xerox Special Information Systems. (1985). *Notecards release 1.2i reference manual.* Pasadena, CA: Author.

The Role of
Human–Computer Interaction
in Intelligent Tutoring Systems

James R. Miller
Microelectronics and Computer Technology Corporation

INTRODUCTION

The study of human–computer interaction is especially germane to research on intelligent tutoring systems (ITSs). The interaction between students and ITSs is inherently complex because the users of these systems are by definition working with concepts they do not understand well. If the interface to the ITS is confusing or poorly designed, the effectiveness of the entire instructional session will suffer. Conversely, a well-designed interface can enhance the capabilities of an ITS in many ways. Being able to specify the interface to an ITS means that the designer has considerable power over the way in which the student will conceptualize the problem domain, and over the vocabulary the student will use to talk about the domain. This is, of course, a two-edged sword—it means that for an ITS to be effective, the designer must be aware of the ITSs interface and must treat its design as a fundamental part of the design of the system.

Human interface techniques affect two aspects of ITSs. First, they determine how students interact with the ITS. A well-designed human interface allows the ITS to present instruction and feedback to students in a clear and direct way. Similarly, it can provide students with a set of expressive techniques for stating problems and hypotheses to the ITS. Second, they determine how students interact with the domain. Many ITSs allow students to work in the domain that is being tutored, through either a simulation of the domain or direct connection to the domain itself. This interaction is generally tied closely to the tutorial component of the system so that actions in the domain are analyzed and acted upon (e.g., Brown, Burton, & deKleer, 1982; Hollan, Hutchins, & Weitzman, 1984; Reiser, Anderson, & Farrell, 1985). For example, students might write computer programs, solve geometry problems, work with computer systems, or repair simulated electronic or mechanical devices, with an ITS monitoring the students' use of the system. A good interface should ease this interaction: It should be easy to carry out actions in the domain and to see and understand the results and implications of those actions. There are, of course, different ways in which a domain can be characterized by an interface, and, as we noted earlier, this is where the real power of a well-designed tutorial interface lies: in defining the way that students think about the concepts in which they are being tutored.

It is easy to talk about what constitutes a good human–computer interface but much harder to build one. The key lies in how we think about human–computer interaction, because this conceptualization will affect how we go about making it good. In fact, *interaction* is perhaps a poor term to use for this process because it connotes a rather mechanical exchange of actions. *Communication* is better; it emphasizes the exchange not of actions but of concepts. By thinking in terms of communication, an inherently semantic process, it becomes evident that interfaces should reflect the semantic nature of this interaction. Good interfaces embody an understanding of and appreciation for the goals and concepts that are important to users and to the domain being tutored; bad ones do not. As a result, it is very difficult to talk about a good or a bad interface without considering the users' cognitive capabilities and limitations, and the domain to which the interface serves as a portal. An important part of this discussion is thus to describe how a user's interaction with an ITS is affected by these essential yet external parts of the overall human–computer communication problem. Many of the examples in this paper are of interfaces that address issues other than ITSs. However, the important issue is not the application area of the interface but the definition of the ways in which good interfaces can support people as they gradually acquire an understanding of a complex semantic domain. This support task is the whole purpose of ITSs, and, as will be shown, it is also central to the more general questions underlying human interface research.

HUMAN–COMPUTER INTERACTION: THE STATE OF THE ART

The importance of the application domain and of user's past experiences for the quality of interfaces means that the critical problems in interface construction lie in the design of these systems. The following three questions raise other important points about interface design, and particularly about the suitability of an interface for a particular task and user community.

What Conceptual Model is Offered of the Underlying System?

All users come to an interface with knowledge that can guide their use of that interface: knowledge about their past use of computer systems, about the kinds of real-world objects that might be manipulated by the application program, and about the kinds of real-world objects that might be portrayed and manipulated as part of the interface. It is clear that this knowledge plays an important role in human–computer interaction and that people combine this knowledge with their observation of the structure and behavior of the interface to construct a conceptual model of the system (Gentner & Stevens, 1983). The value of conceptual models is that they can be used to guide users' interactions with systems: They allow users to make reasonable guesses about likely ways to handle novel problems, about probable reasons for errors, and about good ways to recover from errors.

A good conceptual model of an interface has several characteristics. First, it should offer the user *clarity.* The important concepts, distinctions, and relations in the domain that are under the control of the interface should be clearly and accurately captured by the model. Second, it should offer the user a high degree of *coverage:* It should explain as many aspects of the interface and domain as possible. Third, it should offer a *sound level of abstraction of the system.* The model should be specific enough to allow the user to make strong, correct inferences about the interface and the domain but general enough that the user can accept—or even look for—differences between a literal interpretation of the model and the application domain.

These properties can interact. Simple models can be powerful and clear, but their coverage can be limited and may characterize the domain at an inappropriate level of abstraction. Users who take too literally the analogy that "a word processor is like a typewriter" have no reason to think that such a system would let them cut and paste text, search for and replace strings, or justify paragraphs, and they may never think to search the system for evidence of these capabilities (cf. Douglas & Moran, 1983; Halasz & Moran, 1983; Lewis & Mack, 1981).

Constructing a good conceptual model for a system is not easy but is very important. If a good model is not provided for the users, they are almost certain to build their own, and it will almost certainly be flawed. Unfortunately, picking and building a good conceptual model for a particular domain is difficult. Most domains can be described by alternate models (e.g., the "flowing water" vs. "teeming crowds" models of electricity, Gentner & Gentner, 1983), and these different models can lead users to make very different kinds of predictions about the domain. Insuring the quality of the conceptual model around which an interface is built is an important part of the design of that interface, and good tools to support the incremental development and evaluation of model-based interfaces are badly needed.

How Does the Interface Handle
the External-Internal Task-Mapping Problem?

Users come to a computer system with a set of task-level goals that they want to achieve, such as to "archive all the Scribe manuscript files I created last month." Unfortunately, there is a considerable distance between this goal statement and the actions that most interfaces make available to users. Spanning this gap—solving the *external-internal task-mapping problem* (Moran, 1983)—poses a major design problem for interface construction and a major interaction problem for users. The greater the gap, the more difficult the interface will be to use.

This gap can be minimized by building the interface so that the actions supported by the interface map directly to corresponding actions in the domain. In principle, if users understand the domain, the use of the interface is trivial. There are problems here, though. The resulting interface may be good for its intended domain but useless for others. Other interfaces must be constructed separately for these domains, at the cost of considerable time and money. If the interface is too specialized, users cannot do anything other than what the interface designer thought of during the design process. Finally, the conceptual models that underlie specialized interfaces are critical to their success, which means that the difficulties in identifying appropriate models are especially critical.

Despite these problems, the trend toward building high-level, specialized interfaces for specific domains is becoming predominant. The task-mapping problem is too great to ignore, and the increasing availability of graphic interfaces and powerful tools for interface development is reducing the effort required to implement a well-designed, specialized interface. Simultaneously, the conceptual model problem is diminishing as more knowledge about these models accumulates and as interface development tools allow alternative models to be implemented and experimented with.

What Is the General Style of the Interface?

Laurel's (1986) analysis of interfaces is a good place to start in search of a way to classify systems on the basis of their overall structure and orientation to the user. This analysis divides interfaces into two groups, based on the perceived relationship between the user and the domain addressed by the computer system. In one group, the interface allows users to become direct participants in the domain. In the other, users control the domain by instructing an intermediary to carry out actions in the domain.

First-Person Interfaces

In *first-person* or *direct manipulation* interfaces, the user has a feeling of working directly with the domain. These interfaces almost always make strong use of graphics, allowing users to carry out desired computations by manipulating graphic objects. These interfaces are designed so that the actions and objects relevant to the task and domain at hand map directly to actions and objects in the interface. In this way, designers of first-person interfaces hope to avoid the task-mapping problem altogether, or at least to minimize it.

First-person interface techniques came to prominence in the iconic interfaces of the Xerox Star and the Apple Macintosh. The basic hardware configuration of these systems has not changed very much from the days of the Xerox Alto (Thacker, McCreight, Lampson, Sproull, & Boggs, 1979), the forerunner of this technology. A single-user workstation drives a large bit-mapped display of about 1,000 by 1,000 points and includes some sort of pointing device with which users can refer directly to objects drawn from collections of these points. The mouse has become the pointing device most commonly used with these systems, although joysticks and trackballs have been tried in other systems and applications, with varying degrees of success.

In these systems, small pictures, or *icons,* represent programs and data files on the screen (Figure 6.1). These icons can be selected and activated with the system's mouse, which starts the execution of the desired program (Smith, Irby, Kimball, Verplank, & Harslem, 1982). Notice that the user need not remember the name of the document

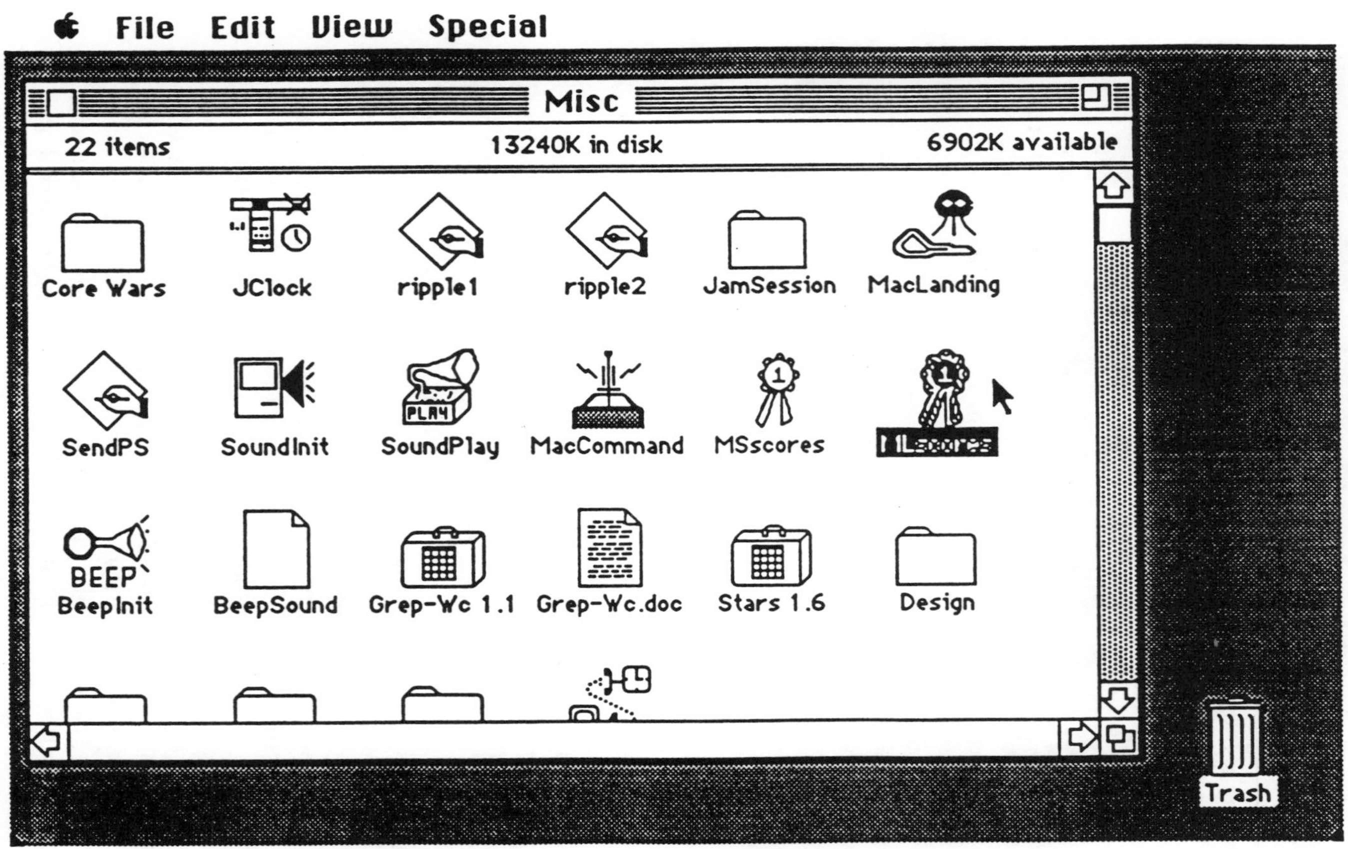

🍎 File Edit View Special

FIGURE 6.1 A typical use of windows and icons on the Apple Macintosh.

to be accessed—it is present on the screen as part of the icon. Further, links are generally established between text files (document icons) and the programs that created them (program icons). Users need not remember what program is used to edit a document or how to access that editor—this information is an intrinsic part of the data structures underlying the icon and is accessed automatically by the system.

Steamer (Hollan, Hutchins, & Weitzman, 1984) is a training system that emphasizes first-person interface techniques. Steamer's graphic display allows students to view a simulation model of a naval steam power plant in ways that emphasize different structural relations among the components of the steam plant. Steam and water tanks are shown interconnected by pipes, with different kinds of gauges and valves displaying and offering control over certain aspects of the plant (Figure 6.2). Many of these devices can be directly manipulated by the student; valves can be closed by clicking the system's mouse on them rather than by issuing a command like CLOSE VALVE-17X. Similarly, when gauges display values associated with parts of the system under the student's control, such as the temperature of a boiler, the student can reset the value by clicking the mouse on the needle of the gauge, and moving the needle to the desired value. The corresponding variable in the simulation model is then given that value, and the model is updated to reflect the modification.

Other projects have used first-person techniques to facilitate procedural tasks such as data manipulation. Miller and Blumenthal (1985; Figure 6.3) and Hutchins, Hollan, and Norman (1986) have independently pursued this problem, with rather similar results: Icons represent data structures and procedures, and links between these objects specify how the procedures are to be applied to the data structures. The overall intent is the same as in Steamer: to use graphic techniques to concretize data and procedures, and to make the procedural relations between data and procedures explicit.

The graphical properties of icons have evoked responses ranging from excitement to antagonism. Some people find the depiction of a document as a little piece of paper to be a convenient memory aid; others find it insulting. However, the graphical representation of icons is ultimately beside the point. What is valuable about iconic systems is the directness of the user's interaction with the system. The objects available to the user are visible on the screen, and when users interact with these objects, they receive immediate feedback about their actions. When a Macintosh icon is clicked upon, it expands into a window containing the appropriate application program; when an icon is deleted, by picking up the icon with the mouse and moving it to the system's "garbage can" icon (see Figure 6.1), it immediately disappears from the screen. It is this immediacy, and the visibility

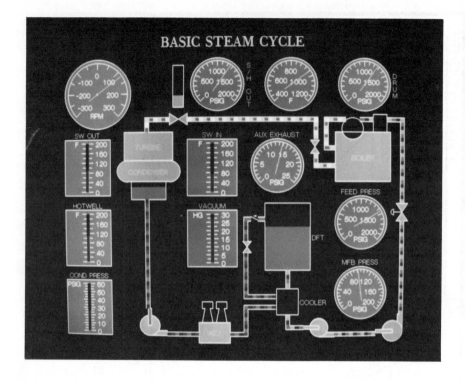

FIGURE 6.2 Steamer's depiction of a steam plant. *Note.* From "Steamer: An Interactive Inspectable Simulation-Based Training System" by J. D. Hollan, E. L. Hutchins, & L. Weitzman, 1984, *AI Magazine, 5,* pp. 15–28. Copyright 1984 by the American Association for Artificial Intelligence. Reprinted by permission.

of the user's actions and the results of these actions that are important, not the details of the graphic presentation.

Although the properties of first-person interfaces appear to offer significant advantages to users, they are not well understood. The systems that exist today have generally been handcrafted through long periods of incremental design and evaluation; it is hard to say in any objective way what types of system functionality can reasonably be offered through direct manipulation techniques. Many of these questions follow from the extensibility issue raised in the discussion of conceptual models. For instance, in the gauge example from Steamer, how would inexperienced users know that clicking the mouse on the needle of the gauge allows them to change the rate of flow of the water? Real gauges certainly don't behave in this way! A tutorial system might explain the different capabilities of the system to the user, but

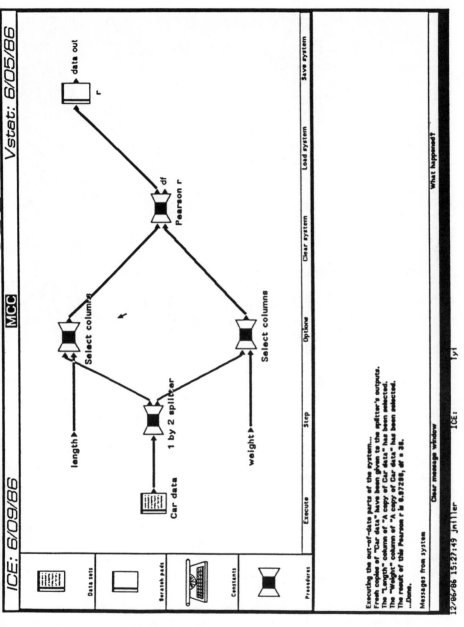

FIGURE 6.3 Computing a Pearson *r* with VSTAT.

the whole point of first-person systems is that they are meant to be self-evident—such a detailed explanation of their use should be unnecessary.

An additional problem is that of conveying through the model enough of the underlying application that users can understand which parts of the system they can directly manipulate. In the Steamer example, the gauge attached to the boiler is a means of controlling the temperature of the boiler, and so can be manipulated by the user. Another gauge might indicate the pressure of the water leaving the boiler, and so would not be manipulable. Understanding which gauges can be manipulated and which cannot is the same problem as was seen before: the link between the semantics of the domain and the semantics of the interface. Direct manipulation techniques are a particularly promising way to approach this problem, but they do not solve it.

Second-Person Interfaces

In *second-person interfaces,* users interact with the domain by giving commands to a computerized intermediary, which then carries out the desired actions. Textual interfaces and some graphical interfaces fall into this category.

Command languages.   These are the keyword-oriented interfaces that were originally developed on and for the teletype-based computer systems of the past. A command consists of a string of words and sometimes special characters that, when processed by the system's command interpreter, specify the action the user wants to carry out. This command typically states the name of an application program that will carry out the user's request, followed by a list of optional arguments that specify either data files on which the application program should operate or modifications to the default operation of the program. The feedback to the command varies, depending on the program that is run as a result of executing the command.

Few ITSs have used command languages. Either the domain of the ITS and the student's options in the domain have been so restricted that menu selection or other highly restricted interaction techniques have been appropriate, or they have used a restricted form of natural language. Both alternatives are discussed later in this chapter. In general, command languages are relevant to this discussion because they may serve as the interface to an application program for which an ITS is being constructed.

The advantages and flaws of command languages are by now

well known. For experts who know the numerous functions that can be accessed by the commands, a command language can be a very efficient way of interacting with a system. However, the number of commands needed to cover the range of functions available on complex systems is large, and mastering this set is an imposing task even for system experts. Further, the names for these commands are rarely derived from a coherent set of rules and are consequently hard to remember or predict (Norman, 1981). The number of commands can sometimes be reduced by collapsing several commands into one, with a set of options that can request the finer-grained behavior. However, this solution merely shifts the user's problem from remembering the name of a specific command to remembering (or deducing) the appropriate set of options that must be specified as part of the more general command.

Countless versions of command languages have been developed, both as interfaces to general operating systems and as more specialized application programs. Some are better than others. However, they have flourished not because they have been good interfaces but, rather, because they have been easy to implement, could be run on many different computers and terminals, and for a long time were the only kind of interface that could be supported by the available hardware.

It is hard to justify more research on the properties of command languages. This does not mean that command languages are inherently bad or that designing a good command language for a specific task is trivial. Quite the opposite: For some applications and users, a command language is a very efficient means of interaction, and the task of designing a command language that provides an adequate interface to a given task can be difficult. But it is not worthwhile to study the fundamental characteristics of command languages themselves, such as alternative syntaxes for specifying command arguments, or good techniques for abbreviating terms describing system functionality. The practical problems that arise from the use of command languages today are not whether one method of specifying arguments is better than another but how to design a particularly good command language for a given task and user population. These task and user constraints are independent of the command languages themselves, and more abstract work on command languages will offer no insights into these issues. It is time for research to move on to problems with higher payoffs.

Menus. Menus first came about as a feature of teletype systems, in which a list of options was shown to the user, who selected the desired option by striking a specific key. This technique was never really satisfactory. Finding a reasonable one-to-one mapping between a set of menu items and alphanumeric characters was generally difficult, and the speed with which the options could be presented was limited. However, the advent of personal computers and bitmapped graphics revived the use of menus. Display speed was no longer an issue because an entire menu could be displayed in a fraction of a second. Because the strings representing the individual items could be arbitrarily long phrases, the clarity and thereby the meaningfulness of the terms used in menus were increased substantially. Further, because an item could be selected by pointing at a string instead of pressing a key, the need for a one-to-one mapping between menu items and keyboard characters disappeared. These types of menus have been frequently incorporated in workstation-based ITSs, such as in Steamer (Hollan, Hutchins, & Weitzman, 1984) and the presentation of proof techniques in the Geometry Tutor (Anderson, Boyle, & Yost, 1985).

Like command languages, menu-based systems have rather well defined advantages and disadvantages. Menus can offer novices a reasonable interface to a system because they have simply to recognize the desired action from its description in the menu rather than to recall the name of the command they need from memory (Shneiderman, 1986). In a sense, menu systems are a middle ground between first- and second-person interfaces: Being presented with information and subsequently selecting some of that information is characteristic of second-person interfaces, but the direct way in which the user can specify the information is more like a first-person interface.

On the negative side, interacting with a menu system can be tedious. Even a simple interaction can require selecting items from several menus. This can be tedious, especially for experts, who generally prefer a more terse form of interaction that takes advantage of—in fact, relies on—their greater knowledge of the system (Savage, Habinek, & Barnhart, 1981). In addition, menus can pose special problems for tutorial systems, inasmuch as allowing students to recognize the solution to a problem instead of requiring them to generate it can defeat the whole purpose of the tutor.

Just as was true with command languages, it is hard to see any large payoff coming from continued research on the basic properties of menu systems, such as the optimal arrangement and number of items in a menu or the colors the menu items should be displayed in. Visually acceptable menu systems can be built with tools available today; the real question is how to tailor a particular menu system to a specific task and user population. Abstract research on menus themselves will not address this question. As before, it is time for the research community to move on.

Natural language interfaces. The image of an interface as a "second person" agent working for the user is perhaps most clearly captured by a natural language interface. Here, so it seems, users can communicate in a language they already know with an agent that will interpret their requests and instruct an application program to carry them out. SCHOLAR (Carbonell & Collins, 1973), WHY (Stevens & Collins, 1977), GUIDON (Clancey, 1982), and SOPHIE (Brown, Burton, & deKleer, 1982) all rely on some form of natural language, and much of their power comes from the naturalness of this style of interaction. However, it is important to be aware of the difference between the kind of natural language interaction we would like to have and the kind of interaction that is possible.

The most significant problem with natural language interfaces is that there are large differences between the kinds of languages that people use—and want to use when talking to computers—and the kinds of languages that current natural language systems can understand. This problem can best be described in terms of the *coverage* a given natural language system provides for certain language phenomena:

- **Lexical and syntactic coverage:** the ability to handle the basic word tokens and sentence structures that are entered by users.
- **Semantic coverage:** the ability of the "front-end" natural language system to map parsed words and phrases into meaningful concepts in the world of the "back-end" application program. For instance, a natural language front end to a company's employee data base would have to understand that a query about "salary" refers to the EMP-SALRY column of the EMPLOYEE table in the data base.
- **Dialogue coverage:** the ability to handle intra- and intersentential references, such as pronouns, ellipses, and anaphora.
- **Action coverage:** the ability to translate the user's statement into an action or set of actions that will carry out the desired operations in the application program to which the natural language system is serving as an interface.

Providing adequate coverage of these phenomena is very difficult, primarily because natural language interfaces so strongly embody the second-person view of interfaces. Because the style of interaction is very much that of speaking to an assistant who will carry out the requested actions, users tend to treat a natural language system as if it had not only a human's understanding of language but all the human's world knowledge and problem-solving capabilities as well.

This has unfortunate implications for natural language systems. Users are likely to adopt a vocabulary that exceeds the lexicon of the natural language system and may make use of obscure or ungrammatical sentence constructs that exceed the capabilities of the natural language system's parser. They will often make considerable use of discourse phenomena such as ellipsis and anaphora, which are very hard for natural language systems to handle. They may also ask the system about things it has no knowledge of, or ask the system to do things either that cannot be done by the application program or that are logically possible but require vast planning capabilities to determine the series of actions required to carry out those actions in the application program.

These shortcomings are unavoidable in an interface that places no constraints on how the user may interact with it. They arise because without training or experience, users have no way of knowing what words and sentences the system can understand, what kinds of things the system might know about, or what actions the application program can carry out. There are two primary ways of addressing this problem, and research on both of them is needed.

The first approach is to improve natural language technology so that natural language interfaces can handle the kinds of language people want to use. This is a difficult and long-term task. However, for short-term projects, this difficulty is lessened somewhat by the inherent constraints of the application program that a given natural language interface serves. Natural language interfaces do not have to know every word in the language, just the words that are relevant to the task served by the interface. If a user refers to an unknown word, it may be possible to allow the user to add the missing word to the system's lexicon by defining it in terms of words the system already understands (Ballard & Stumberger, 1986). This may be especially feasible in the technical areas served by most natural language systems, where a well-defined, highly interrelated set of terms often exists. The limitations to understanding ungrammatical language can be addressed by natural language techniques that pay special attention to ungrammaticality (Carbonell & Hayes, 1983) or that are designed to be less sensitive to these problems (Granger, 1983). Handling complex requests that result in sequences of application program actions will require planning facilities, so research in natural language must also be aware of ongoing work in planning (Allen & Perrault, 1980; Littman, 1986).

Many of the usability problems with natural language systems became evident when these systems were applied to real-world problems such as tutoring (Brown, Burton, & deKleer, 1982) and data-base retrieval (Tennant, 1979). These practical attempts to use natural language have led to the second approach to this problem, which is to acknowledge that all natural language systems are designed to handle only a very specific subset of the user's language. Furthermore, people will not be able to use a system that implements such a sublanguage unless they are aware of the boundaries of that language. Acknowledging this problem leads to a rather different research agenda than that derived from the technological approach. The important issues in this second, user-oriented approach are finding ways of defining a sublanguage so that the boundaries are as obvious as possible, identifying interface techniques that make the boundaries of the sublanguage evident, and developing ways of allowing users to investigate the boundaries and capabilities of the natural language interface and the application system.

The NLMenu system, marketed for personal computers by Texas Instruments, Inc., as *NaturalLink,* is an example of this pragmatic approach. It presents users with means that control and are controlled by a natural language system running beneath the menu interface (Tennant, Ross, Saenz, Thompson, & Miller, 1983). A user constructs a query in natural language by repeatedly selecting items from these menus. After each selection, the system updates the list of menus from which items can be selected and the contents of the menus themselves so that only permissible continuations of the query are possible. As shown in Figure 6.4, users are permitted to select items only from the windows with the light background. The items in those menus correspond to legal continuations of the query in progress. As a result, any query constructed with the system is guaranteed to be interpretable. This kind of interface is not appropriate for all areas where natural language might be considered. However, for those areas in which it is appropriate, its constraints offer significant advantages in understandability and ease of use.

The second problem with natural language interfaces is the amount of work required to implement one. Two basic approaches can be taken to this problem. One approach is to capitalize on the constraints in the domain addressed by the application program and to build the system in such a way that it relies upon these constraints. This "semantic grammar" approach (Brown, Burton, & deKleer, 1982; Hendrix, 1979) can produce a natural language system relatively quickly. Additionally, the techniques used to build such systems typically place more emphasis on the concepts underlying the domain than on syntactic issues. Consequently, these systems can handle a greater variety of sentence forms than can syntactic natural language systems, and are typically less sensitive to ungrammaticality. The disadvantage of this approach is that the resulting system is so closely tied to the targeted domain that very little of it can be reused when building a natural language system for a new domain.

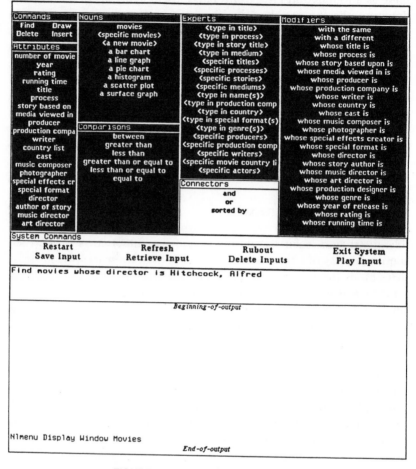

FIGURE 6.4 A typical NLMenu screen.

The second approach to implementation is to base the system in linguistics theory and to implement components to handle the lexicon, syntax, semantics, and pragmatics of the chosen language. This work requires more effort than the semantic grammar approach, but it can result in a system that is largely domain-independent. For example, although different domains have specialized lexicons, these can be viewed as extensions of a large, basic lexicon that is shared by all domains. Similarly, the syntax of language varies little, if at all, across different problem domains. As a result, the formal linguistic approach offers the hope of producing not only a natural language system that is as flexible as the domain-bound systems previously described, but also a set of tools and knowledge structures that can serve as a foundation for natural language systems for many different domains, thereby greatly reducing the effort required to implement a new system. To be fair, it should be noted that techniques for designing and implementing these systems so that their portability is maintained is still a research issue (cf. Ballard & Stumberger, 1986; Hendrix & Lewis, 1981; Grosz, Appelt, Martin, & Pereira, 1987). However, such portability is an inherent part of their design, which is not the case for the domain-specific systems. Middle-ground systems, such as IRUS (Bates & Bobrow, 1983) that employ both semantic grammar and formal linguistic approaches are also being studied.

Tradeoffs Between First- and Second-Person Interfaces

The discussion so far should not be taken as an attempt to establish the superiority of either first- or second-person interfaces. What really determines the utility of a particular interface technique is the task for which it is being used, and this interaction between the task and the interface can shift the scales from first-person to second-person very capriciously. For instance, the direct manipulation techniques of the Macintosh make moving files from one disk directory to another very easy. All a user must do is select the file by clicking on its icon with the mouse, move the icon into the desired destination "folder" (an iconic representation of a disk directory), and release the mouse button, "dropping" the file icon into its new directory. This is much easier than the corresponding operation in a Unix system, which requires learning the name and syntax of the corresponding command, "mv."

Suppose, however, a user wants to move all the Scribe manuscript files in one directory to another. On the Macintosh, the user must identify each file and individually select, move, and drop it into the target folder. This direct manipulation technique now becomes tedious, and the Unix user has the easy job. Because the names of Scribe manuscript files are required to end with the characters "mss," the Unix "wildcard" feature can be used to refer to all the desired files in an abstract, parameterized way. They can then be moved with a single command: "mv * .mss new-folder." This ability to describe an arbitrary set of system objects in terms of the properties of those objects is relatively easy to do in second-person interfaces but difficult or impossible in first-person interfaces.

Second-person interfaces also give the user more precise control over system functionality than the first-person interfaces do. In Steamer, for example, it is easy to change the rate of flow of water through a valve by adjusting the needle on the gauge. However, if the user wants to set the flow rate to be exactly 78.85492 gallons per minute, typing that number would be preferable to trying to adjust the needle on the gauge by moving the mouse. Note that this shortcoming of direct manipulation techniques comes from both the difficulty of precise control with the mouse and the difficulty of precisely reading a number from a gauge.

These interface styles also differ in how they expose users to the capabilities of their systems. The basic model of a second-person interface, especially a command language, is clear. The user types in the name of the desired command, followed by some arguments, and waits for the specified function to compute its results. Most of these systems have some simple but reasonably effective way to inform the user of the available commands (e.g., typing HELP), as well as ways for the user to find out what a given command does (e.g., typing HELP *command-name*). These techniques are not ideal—finding the desired command can require searching through the documentation of several commands, and the difficulties of the external–internal task-mapping problem discussed earlier complicate the search. However, they are better than nothing. In contrast, it is unclear how the user of a first-person interface can discover what can be done with it, especially those things that are not self-evident in the design of the interface. Because there are no keywords in a first-person interface, there are no easy ways to get at information about the system. How does the user find out what it means to double-click and drag the mouse? Why should the user think that doing this would cause something interesting to happen in the interface? How can the system help the user learn these things? Because this interface style is new, little is known about these problems. One promising approach to investigating them is to develop systems that allow students to work with a domain from several different perspectives, including the external interface the system presents to the world as well as some independent view of the knowledge underlying the domain. Burton (chapter 5), describes several examples of this *meta-world* approach.

As usual, when there is a choice between two attractive alternatives, the right solution is to try to have both. First-person interfaces reduce the external–internal task-mapping problem and thus greatly enhance ease of use and learning. However, they are inherently very specific: Steamer's interface is good for steam plants but little else. As a result, two things are needed. One is a good set of tools for building first-person interfaces. Because these interfaces are unavoidably tied to the domain they address, and new ones must be built for different domains, their construction must be made as efficient as possible. Second, their capabilities need to be augmented with second-person, assistantlike capabilities, which can inform the user about the capabilities of the system and offer advice on how task-oriented goals can be achieved. More will be said about these combinations of technologies later.

Alternative Interface Technologies

The hardware platforms on which these interfaces are presented have not yet been discussed. Most of the interfaces described previously could be implemented on the now-common combination of monochrome bitmapped display, keyboard, and mouse, if not on the even simpler teletype. This omission should be corrected, for many of the advances in display and interaction technology have the potential to change the nature of interfaces dramatically. Furthermore, many of these changes are likely to be especially relevant to the communication needs of tutoring systems and to allow information to flow much more directly between a tutoring system and a student. These developments can then contribute to the primary design goal of a good interface: to make the semantics of the domain evident and manipulable.

Graphics. The increasing availability of high-quality graphics has already significantly enhanced the quality of computer interfaces. It is now possible to develop interfaces assuming the availability of a bitmapped display of reasonable resolution—at least 600 by 200 pixels on personal computers, and probably 1,000 by 1,000 pixels on workstations—and some sort of software support for the creation of windows, menus, and icons. Graphics technology has been used to excellent effect in many ITS interfaces, as described earlier in this chapter and by Burton (chapter 5). Color displays are often but not yet universally available. In addition, the level of hardware support for complex graphics procedures is rapidly increasing. Many systems now have hardware assists for line or curve drawing, and this technology is extending into support for real-time animation and the coloring and shading of complex two- and three-dimensional images. These developments increase the ability to use dynamic, highly realistic images in interfaces.

Sophisticated graphics technology should have great potential value for ITSs. If used well, color can clarify the relationships among the components of a complex structure. Steamer has made good use of color, as have a number of CAD/CAM systems (Hertzog, 1985). Animation has also played a useful role in several systems, including several of the PLATO applications (Bitzer & Easley, 1965) and Steamer, in which animation indicates the direction and rate of flow of steam through pipes.

Nevertheless, graphic techniques do not always enhance the quality of an interface. When the precise role of graphics or color can be well defined, there is much to be gained. However, it is also easy to use graphical techniques in ways that are unmotivated, that add little to the interface, and that may even detract from its quality. Some guidelines are available for insuring that the use of graphics and color produce maximum perceptibility (Christ, 1975; Marcus, 1985; Tufte, 1983), but knowledge about using color to enhance the semantics of the interface is little more than anecdotal. There simply is no general theory for directing the effective use of sophisticated graphics techniques in human interfaces. Until such a theory is found—and finding one will be difficult—it is likely that the field will have to muddle through by experimenting and prototyping.

Large displays. Even though many current workstations offer 17-inch, 1,000 by 1,000 pixel displays, most users and system designers want more. To deal with the problem of allocating the existing screen space, techniques exist for presenting multiple overlapping windows of varying sizes and shapes (Teitelman, 1984a) or for "tiling" windows together so that they do not overlap but still occupy all the space available on the screen (Teitelman, 1984b). The more basic alternative to these approaches, of course, is to increase the size of the screen so that there is room for more windows and more information.

However, the screen size issue does not refer simply to the physical size of the screen, which can be easily increased with projection systems now available. Rather, the number of pixels on the screen as well as the physical size of the screen must also be increased to accommodate a greater amount of information. This task is harder. Plasma and liquid crystal technologies, which offer both higher resolution and larger size, are becoming available. However, they are still quite expensive. An 18 by 22 inch LCD display currently costs about $40,000, and a 30-inch plasma display with a resolution of about 100 pixels/inch was recently marketed at $250,000.

Of course, these prices will eventually drop, and these technologies will become cost-effective for at lest some applications. In the meantime, the psychological implications of these displays should be considered. A significant increase in the size of a display is likely to produce problems of attention and salience: It will do little good to put large amounts of information on a display if users can't find the information they need. This is not to argue against the potential value of large displays, but only to note that the user-oriented aspects of the technology must also be considered.

Small displays.   A small, portable, high-resolution display would be valuable in such situations as the field placement of ITSs for maintenance and on-the-job training. The LCD displays of portable computers are limited in resolution, speed, and the availability of color, but they are adequate for the field placement of ITSs that do not make extreme demands on display technology (assuming that the computing power in the machine is sufficient to support the ITS). A portable version of the LISP tutor (Reiser, Anderson, & Farrell, 1985) or of Johnson's fault diagnosis system (Johnson, 1987) would be straightforward from the perspective of the interface; a portable version of Steamer is further away but possible. The main bottleneck at the moment—the limited computing power of portable computers (compared to LISP machines and 68020-based workstations, that is)—will eventually disappear.

A secondary area of interest is much smaller displays—perhaps 1 or 2 inches wide— that might be embedded in specialized maintenance or job-training devices that incorporate ITS technology. Color, high-resolution LCD displays of this type are already available, as seen in the pocket television sets from several manufacturers. The limiting factor in the use of these displays is the visual acuity of the user; they are suitable for the display of a small amount of text or for graphic displays that are not too complex. These displays may be useful in certain classes of ITSs, but their limitations need to be kept in mind.

Videodisks.   One of the problems with graphics technology noted earlier is the difficulty of generating real-time animation and highly realistic images. In many cases, this problem can be finessed by creating the desired animation or images ahead of time and encoding them on a videodisk. These sequences can then be merged with computer-generated information to produce the desired effects. The capacity of these disks should be sufficient for many tutorial purposes: A 12-inch videodisk can hold up to 54,000 images, which results in up to an hour of video (Brewer, 1986). Several tutorial systems have already used videodisks with promising results, especially in the demonstration of procedures involving real-world devices (Bonissone & Johnson, 1984). There is no strong theory to guide and motivate the use of video as part of interfaces and ITSs. However, the body of experience with these systems is growing, and opportunities for effectively using this technology are becoming known.

The primary limitation of videodisk technology is that at present these disks are read-only devices. All the information that the designer wants to present via a videodisk must be anticipated, created, and stored on the disk as part of the development of the system. This limitation has two implications for ITSs. First, it may not be possible or practical to identify all the unique states into which a student might enter. In such cases, it will be necessary to generate the desired images with real-time graphic techniques during the execution of the system. As noted earlier, however, this solution is becoming increasingly feasible. Second, constructing a master disk from a videotape containing the desired images is both time-consuming and expensive enough to limit the number of prototypes and experiments that can be made with different disks: A test disk currently costs about $400, and a production master costs at least $800. Some prototyping can be done with the videotape that is ultimately used to produce the videodisk, but this work is feasible only when the time required to find the relevant part of the program on the videotape does not interfere with the user's interaction with the system. The prototyping problem will be partially relieved by WORM disks (write once, read many times), which will allow instructional developers much more flexibility in experimenting with different programs, while preserving the random-access capabilities of videodisks.

As an adjunct to videodisk technology, there is much interest throughout the computing industry in CD-ROMs (Lambert & Ropiequet, 1986). CD-ROMs use the technology that produces audio compact disks to store and retrieve large amounts of digitized information. At present, CD-ROMs can hold about 550 megabytes, which makes them an appealing alternative for storing large documents such as dictionaries and encyclopedias, documentation, and source code, as well as single digitized images.

However, creating moving images from CD-ROMs is difficult. Substantial external hardware is required to reconstruct the image from the bits that encode it, and the data transfer rate of current CD players is not high enough to support live video. The current capacity of 550 megabyte is enough to store only 5 or 6 minutes of video. Nevertheless, all of these problems are being addressed because of their importance for the audio entertainment industry. This work will result in increased capacity and retrieval speed, and advanced techniques for encoding and compressing video images (Brewer, 1986). In addition, work on digital television, which is required to regenerate the video from the encoded signal on the disk, is well underway.

Touch screens and tablets. In some circumstances, touch technology can be a useful alternative to mice or other pointing devices. Various techniques exist for sensing the position of fingers on a computer display; alternatively, a special-purpose tablet can be used that contains a predefined set of options. Touch screens can be very useful when a separate pointing device is undesirable, as in field placement of portable systems. At one time, the designers of SOPHIE experimented with the use of touch panels by placing a schematic of the circuit being repaired on a touch panel. This allowed users to specify circuit components by touching the schematic (Soloway & VanLehn, 1985).

The primary shortcomings of these systems are the limited resolution available in the detection of finger position and the parallax problems that result from the curved shape of the display and the changing viewing angle as the user points at different parts of the screen. The resolution problem can be addressed through the use of a stylus, but adding an external device defeats much of the purpose of touch systems. If an interface can be designed so that these problems can be minimized, a touch screen may be a reasonable alternative to other pointing techniques.

Speech recognition and understanding. The ability to talk to a computer instead of typing has been a long-held dream. Many people cannot or do not want to type, and keyboards are sometimes impractical, as they are when the user's hands are busy performing other tasks. In these cases, speech recognition seems like the ideal solution. However, as with natural language, reality has not caught up with the dream. Analyzing real-time speech is very difficult, and the technology is still inadequate.

Current speech systems differ in whether they are *speaker-dependent* or *speaker-independent*. If the system is speaker-dependent, it must be pretrained on the speech of a specific person. The tradeoff between these two characteristics, as one might expect, lies in the size of the vocabulary that the systems can handle. At present, low-cost speaker-dependent systems are available that can handle vocabularies of about 100 to 300 words with reasonable accuracy (about 70%). More powerful and more expensive systems are beginning to reach levels of 1,000 words. In contrast, speaker-independent systems are restricted to much smaller and more specialized vocabularies, often the digits from 0 to 9 and the words *yes* and *no* (cf. Cater, 1984).

Systems also differ in whether they are capable of *discrete* or *continuous* recognition. When speaking, people normally do not pause between words. Rather, words flow into each other, forming blocks of continuous speech sounds. This obscures the boundaries between words and greatly complicates the recognition process. Most existing systems require that speakers segment their speech so that the recognition algorithm does not have to deal with the word-boundary problem. Systems capable of continuous recognition require more complex algorithms and are typically less successful than those with discrete recognition. Most commercial systems assume discrete speech, and continuous systems are currently limited to vocabularies of about

75 to 100 words. Conveniently, some evidence suggests that people can adapt to the requirements of discrete speech rather easily (Biermann, Fineman, & Gilbert, 1985; but see Gould, Conti, & Hovanyecz, 1981). The word-boundary problem may then not pose a serious barrier to the use of this technology.

The foregoing discussion is meant to characterize what is generally referred to as *speech recognition*—identifying which member of a rather small set of words was just spoken. This task is very different from what is usually thought of as "talking to a computer." This latter, more complex process is better thought of as *speech understanding*, in which the speech being analyzed is not a word or two but a longer, more meaningful utterance. This complicates the interpretation task greatly, for it presupposes a natural language understanding system capable of interpreting the meaning of the utterance once the words have been identified. Consequently, speech understanding inherits all the problems of natural language understanding. In addition, spoken language has long been known to be much less grammatical and well structured than written or typed language (Dreiman, 1962; Horowitz & Newman, 1964). Thus, the natural language understanding task is complicated even more.

Further, regardless of the complexity of speech understanding, speakers are likely to want to use much larger vocabularies than most current systems can handle. One way around this limitation is to partition the complete vocabulary into several smaller vocabularies and to use a predictive parser to select the specific vocabulary that is in use at any instant. That is, when the parser is expecting a verb, the vocabulary containing verbs would be loaded into the speech system. This approach is reasonable for simple grammars where such accurate predictions of word types are possible, but it breaks down when language is richer and predictability decreases. Speakers are also likely to tend more toward continuous speech, further complicating the speech-processing component.

The most promising work in speech understanding (Adams & Bisiani, 1986; Erman, Hayes-Roth, Lesser, & Reddy, 1980) has integrated speech and natural language processing so that the attempts at understanding one level can influence and be influenced by attempts to understand the other. Although there is promise for the future, speech technology can be a useful part of present-day interfaces if it is used in ways that reflect its limitations. In some situations, it can be a good way to enter simple, short commands or to select items from menus. Much more research will be required before the more complex and desirable uses of speech and spoken language are possible.

Speech coding and speech synthesis.   These techniques have a much less ambitious goal than speech recognition and understanding. They are not meant to identify or extract the meaning of an utterance. Instead, they are concerned with storing and reproducing speech sounds as part of an interface.

The most straightforward way to produce voice sounds is to digitize and store the analog speech waveform. At a later time, these samples can be passed through a digital-to-analog converter and turned back into sound. If the sampling rate is high enough—at least 40,000 samples per second—very high-quality speech can be obtained. Unfortunately, sampling at such high rates produces a very large amount of data: 5 seconds of sound would require about a half megabyte of storage.

The alternative, of course, is to encode the speech waveform in some way. Techniques for doing this can reduce the size of the stored waveform considerably, but the quality of the reproduced speech is also somewhat reduced. The simplest of these techniques, linear predictive coding (LPC) and adaptive delta pulse code modulation (ADPCM), perform relatively straightforward transformations on the waveform and can reduce the size of the stored waveform by several orders of magnitude.

The next step beyond *speech coding* is *speech synthesis.* Techniques for speech synthesis represent a speech waveform in a more abstract form than the waveform itself, typically as phonemes or words. The playback system is then responsible for translating this representation into speech. This is true synthesis: The user can specify a novel set of phonemes or words to the system and produce novel speech. Several techniques are available, primarily *phoneme synthesis,* in which the user specifies the phonemes that are to be "spoken," and *synthesis by rule,* in which the user can specify a string of words that are to be spoken and then rely on transformation rules to convert the words into the proper set of phonemes. Both of these techniques can produce acceptable but identifiably synthetic speech. The major benefit is that the data rates that are required to produce this speech are greatly reduced, often to as low as 70 to 100 bits per second.

At present, speech-synthesis technology is rather good; as in other areas, it is much more advanced than is the knowledge about how to use it wisely. Little work has been done on the kinds of messages that should or should not be presented by speech. Nevertheless, the advantages to speech are clear. It takes advantage of a powerful communication channel, and it can pass information to users without cluttering up the display with a message of possibly only temporary relevance. Also, it does not require users to divert their eyes from some part of the display that might be critical to their interaction. These techniques have been used by Nakatani, Egan, Ruedisueli,

Hawley, and Lewart (1986) to develop a speech-oriented tutoring system for the Unix *vi* text editor. This system uses synthetic speech to present tasks to the user, report user errors, and offer hints and suggestions. The focus of this work has been on how speech can be used effectively in training tasks; more work of this sort should help clarify the true value of speech output in the interface.

A brief note on the dangers of technology projections. Predicting trends in computer technology is very risky. Many of these predictions are probably very conservative, and readers of this chapter several years from now may well be shaking their heads and wondering how the speed of these developments could not have been foreseen.

Such is life. However, pretend for the moment that tomorrow everything described so far—three-dimensional graphics, large-vocabulary continuous speech recognition, huge displays, and the like—will be widely available. It is still unclear that we would know how to use this technology wisely. Right now, we are actually in a very good position from a research perspective. These technologies are more or less available now, although not in forms as cheap or convenient as we would like. We have the opportunity to experiment with them from the user's perspective, to understand their strengths and weaknesses, and to learn what opportunities they offer to us. This is not to say that these technologies are all "solutions in search of problems," but we must be careful to look beyond the simple technologies to the larger question of how to use them to enhance the interface and the user's capabilities.

GOING BEYOND INTERFACE TECHNOLOGY: TOWARD INTERFACE SEMANTICS

It is easy to list the developments in interface technology and to speculate about their influence on interfaces and ITSs. However, it is difficult to go much beyond speculation because the problem these developments address is underconstrained. If the issue is really the quality of the interface—its power, ease of use, and ease of learning—we must ultimately be concerned not with the outward appearance of the interface but with the underlying structure of the interface and the application program. What is most important is not how the interface looks but how it allows the user to understand the capabilities of the underlying application program. Because these capabilities are inherently constrained by the domain that the application addresses, it is also important that the interface convey the important properties of the domain. Clearly, the appearance of the interface and the technologies that can contribute to this appearance are an important part of this process. However, the physical appearance of the interface should never be the driving factor in the development of an interactive system. That role must be played by the semantic constraints inherent in the application and the domain.

If the proper role of the interface is to help the user understand the semantics of the application and the domain, there would seem to be two ways to do this:

Make the Constraints Self-Evident
in the Interface

This is the first-person approach to interfaces. Graphics can be used to create an interface with objects and relations that express the semantic constraints of the domain. Things that are manipulatable in the domain are manipulatable in the interface, and in much the same ways. As a result, users do not have to learn how to use a general-purpose interface; their knowledge about the domain will constrain and guide their use of the system.

Let the Interface Reason About
and Explain Its Constraints

As noted earlier, first-person techniques are not always desirable, possible, or completely effective. In these cases, second-person techniques are required. The interface must be given the ability to inform the user about the capabilities of the system, the actions that can be carried out, the conditions under which they are possible, and their consequences. This advice can be given to users in several ways, corresponding to the different tutorial strategies discussed elsewhere in this volume: question answering, coaching, guided exploration, and the like.

An ideal interface would combine these techniques to cover all of the constraints present in the system. Users would therefore always be able to induce a certain characteristic of the system from the appearance of the interface or to enter into a dialogue with the system advisor to resolve a problem. All of this is, of course, easier said than done. Much is not understood about the construction of self-evident interfaces, and the development of first-person techniques depends on progress in this area. Similarly, the second-person techniques depend on substantial progress in artificial intelligence technology, especially knowledge representation, reasoning, and natural language understanding.

The entire set of constraints that affect the relationship between a user, an interface, and an application domain is hard to enumerate and address. The following sections present an initial categorization of these constraints and an attempt to identify some of the most challenging problems facing the development of good user interfaces.

Task Constraints

The real issue here is mental models (Gentner & Stevens, 1983), that is, understanding how people think about semantically rich domains. How are these domains broken up into meaningful components, and how are these components related to each other to reflect the constraints of the task and the domain? How do people resolve apparent or real inconsistencies in mental models, and how do they choose among alternative representations of a task? What are effective ways of embodying constraints in an interface, and how can users best be given control over them? Answers to these questions are critical if we are to build interfaces that do a good job of reflecting domain semantics and helping users understand and manipulate them.

User Constraints and Cognitive Limitations

One of the most important properties of a good user interface is that it can augment and compensate for weaknesses in the users' cognitive abilities. For instance, a good interface is in many ways an external memory system. Menus support recognition over recall, and iconic techniques such as those used in Steamer (Hollan, Hutchins, & Weitzman, 1984) and VSTAT (Miller & Blumenthal, 1985) capture and preserve information that users would otherwise have to keep in working memory or retrieve from long-term memory (Anderson, Boyle, Farrell, & Reiser, 1984; Anderson & Jeffries, 1985). Similarly, the display of the Geometry Tutor (Anderson, Boyle, & Yost, 1985; Figure 6.5) maintains a concrete representation of the current state of the proof process. This display relieves the student of the need to maintain a well-organized representation of the proof in working memory, a difficult task when, as is inherently the case in a tutoring situation, the student does not have a sound understanding of the information being worked with. The display also reifies the proof process: It makes the student's thought processes themselves a subject of study. A good interface can also help users understand the results of complex processes. Rather than requiring users to infer or guess the effects of their actions, these effects can be made an explicit and visible part

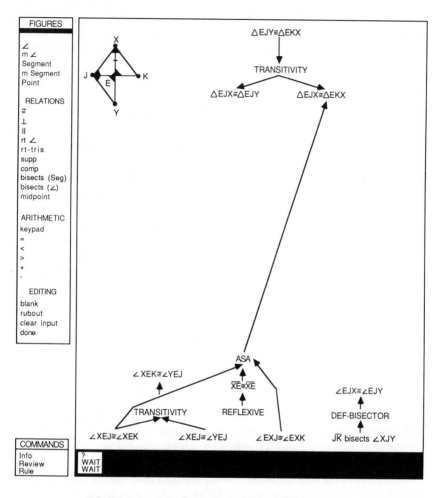

FIGURE 6.5 Anderson, Boyle, and Yost's Geometry tutor.

of the interface, especially through direct manipulation techniques (cf. Norman, 1986).

Designing interfaces that help users with these limitations will require good models of the sources of these limitations: basic human cognitive processes. An appropriate division of labor must be established between the user and the system, and it must be based on a good understanding of what people are capable of and how their cognitive capabilities complement those of computer systems.

Instructional Constraints

The domain being tutored and the instructional role played by the ITS inevitably drive the form of a tutorial system's interface. Instruction that entails continuous dialogue between the student and the ITS would call for a strong natural language understanding component, whereas a coaching system that monitors user actions and offers advice about more efficient use of the system would not. Intead, for this coaching system, a first-person interface that supports high-level, semantically meaningful user actions and thereby eases the diagnosis problem would be more desirable. A domain that requires mastery of a large and complex body of knowledge could benefit from powerful and flexible tools for browsing and editing, such as those available in GUIDON-WATCH (Richer & Clancey, 1985; Figure 6.6), an exploratory system for medical knowledge. Designing the "face" of the ITS requires identifying the kinds of information that are relevant to the instructional task the system is dealing with, and making sure that interface techniques capable of conveying this information are available and are used. Ultimately, the choice of interface techniques is an issue of pedagogy and tutorial strategies.

A second instructional issue is how the ITS presents information to the student. This is a matter of deciding in which of several different ways a specific piece of information should be presented: as a table, graph, piece of text, or diagram. The nature of the interface controlling the application should direct this choice, of course: Consistency of presentation is important. However, when no such constraints exist, the user often benefits when different kinds of information are presented in ways that emphasize their most important properties. Some relationships are best shown graphically; others require a table for greatest clarity. The simultaneous presentation of the same body of information in several different formats is another pragmatic middle ground. The real questions are what point is this information trying to make, and what presentation techniques are best for conveying this point? At the moment, the presentation of information must be determined either by the system designer, who can "hard code" a few alternatives into the system, or by the users, who might be allowed to vary the presentation format according to their own preferences and the ongoing requirements of the task. However, work has begun on automated techniques for examining a set of data and a situational context and choosing an appropriate display format (e.g., Mackinlay, 1986; Myers & Buxton, 1986), so some of this effort may ultimately be taken on by the interface itself.

A third issue concerns the interpersonal spirit in which the information offered by the ITS is ultimately presented. An ITS could

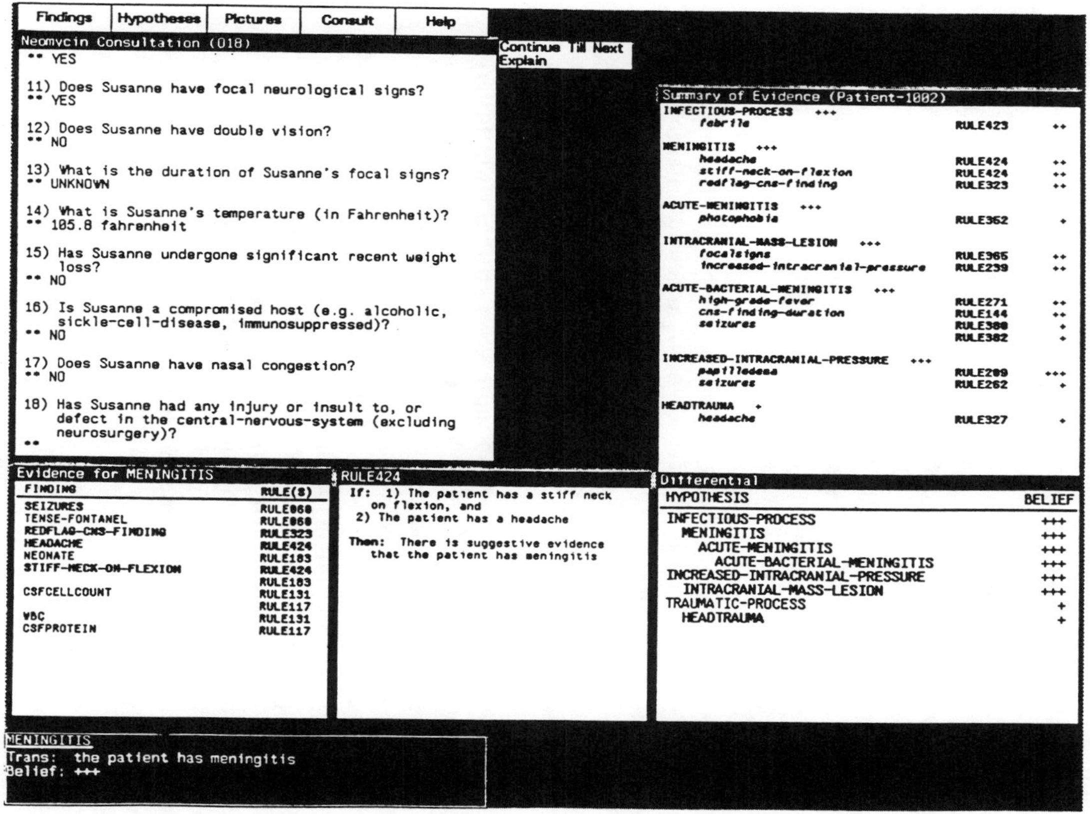

FIGURE 6.6 A sample screen from GUIDON-WATCH, which supports exploration of large knowledge bases.

present information to the student in a very unemotional way, emphasizing that the tutor is really just a computer system; or the ITS could attempt to portray a human teacher and present information in a friendly and encouraging way.

Both styles have benefits and dangers. Bloom (1984) has argued that much of the benefit perceived in individual human tutoring comes from the cooperative and empathetic style of interaction. The "humanized" ITS should, in principle, be less threatening and more motivating. However, a human style of communication should follow from the principled design of the interface and from the knowledge-driven, strategic capabilities of the intelligence at the heart of the ITS. Simply writing all the PRINT statements in the system in a "Now, Johnny" tone will not work. Most students quickly see that such statements are artificial, and what is meant to be helpful and motivating soon becomes a distraction.

We should also remember the problems seen with natural language systems whose capabilities are limited: Because of their ability to handle some instances of language, their users will sometimes assume far greater capabilities than are actually present, and the overall effectiveness of the interface declines as a result. Similar problems could arise in ITSs built with a strong facade of friendliness: Users might inappropriately presume that the system understands them more thoroughly than it really does. The "impersonal computer" style may clarify the capabilities of the system more successfully; it would fail because it leads the user to expect too little.

The most realistic approach to the issue of style is to accept the fact that ITSs are implemented on computer systems and to minimize human characteristics in the interaction. This does not mean that interaction in ITS should be as primitive as that common in the computers of the 1950s. In fact, one of the attractive aspects of using graphics in an interface is that they can increase users' interest and motivation (Malone, 1981). Motivation is certainly an important part of education and tutoring; so important, in fact, that designers should consider it in its own right and not try to add it to a system like a coat of paint.

Physical Constraints

In many ITSs, the application domains being tutored by the system are highly symbolic and conceptual, such as basic cognitive skills or computer programming. In these cases, as long as the systems' interfaces provide good models of the domains, they can typically rely on relatively simple graphic or textual presentation techniques for communicating with the student; the usual bitmapped display, mouse, and keyboard combination are often sufficient. However, for a tutorial task that deals with a real-world device and environment, these techniques may not be enough. Instead, a highly realistic depiction of the device or environment and equally realistic techniques for interacting with this interface may be necessary for the student to understand and learn the domain. This belief has led to the development of flight simulators and maintenance training systems that are based on real-world devices, and that give students direct experience with both the devices and the problem domain on which they are used.

An alternative view of instruction for real-world devices and environments is that highly realistic interfaces are not required. Students certainly need to understand the concepts in the curriculum, but these can often be presented in relatively abstract ways that not only are less expensive and easier to implement but also may improve the learning environment in the process. Thus, in Steamer, abstract illustrations replace much of the real-world appearance of the components of the steam plant. Water tanks appear as boxes or cylinders, and pipes as rectangular conduits between tanks, but no attempt has been made to make a tank or pipe look exactly as it does in a real steam plant. Doing so would actually impair the student's ability to understand the operation of the steam plant, because the student would no longer be able to see the water levels in the tank or the direction and rate of flow of water and steam in the pipes. There is no question that students ultimately need to become familiar with real steam plants, but the claim here is that it is possible to separate the physical aspects of the problem from the cognitive aspects and to teach them separately, using whatever techniques are most appropriate.

Of course, hybrid systems are possible. As noted earlier, real-time, three-dimensional animation is rapidly becoming feasible. The displays in a flight simulator may soon completely simulate a pilot's environment with computer graphics techniques. Research at Wright-Patterson Air Force Base has been exploring stereoscopic display techniques to generate and project, via a helmet incorporating small television screens positioned in front of the student's eyes, an animated, three-dimensional flight scene. The system reacts to both the student's head movements and the student's control of the simulator. However, the displays are still highly schematic. Hills and rivers do not look exactly like real hills and rivers, and the display is filled with symbols that denote and describe especially important objects (e.g., friendly and enemy aircraft) in the student's field of vision. This work is a good example of a system that identifies the physical and cognitive components of the task and applies appropriate techniques to each.

Another advantage of the middle ground between the abstract and representational positions is that it can accommodate change in the users' requirements as their understanding of the domain changes. Johnson (1987) has found that novices can benefit from concrete representation of the devices they are learning about. However, once they understand the basic properties of the devices, they are better off with a representation of the device that is more abstract and emphasizes the domain semantics, the primary focus of their learning at this point.

The key to designing a good interface is to understand the task, the information that must be presented, and the ways in which students might interact with it. In many situations, highly realistic interfaces may not be desirable because one or more of these requirements would be violated. For instance, it would probably be possible to build a new version of Steamer with a highly realistic, three-dimensional computer graphic model of a steam plant. However, the user of such a system would need to manipulate and control this model: to reach into it and change its orientation, open and close valves, and inspect the contents or status of the device. This leads to two problems, one technological and one psychological. The technological problem is that the system would have to track the position of the user's hands with respect to the perceived position of the image. Two-dimensional pointing devices such as joysticks or mice are not particularly effective for this task because they do not provide for movement in the third dimension. One alternative is to use small sensors that can be attached to the user's hand, similar to the Pohemius device used in the "Put That There" system (Bolt, 1980; Schmandt & Hulteen, 1981). More recently, a glove has been developed for use with personal computers, which senses the position of the user's hand in three-dimensional space, the tilt of the hand, and whether the user's fingers are straight or bent (Zimmerman, Lanier, Blanchard, Bryson, & Harvill, 1987). Relating the tracking information produced by these devices to the image is complex but possible.

The real problem, of course, lies in what the student takes away from the interaction. In Steamer, the important concepts to be acquired by the user are not physical but functional. Depending on the student's needs (cf. Burton, chapter 5; Johnson, 1987), highly realistic presentation techniques may even impair learning. However, these techniques may be very useful in problem areas such as molecular modeling (Feldmann, 1985), in which a three-dimensional model of molecular structure is the most appropriate way of characterizing and manipulating the information to be acquired by the student. As before, the real task is to understand the goals and needs of the student, and to make sure that the interface offers a good match to these.

Tutorial Constraints

There is a crucial relationship between the interface and the capabilities of the ITS. One part of this problem is the extent to which the interface can ease the diagnosis and remediation tasks of the ITS. First-person interfaces can present students with a good picture of the underlying application, one that provides a meaningful context for explaining and discussing the domain and a student's possible problems with it. First-person interfaces can also enhance ITSs through their reliance on the manipulation of semantically rich graphic objects. In an interface built around such objects, the user's actions are also high-level and semantically rich. The semantic basis of these actions can make diagnosing problems and hypothesizing about the student's knowledge much easier. Another possibility is to embed "bug objects" in the interface; manipulation of these objects indicates that the user harbors a particular misconception.

The advantages of these high-level interfaces can be seen by comparing two different types of tutoring systems. In the Geometry Tutor (Anderson, Boyle, & Yost, 1985; Figure 6.5), students make very high-level assertions about the domain. They focus on specific parts of the proof and identify some of them as being especially significant and worthy of elaboration. As a result, the tutorial system underlying this interface can reason directly about the student's assumptions and beliefs about the high-level geometric concepts that are being manipulated. The system can therefore make inferences about misconceptions and future actions, and explain past actions in a meaningful way.

In contrast to the Geometry Tutor, consider several coaching systems for text editors such as Emacs (Fischer, Lemke, & Schwab, 1985; Miller, 1982; Zissis & Witten, 1985). These systems monitor a user's keystrokes and offer suggestions for making the user's interaction more efficient. For instance, if a user moves the cursor forward character by character over several words, the coach might suggest using the editor's "forward word" command.

The problem with these coaching systems is that the interface actions do not carry with them much in the way of semantics—they do not constrain the domain enough to support strong inferences about future or past actions. For example, in a text editor, moving the cursor forward by a character does not limit a user's subsequent actions much, if at all. Consequently, the inferencing and advising that the system can do is very limited. About the most it can do is suggest more powerful commands that subsume several recently observed actions, as in the "forward-character, forward-word" example. This problem lies not in the system but in the domain: People who look over the shoulder of text editor users and try to infer high-level editing plans do not seem to be much more successful than these programs.

The utility of Emacs coaches and other systems such as operating systems interfaces (cf. Shrager & Finin, 1982) that apply to semantically unconstrained domains is an empirical question. It may be that the low-level advice they make available is useful enough to warrant their development. However, the more general point is that systems with low-level, semantically weak interface actions complicate the diagnosis problem greatly and are probably not good candidates for the application of these low-level coaching techniques. In general, interfaces should be built at as high and semantically rich a level as is appropriate for the task and the needs of the user. This should make the system easier to learn and use, and also enhance the ability of the ITS to make powerful inferences that lead to useful advice and tutoring.

Another crucial relationship between the components of an ITS is whether the intelligent component of the ITS—the agent capable of reasoning about the domain addressed by the interface—can influence the design and the capabilities of the interface. The presence of an active, knowledgeable agent could allow a graphical, first-person interface to insure that the user could carry out semantically acceptable actions. Consequently, major classes of user errors could be eliminated simply by preventing the user from making them.

However, as the power and the subtlety of controlling the interface increases, preventing user errors becomes a more controversial issue in the basic design of the system. In some cases, letting the user make mistakes can be useful because it allows misconceptions to be identified and corrected in a specific, problem-oriented context. If these mistakes are prevented, the misconceptions may linger and need to be detected later by techniques that are computationally more costly and complex, and less certain to succeed. Better results may be achieved in the system as a whole by intentionally reducing the level of intelligence that is playing an explicit role in the interface. The appropriate level of intelligence in the ITS certainly depends on the specifics of the task. The point is, however, that issues of interface design and implementation can quickly slip into the area of tutorial strategy, and vice versa. Consequently, a system-wide approach to the development of an ITS is essential to ensure that the parts of the system complement one another.

Implementation Constraints

An ITS is really three things: an educational instrument, an interface to an application program, and a knowledge-based system. The discussion thus far has focused on issues related to the educational and tutorial aspects of these systems and the ways that interface and artificial intelligence technologies can improve education and ease of use. The issues related to the latter two aspects focus on how these systems are implemented, and, although these issues are more pragmatic than theoretical, they cannot be ignored.

Interface implementation. The tools that are commercially available for implementing powerful graphical interfaces, such as SunTools for the Sun workstation, the window systems on LISP workstations, and the Macintosh Toolbox, are very limited. They typically support basic window properties and operations (e.g., sizing, scrolling, and refreshing), multiple text fonts, menu presentation and selection, and simple graphics functions (e.g., line and curve drawing and sometimes region filling). Unfortunately, there is a great distance between these capabilities and those needed to implement a system with the graphic capabilities of Steamer or Trillium (Henderson, 1986). As a result, many research projects are actively concerned with extending these capabilities in ways that provide the interface designer—and thereby the ITS designer—with significantly more power.

These efforts take two rather different approaches. The *user interface management system* (UIMS) strategy attempts to separate the interface component of an application program from the more direct computational part. The idea here is that the UIMS should serve as a high-quality interface to a preexisting application program. It should be responsible for translating users' interface actions— perhaps menu and icon selection—into whatever form is required by the application program—perhaps a command language designed 10 years before the integration of the system with the UIMS. If the UIMS is kept separate from the application program, the same UIMS can be used with many different applications, yielding a consistent and high-quality interface across all these applications. Examples of the UIMS approach include FLAIR (Wong & Reid, 1982), COUSIN (Hayes, Szekely, & Lerner, 1985), and ADM (Schulert, Rogers, & Hamilton, 1985).

The problem with the UIMS approach is that the communication channel between the UIMS and the application program is very narrow. Typically it is either a character stream across which command language statements and results are passed, or a very limited set of system calls. If the interface needs to know a great deal about the ongoing state of the application program in order to carry out its operations, this narrow band of communication may be inadequate. This gap is likely to widen as application programs become more powerful and intelligent and the interface to these programs must display the internal state of the programs in even greater detail. ITSs and the computer-based applications for which ITSs are being developed certainly fall into this category.

One approach to this problem is for the UIMS to maintain a simulation model of the application program so that information about the state of that program is available to it. However, these models are very difficult to develop and to synchronize with the application programs. The alternative to the UIMS approach is to abandon a strong separation between the application and the interface tools and instead to integrate the interface and the application. In this way, access to the information about the state of the application program is made available in the values of global variables of function calls. The large, common address space of LISP environments supports this communication in a very direct way, and designers of many of the systems with powerful interfaces and complex application programs have chosen this route (Bocker, Fischer, & Nieper, 1985; Henderson, 1986; Hutchins, Hollan, & Norman, 1986; Mackinlay, 1986; Miller & Blumenthal, 1985; Myers & Buxton, 1986; Weitzman, 1986). High-level interface tools are just as central to this work as they are to the UIMS approach. If these tools are good, they can provide much of the application independence that is available with UIMSs, although some recoding of the application is inevitable. The integrative approach to intelligent interface development expands the communication path between the interface and the application, and allows rich communication between a complex system and its interface.

Knowledge acquisition. The absence of good design and development tools is also evident when ITSs are available as knowledge-based systems. Commercial expert system shells may be useful in implementing the underlying mechanics of ITSs, but they offer little help on the knowledge acquisition problem itself. Collecting and encoding the knowledge needed to build an ITS is still a long and difficult task, and substantial project resources must still be allocated to this stage. Of course, the lack of good high-level tools for knowledge acquisition is a serious problem not merely for development, but for testing and maintenance as well.

The interface construction and knowledge acquisition problems ultimately merge when implementation finally begins. Many ITSs, especially those that provide training on specific application programs or simulated devices, require two virtually identical stages of implementation. First, the running application program that is the basis of the training system must be built. Once it is completed, what amounts to a second version of that program must be built. This version, the knowledge component of the ITS, is essentially a symbolic representation of the application, which captures the important aspects of that application program in such a way that the ITS can reason about it. The development of an ITS is therefore a difficult and time-consuming task with significant opportunities for error.

Something must be done about the difficulties of implementing these systems. Ultimately, tools like the authoring languages for traditional computer-aided instruction systems (Bitzer & Easley, 1965) are needed, but they must appreciate the knowledge requirements of ITSs and the likelihood of a link between the ITS and the more advanced interface techniques that are now important parts of these systems. Bonar's Bite-Size Tutor (Bonar, 1985) and Anderson's PUPS Tutoring Architecture (Anderson & Skwarecki, 1986) are initial steps toward splitting the knowledge relevant only to tutoring apart from domain-specific knowledge. Other researchers are seeking a merger of the interface and knowledge components of the problem so that some of the effort of defining knowledge about the application area can be used to define the interface, and vice versa (Miller & Blumenthal, 1985; Sibert, Hurley, & Bleser, 1986).

WHERE CAN WE BEGIN?

The preceding discussion has enumerated some important research topics in human–computer interaction that pertain to ITSs. In view of the complexity of these topics and the rapidity with which developments in both fields are occurring, it should not be surprising that the list is long. Given the current state of knowledge about these topics, however, progress in certain areas looks especially promising for ITSs.

Making domain semantics visible. Solving this problem is critical to the success of first-person interface techniques. An especially important part of this problem is to find ways to identify appropriate mental models for complex domains, and to convey these models to the users of the systems. Similarly, designers need some basis for choosing between alternative models, for choosing the proper level of abstraction for a successful model, and for implementing a graphic representation of a model.

Another aspect of this problem is understanding the various stages of users' conceptualizations of systems and domains. The ways in which people conceptualize a problem gradually change (cf. Chi, Feltovich, & Glaser, 1981), and interface designers need to understand these stages of conceptualization, how the movement from one stage to another takes place, and how these changes would constrain interface design and development. Finally, as these changes take place, the relative importance of cognitive and physical fidelity needs to be understood.

Dealing with domain semantics is hard; it requires much work that is specific to a particular domain and that is not reusable in other areas. An important direction this work could take is to follow on the PUPS and Bite Sized Tutor projects and consider whether some abstract system can be defined that would be capable of representing the semantics of many different domains, generalizing as much of this semantic information as possible. Such a system would ease the implementation of ITSs and would have value for other areas of artificial intelligence as well.

The dichotomy between first-person and second-person interfaces. This distinction appears to be a valuable way to think of interfaces, but a better understanding of these classes of interfaces is needed. For instance, the limitations of first-person interfaces are not well understood. We need a better understanding of when they are most appropriate from a tutorial or interaction perspective, and how far they can be pushed before the illusion of direct interaction or cooperation with an agent begins to break down. We also need to address the problem of understanding the coverage of the domain offered by a particular interface. As noted in the discussion of natural language interfaces, serious problems arise when users misunderstand the limitations of the application programs behind the interface. This calls for identifying interface techniques that communicate the capabilities of these application programs as clearly as possible. Finally, we need to understand how to integrate first- and second-person interface styles, so that the power and flexibility of this integration can be maximized. For instance, it should be possible for a student to ask a question about a graphical object in the interface's display by combining a typed or perhaps spoken statement to the tutor with a mouse click or some similar manipulation of that object. Such possibilities imply a whole class of research projects on how to combine multiple interface technologies in fruitful, synergistic ways.

Interface design aids. Except in a few limited areas, there is not a strong scientific component to the design of interfaces. This lack of knowledge points to work in two basic areas. First, more knowledge about interface design is needed. The research cited earlier has primarily explored screen layout and information presentation; other guidelines exist regarding color, fonts, and window proportions (Marcus, 1985) that could similarly be codified. There has been some study of the command structure of interfaces, with the goal of predicting the ease of use and learnability of these interfaces (Payne & Green, 1986; Polson & Kieras, 1985), this work should continue and move into the more complex, semantic aspects of domains and interfaces.

Second, to fill in the gaps in our knowledge about interface design, powerful interface prototyping tools are also needed. These tools would allow designers to experiment with different designs and rapidly converge on a good design. These tools should increase the level of support for interface designers so that they can work directly with the objects that will appear on the screen and the behaviors that will be associated with them. Designers must be freed from worrying about plotting points and tracking mouse positions.

Knowledge acquisition environments. Help is also needed in the design of the knowledge component of ITSs. Tools supporting this design process need to go beyond the currently available expert system shells and to address the link between interface development and knowledge acquisition. In particular, it would be useful to learn how much knowledge about the use of an interface and about the domain it controls can be derived from a representation of the interface itself, and how much help can be offered toward filling in the knowledge that cannot be derived from these representations. The problem of domain specificity is again relevant here: One would like a development environment that both addresses the knowledge acquisition problem and also supports the development of interfaces of many different styles and for many different domains. However, this may not be feasible: It may instead be necessary to build many different interface toolkits, each of which has been specialized to reflect the interface and knowledge requirements of a particular domain.

Cognitive limitations. An important step in building better interfaces is knowing more about basic cognitive processes and the limitations inherent in these processes. For instance, if we learn more about how working memory is managed, we can begin to design interface techniques that offer minimal interference with working memory and that serve as useful external memory systems. Similarly, attention and salience are also important problems for interface design because of the problems people have in organizing their displays and the information on them so that they can later find what they need. This problem is somewhat manageable now but only because the size and resolution of current displays limit the amount of information a display can contain. As displays become larger, it will be especially important to understand how large amounts of information can be organized to insure the clarity of the information, and to find ways for the application program to alert the user to changes on some part of the screen.

Intelligent interface capabilities.   Two areas of research are especially important here. First, there is a practical need for better intelligent system development environments. Interface designers are rarely expert in the development of knowledge-based systems, and toolkits to aid the development of knowledge components of interfaces and tutoring systems are badly needed. Second, basic research on the role of intelligence in interfaces is needed. How can an intelligent system make its powers and limitations clear to its users? Systems like NLMenu offer one solution for one class of problems, but the more general question remains. Until better answers for these questions exist, much of the effort devoted to putting intelligence into interfaces and ITSs may go unused.

Educational and psychological utility of interface technologies. What is the relative value of graphics versus text and voice versus typing? What is the utility of color, animation, and other high-realism graphic techniques? The evaluation of these specific technologies will be difficult. One can often be shown to be better than another, but it is hard to determine whether this advantage is inherent in that technology, or if it is the result of better implementation or of the specific domain or task that was chosen for the evaluation process. Nevertheless, a better understanding of the real values of alternative technologies is badly needed. It brings us back to the real problem surrounding the development of interfaces for ITSs: that of making the application domain clear and easily understood. Ultimately, this is the real role of all these techniques: to serve the user and improve the total educational experience.

REFERENCES

Adams, D. A., & Bisiani, R. (1986). The Carnegie-Mellon University distributed speech recognition system. *Speech Technology, 12,* 14–23.

Allen, J. F., & Perrault, C. R. (1980). Analyzing intention in utterances. *Artificial Intelligence, 15,* 143–178.

Anderson, J. R., Boyle, C. F., Farrell, R., & Reiser, B. (1984). Cognitive principles in the design of computer tutors. *Proceedings of the Sixth Cognitive Science Conference* (pp. 2–9). Boulder, CO: University of Colorado.

Anderson, J. R., Boyle, C. F., & Yost, G. (1985). The geometry tutor. In A. Joshi (Ed.), *Proceedings of the Ninth International Joint Conference on Artificial Intelligence* (Vol. 1, pp. 1–7). Los Altos, CA: Morgan Kaufmann.

Anderson, J. R., & Jeffries, R. (1985). Novice LISP errors: Undetected losses of information from working memory. *Human–Computer Interaction, 1*, 107–132.

Anderson, J. R., & Skwarecki, E. (1986). The automated tutoring of introductory computer programming. *Communications of the ACM, 29*, 842–849.

Ballard, B. W., & Stumberger, D. E. (1986). Semantic acquisition in TELI: A transportable, user-customized natural language processor. *Proceedings of the 24th Annual Meeting of the Association for Computational Linguistics* (pp. 20–29). New York: Association for Computing Machinery.

Bates, M., & Bobrow, R. J. (1983). A transportable natural language interface. *Proceedings of the 6th Annual International ACM SIGIR Conference on Research and Development in Informtion Retrieval*. Bethesda, MD: Association for Computing Machinery.

Biermann, A. W., Fineman, L., & Gilbert, K. C. (1985). An imperative sentence processor for voice interactive office applications. *ACM Transactions on Office Information Systems, 3*, 321–346.

Bitzer, D. L., & Easley, J. A., Jr. (1965). PLATO: A computer-controlled teaching system. In Sass & Wilkinson (Eds.), *Computer augmentation of human reasoning*. Washington, DC: Spartan Books.

Bloom, B. S. (1984, June/July). The 2 sigma problem: The search for methods of group instruction as effective as one-to-one tutoring. *Educational Researcher*.

Bocker, H., Fischer, G., & Nieper, H. (1986). The enhancement of understanding through visual representations. In M. Mantei & P. Orbeton (Eds.), *Proceedings of the CHI '86 Conference on Human Factors in Computing Systems* (pp. 44–50). Boston, MA: Association for Computing Machinery.

Bolt, R. A. (1980). Put That There: Voice and gesture at the graphics interface. In *Computer Graphics: Proceedings of ACM SIGGRAPH '80* (pp. 262–270). New York: Association for Computing Machinery.

Bonar, J. (1985, Newsletter 85-3). *Bite-Sized Intelligent Tutoring*. Pittsburgh, PA: University of Pittsburgh, Learning Research and Development Center.

Bonissone, P. P., & Johnson, H. E., Jr. (1984). DELTA: An expert system for diesel locomotive repair. In *Artificial intelligence in maintenance: Proceedings of the joint services workshop* (pp. 181–195). Brooks Air Force Base, TX: Air Force Systems Command.

Brewer, B. (1986). Video on CD: The big picture. In S. Lambert & S. Ropiequet (Eds.), *CD ROM: The new papyrus* (pp. 291–294). Redmond, WA: Microsoft Press.

Brown, J. S., Burton, R. R., & deKleer, J. (1982). Pedagogical natural language, and knowledge engineering techniques in SOPHIE I, II, and III. In D. Sleeman & J. S. Brown (Eds.), *Intelligent tutoring systems* (pp. 227–282). New York: Academic Press.

Carbonell, J. G., & Collins, A. M. (1973). Natural semantics in artificial intelligence. *Proceedings of the Third International Joint Conference on Artificial Intelligence* (pp. 344–351). Stanford, CA: Stanford Research Institute.

Carbonell, J. G., & Hayes, P. J. (1983). Recovery strategies for parsing extragrammatical language. *American Journal of Computational Linguistics, 9*, 123–146.

Cater, J. C. (1984). *Electronically hearing: Computer speech recognition*. Indianapolis, IN: Sams.

Chi, M. T. H., Feltovich, P. J., & Glaser, R. (1981). Categorization and representation of physics problems by experts and novices. *Cognitive Science, 5,* 121–152.

Christ, R. E. (1975). Review and analysis of color coding research for visual displays. *Human Factors, 17,* 542–570.

Clancey, W. J. (1982). Tutoring rules for guiding a case method dialogue. In D. Sleeman & J. S. Brown (Eds.), *Intelligent tutoring systems* (pp. 201–226). New York: Academic Press.

Douglas, S. A., & Moran, T. P. (1983). Learning text editor semantics by analogy. In A. Janda (Ed.), *Proceedings of the CHI '83 Conference on Human Factors in Computing Systems* (pp. 207–211). Boston, MA: Association for Computing Machinery.

Dreiman, G. H. J. (1962). Differences between written and spoken language: An exploratory study. *Acta Psychologia, 10,* 36–100.

Erman, L. D., Hayes-Roth, F., Lesser, V. R., & Reddy, D. R. (1980). The Hearsay-II speech understanding system: Integrating knowledge to resolve uncertainty. *ACM Computing Surveys, 12,* 213–253.

Feldmann, R. (1985). Interfaces for molecular modeling systems. Paper presented at the MCC Symposium on Computer Graphics and Human Interfaces: MCC, Austin, TX.

Fischer, G., Lemke, A., & Schwab, T. (1985). Knowledge-based help systems. In L. Borman & B. Curtis (Eds.), *Proceedings of the CHI '85 Conference on Human Factors in Computing Systems* (pp. 161–167). San Francisco, CA: Association for Computing Machinery.

Gentner, D., & Gentner, D. R. (1983). Flowing water or teeming crowds: Mental models of electricity. In D. Gentner & A. L. Stevens (Eds.), *Mental models* (pp. 99–130). Hillsdale, NJ: Lawrence Erlbaum Associates.

Gentner, D., & Stevens, A. L. (Eds.). (1983). *Mental models.* Hillsdale, NJ: Lawrence Erlbaum Associates.

Gould, J. D., Conti, J., & Hovanyecz, T. (1981). Composing letters with a simulated listening typewriter. *Proceedings of the First Conference on Human Factors in Computing Systems* (pp. 367–370). Gaithersburg, MD: Association for Computing Machinery.

Granger, R. H. (1983). The NOMAD system: Expectation-based detection and correction of errors during understanding of syntactically and semantically ill-formed text. *American Journal of Computational Linguistics, 9,* 188–196.

Grosz, B. J., Appelt, D., Martin, P., & Pereira, F. (1987). TEAM: An experiment in the design of transportable natural language interfaces. *Artificial Intelligence, 32,* 173–244.

Halasz, F., & Moran, T. P. (1983). Analogy considered harmful. In A. Janda (Ed.), *Proceedings of the CHI '83 Conference on Human Factors in Computing Systems* (pp. 45–49). Boston: Association for Computing Machinery.

Hayes, P. J., Szekely, P. A., & Lerner, R. A. (1985). Design alternatives for user interface management systems based on experiences with COUSIN. In L. Borman & B. Curtis (Eds.), *Proceedings of the CHI '85 Conference on Human Factors in Computing Systems* (pp. 169–175). San Francisco: Association for Computing Machinery.

Henderson, D. A., Jr. (1986). The Trillium user interface design environment. In M. Mantei & P. Orbeton (Eds.), *Proceedings of the CHI '86 Conference on Human Factors in Computing Systems* (pp. 221–227). Boston: Association for Computing Machinery.

Hendrix, G. G. (1979). *The LIFER manual: A guide to building practical natural language interfaces* (Tech. Note 138). Palo Alto: SRI International AI Center.

Hendrix, G. G., & Lewis, W. H. (1981). Transportable natural-language interfaces to databases. In *Proceedings of the 19th Annual Meeting of the Association for Computational Linguistics* (pp. 159–165). New York: Association for Computing Machinery.

Hertzog, B. (1985). Three-dimensional computer graphics for CAD/CAM. Paper presented at the MCC Symposium on Computer Graphics and Human Interfaces: MCC, Austin, TX.

Hollan, J. D., Hutchins, E. L., & Weitzman, L. (1984). Steamer: An interactive inspectable simulation-based training system. *AI Magazine, 5,* 15–27.

Horowitz, M. W., & Newman, J. B. (1964). Spoken and written expression: An experimental analysis. *Journal of Abnormal and Social Psychology, 68,* 640–647.

Hutchins, E. L., Hollan, J. D., & Norman, D. A. (1986). Direct manipulation interfaces. In D. A. Norman & S. W. Draper (Eds.), *User centered system design* (pp. 87–124). Hillsdale, NJ: Lawrence Erlbaum Associates.

Johnson, W. B. (1987). Development and evaluation of simulation-oriented computer-based instruction for diagnostic training. In W. B. Rouse (Ed.), *Advances in man-machine systems research* (Vol. 3, pp. 99–127). Greenwich, CT: JAI Press.

Lambert, S., & Ropiequet, S. (Eds.). (1986). *CD ROM: The new papyrus.* Redmond, WA: Microsoft Press.

Laurel, B. K. (1986). Interface as mimesis. In D. A. Norman & S. W. Draper (Eds.), *User centered system design* (pp. 67–86). Hillsdale, NJ: Lawrence Erlbaum Associates.

Lewis, C., & Mack. R. (1981). Learning to use a text processing system: Evidence from "thinking aloud" protocols. *Proceedings of the First Conference on Human Factors in Computing Systems* (pp. 387–392). Gaithersburg, MD: Association for Computing Machinery.

Littman, D. J. (1986). Linguistic coherence: A plan-based alternative. *Proceedings of the 24th Annual Meeting of the Association for Computational Linguistics* (pp. 215–223). New York: Association for Computing Machinery.

Mackinlay, J. (1986). *Automatic design of graphical presentations.* Unpublished doctoral dissertation, Palo Alto, CA: Stanford University.

Malone, T. W. (1981). Towards a theory of intrinsically motivating instruction. *Cognitive Science, 4,* 333–370.

Marcus, A. (1985). Screen design for iconic interfaces. In L. Borman & B. Carter (Eds.), *CHI '85 Conference on Human Factors in Computing Systems.* San Francisco: Association for Computing Machinery.

Martin, P., Appelt, D., & Pereira, F. (1983). Transportability and generality in a natural language interface system. *Proceedings of the Eighth Intrnational Joint Conference on Artificial Intelligence* (Vol. 1, pp. 574–581). Los Altos, CA: Morgan Kaufmann.

Miller, J. R. (1982). *System-initiated user assistance: More than just a luxury* (Tech. Rep.). Dallas, TX: Texas Instruments Artificial Intelligence Laboratory.

Miller, J. R., & Blumenthal, B. (1985). *An architecture for generalized intelligent user assistance systems* (Tech. Rep. HI-085-85). Austin, TX: Microelectronics and Computer Technology Corporation.

Moran, T. P. (1983). Getting into a system: External-internal task mapping analysis. In A. Janda (Ed.), *Proceedings of the CHI '83 Conference on Human Factors in Computing Systems* (pp. 45–49). Boston: Association for Computing Machinery.

Myers, B. A., & Buxton, W. (1986). Creating highly interactive and graphical user interfaces by demonstration. *Computer Graphics: Proceedings of ACM SIGGRAPH '86* (pp. 249–258). Dallas: Association for Computing Machinery.

Nakatani, L. H., Egan, D. E., Ruedisueli, L. W., Hawley, P. M., & Lewart, D. K. (1986). TNT: A talking tutor 'n trainer for teaching the use of interactive computer systems. In M. Mantei & P. Orbeton (Eds.), *Proceedings of the CHI '86 Conference on Human Factors in Computing Systems* (pp. 29-34). Boston, MA: Association for Computing Machinery.

Norman, D. A. (1981). The trouble with Unix. *Datamation, 27,* 139-150.

Norman, D. A. (1986). Cognitive engineering. In D. A. Norman & S. W. Draper (Eds.), *User centered system design* (pp. 31-61). Hillsdale, NJ: Lawrence Erlbaum Associates.

Payne, S. J., & Green, T. G. R. (1986). Task-action grammars: A model of the mental representation of task languages. *Human–Computer Interaction, 2,* 93-134.

Polson, P. G., & Kieras, D. E. (1985). A quantitative model of the learning and performance of text editing knowledge. In L. Borman & B. Curtis (Eds.), *Proceedings of the CHI '85 Conference on Human Factors in Computing Systems* (pp. 207-212). San Francisco: Association for Computing Machinery.

Reiser, B. J., Anderson, J. R., & Farrell, R. G. (1985). Dynamic student modeling in an intelligent tutor for LISP programming. In A. Joshi (Ed.), *Proceedings of the Ninth International Joint Conference on Artificial Intelligence* (Vol. 1, pp. 8-13). Los Altos, CA: Morgan Kaufmann.

Richer, M. H., & Clancey, W. J. (1985). GUIDON-WATCH: A graphic interface for viewing a knowledge-based system. *IEEE Computer Graphics and Applications, 5,* 51-64.

Savage, R. E., Habinek, J. K., & Barnhart, T. W. (1981). The design, simulation, and evaluation of a menu-driven interface. *Proceedings of the First Conference on Human Factors in Computing Systems* (pp. 36-40). Gaithersburg, MD: Association for Computing Machinery.

Schmandt, C., & Hulteen, E. A. (1981). The intelligent voice-interactive interface. *Proceedings of the First Conference on Human Factors in Computing Systems* (pp. 363-366). Gaithersburg, MD: Association for Computing Machinery.

Schulert, A. J., Rogers, G. T., & Hamilton, J. A. (1985). ADM: A dialog manager. In L. Borman & B. Curtis (Eds.), *Proceedings of the CHI '85 Conference on Human Factors in Computing Systems* (pp. 177-184). San Francisco: Association for Computing Machinery.

Shneiderman, B. (1986). *Designing the user interface.* Reading, MA: Addison-Wesley.

Shrager, J., & Finin, T. (1982). An expert system that volunteers advice. *Proceedings of the National Conference on Artificial Intelligence* (pp. 74-78). Los Altos, CA: Morgan Kaufmann.

Sibert, J. L., Hurley, W. D., & Bleser, T. W. (1986). An object-oriented user interface management system. *Computer Graphics: Proceedings of ACM SIGGRAPH '86* (pp. 259-268). Dallas, TX: Association for Computing Machinery.

Smith, D. C., Irby, C., Kimball, R., Verplank, W., & Harslem, E. (1982). Designing the Star user interface. *Byte, 7,* 242-282.

Soloway, E., & VanLehn, K. (1985). Tutorial notes for AI applications for education. *International Joint Conference on Artificial Intelligence,* Los Angeles, CA.

Stevens, A. L., & Collins, A. (1977). *The goal structure of a socratic tutor* (Tech. Rep. 3518). Cambridge, MA: Bolt Beranek and Newman.

Teitelman, W. (1984a). A display-oriented programmer's assistant. In D. R. Barstow, H. E. Shrobe, & E. Sandewall (Eds.), *Interactive programming environments* (pp. 240-287). New York: McGraw-Hill.

Teitelman, W. (1984b). A tour through Cedar. *Proceedings of the Seventh International Conference on Software Engineering* (pp. 181-195). Orlando, FL: IEEE.

Tennant, H. (1979). Experience with the evaluation of natural language question answerers. *Proceedings of the Sixth International Joint Conference on Artificial Intelligence* (Vol. 1, pp. 8–13). Tokyo: Morgan Kaufmann.

Tennant, H. R., Ross, K. M., Saenz, R. M., Thompson, C. W., & Miller, J. R. (1983). Menu-based natural language understanding. *Proceedings of the 21st Annual Meeting of the Association for Computational Linguistics* (pp. 151–158). New York: Association for Computing Machinery.

Thacker, C., McCreight, E., Lampson, B., Sproull, R., & Boggs, D. (1979). *Alto: A personal computer* (Tech. Rep. CSL-79-11). Palo Alto: Xerox Palo Alto Research Center.

Tufte, E. R. (1983). *The visual display of quantitative information.* Cheshire, CT: Graphics Press.

Weitzman, L. (1986). *Designer: A knowledge-based graphic design assistant* (Tech. Rep. 138). La Jolla, CA: University of California, San Diego, UCSD Institute for Cognitive Science.

Wong, P. C. S., & Reid, E. R. (1982). FLAIR: User interface dialog design tool. *Computer Graphics, 16,* 87–98.

Zimmerman, T. G., Lanier, J., Blanchard, C., Bryson, S., & Harvill, Y. (1987). A hand gesture interface device. In J. M. Carroll & P. Tanner (Eds.), *Proceedings of the CHI '87 Conference on Human Factors in Computing Systems and Graphics Interface* (pp. 189–192). Toronto: Association for Computing Machinery.

Zissis, A. Y., & Witten, I. H. (1985). User modeling for a computer coach: A case study. *International Journal of Man-Machine Studies, 23,* 729–750.

7

Pragmatic Considerations in Research, Development, and Implementation of Intelligent Tutoring Systems[1]

William B. Johnson
Search Technology, Inc.

INTRODUCTION

The previous chapters in this volume have elaborated on various aspects of intelligent tutoring systems (ITSs). Topics discussed thus far include expert and student modules, design of curriculum, hardware interfaces, and programming environments. The substantive issues and state of the art have been discussed for each of these topics. As the basic research issues are addressed and the applied technical and engineering issues evolve toward solutions, ITSs have the potential for affecting training in business, industry, schools, and the military. However, good science and technology do not in themselves guarantee that ITSs will be successfully integrated into training environments. There are many people-oriented and organizational issues that interact with science and technology. These issues affect whether innovations like ITSs result in successful applications.

ITSs potentially have a wide range of applications across a multitude of disciplines and subject areas. Training related to tactical planning, business decision making, and interpersonal communications are only a few examples of candidates for ITSs. This chapter focuses on technical training for system maintainers and operators. The pragmatic issues related to development and implementation of ITSs are also considered. This chapter complements the previous chapters with a straightforward and practical discussion of the

---

[1]This chapter is complemented by Johnson, W. B. (in press).

personnel who will develop, implement, and evaluate ITSs.

To examine the real-world issues of ITSs, this chapter first considers the users and developers of ITSs by answering the question: *Who* are ITSs for? Second, the chapter addresses the question of what each of these users can expect from ITSs. The expectations section considers not only the formal environments of school and training but also other applications of ITSs. After discussing what ITSs can do and for whom, the chapter takes up the next question: *How* ITSs can be effectively developed and implemented. Implementation issues discussed include not only scientific issues but also organizational considerations and constraints.

Experience with ITS Development

This chapter is based on over a decade of experience with the development, implementation, and evaluation of computer-based training systems (Johnson, 1987, in press), including Framework for Aiding the Understanding of Logical Troubleshooting (FAULT) and Troubleshooting by Application of Structural Knowledge (TASK). During that 10-year period, the developments were in such domains as automotive and aviation mechanics, communication electronics, and nuclear safety systems. These research efforts, conducted by W. B. Johnson, W. B. Rouse, and R. M. Hunt, involved extensive interactions with curriculum developers and instructors, students, and managers in the Army, Navy, electric utility industry, and postsecondary technical training environments. The work ran the gamut from basic research on human problem solving (Johnson, 1981; Rouse & Hunt, 1984) to training applications in an operational environment (Maddox, Johnson, & Frey, 1986). The work involved transfer of training evaluations and early experimentation with intelligent computer-based instruction (Johnson, 1981, 1987). These varied experiences with computer-based instruction projects permit this author to discuss the pragmatic issues associated with the development and implementation of ITSs.

Researchers and developers of ITSs must consider a host of practical issues. These include:

1. Obtaining funding for research and development.
2. Obtaining support across multiple organizational levels.
3. Winning the cooperation of subject matter experts.
4. Conceptualizing and developing usable software within time and budget constraints.
5. Integrating instructional software into the existing curriculum.
6. Evaluating software in the operational training environment.

An experience that this author had early in a project on instructional software development for the military exemplifies these real issues. During the kickoff meeting the commanding officer, a two-star general, commented that computer-based instruction was "high priority" for his post and that we could expect full cooperation from him. In the same day, the subject matter experts and instructors said that they were opposed to computer-based instruction and were reluctant to cooperate. The cooperation of the experts was far more critical than the enthusiasm of the general. Although the general opened the door, the experts and instructors were the key to the development of effective instructional software. Therefore, as that project began, it was an organizational issue, rather than one of science or technology, that threatened the development effort.

EXISTING INTELLIGENT SYSTEMS FOR TRAINING

Artificial intelligence research has been around for over 20 years (Newell, Shaw, & Simon, 1960) and has been followed more recently by research with expert systems. The applications of the technology have influenced such fields as medicine (e.g., INTERNIST/ CADUCEUS, MYCIN, PUFF); chemistry (e.g., DENDRAL); biology (MOLGEN); geology (PROSPECTOR, DRILLING ADVISOR); communications diagnosis (ACE); and locomotive repair (DELTA/ CATSI). These examples of systems in development and evaluation were designed not primarily as instructional or intelligent tutoring systems but as job decision aids that try to bring an expert to any job site, laboratory, or clinic.

As Anderson explains in this volume, when users attempted to validate these expert systems, they wanted to know how the system made decisions. Users who could not obtain and understand the expert system's path to a decision had difficulty accepting the decision. Although expert systems do typically have an exploration facility, this feature is closely tied to the knowledge base and the way it has captured expertise. Often, as was the case with MYCIN, expertise was captured in a highly refined, compiled state. The knowledge was immediately meaningful to experts but obscure or meaningless to novices. Because the structure of the knowledge base could not be easily demonstrated to the user, it was not suitable as a basis for training (Clancey, 1982).

Developers who attempted to improve the explanation of the system's expert decisions began to understand that more than an expert model was needed. It became clear that knowledge had to be represented in an organized way that made explicit the important relations and principles of the content discipline. The system also needed to understand the user (which required a student model) and to know when and how to offer explanation (which required an instructor-curriculum model). Researchers from instructional disciplines became involved with the specification of additional system characteristics for ITSs.

Although there are a number of new ITSs in development today, for example, IMTS, the Navy's Intelligent Maintenance Training System (Towne, 1987), the expert systems that have been developed to provide instruction are relatively few. Further, many of the new systems are proprietary or simply have not yet been extensively described in the available literature. A table of the systems discussed in this volume is given in Appendix I. For the most part, the systems were developed as laboratory tools to test various hypotheses related to specific aspects of learning via ITSs. These early research efforts were constrained by the limits of existing hardware and software. Since then, computational capability has dramatically increased, and the trend is continuing. The impact of these early efforts can be seen in the software and hardware that exist today (Burton, chapter 5).

Limitations of Laboratory ITSs

ITS research conducted in the controlled confines of the laboratory is basic research that paves the way for the development efforts ultimately carried out in the real world. While one laboratory project concentrates solely on student modeling, another project may be devoted to understanding expert diagnostic performance. Other projects may be focusing on processor and interface issues. Ultimately, the fragmented portions of basic research and development must be integrated and tested in real-world applications.

These remarks may sound critical of laboratory research on ITSs, but they are not meant to be. Early development efforts must take place in the research centers of the universities, industry, and military. But these efforts have been underway since the 1960s, and the time has come to concentrate more effort on developing real applications for ITSs. The findings of basic research should be tested against the constraints and unpredictable problems of real training environments. These projects can begin with laboratory prototypes of ITSs; but they must be developed, implemented, and tested in operational training centers. The following sections of this chapter provide guidance for proceeding with real applications.

DESIGNING THE SYSTEM
TO MEET USER NEEDS

The term *tutoring* implies that learning will take place. It follows that the user of an ITS is the student in a classroom; and the student in a classroom is definitely the principal ITS user. However, users also include instructors, curriculum developers, designers, job incumbents, and managers. These groups and their special needs must be considered as ITS research and development continues.

When a system is designed, the needs of the various users must be at the forefront of the designer's attention. In reality, these needs are not necessarily aligned. For example, if the ITS knowledge base is designed to be very easy for the instructor or content expert to develop, the result may be a training system that is not robust enough to meet students' needs or expectations. If the ITS is made to run on an inexpensive, off-the-shelf personal computer, the resulting system may be too slow to meet minimum requirements for multitask processing or response time. On the other hand, when the requirements for the system are a very robust response, sophisticated graphics, fast response, and an interactive knowledge base editor for the expert, the ITS may be so expensive that development is not practical or even possible with present technology. Therefore, successful development and implementation of ITSs depend on setting priorities among users' needs and integrating their requirements. This section considers the requirements of each group of users.

ITSs for Adult Learners

There is likely to be extensive variance within the user population of any ITS. This is particularly true for adult learners in industry and in technical training situations in the military. ITSs must be capable of addressing these conflicting characteristics. For example, some adult learners are impatient with too much review; others are upset with too little review. Some like the "nice to know" facts; others want only the pertinent information. Some are embarrassed to ask questions, and others waste time by asking too many questions. Adults are often outspoken about the time spent reviewing or the time spent teaching theory rather than practice. For example, adults in technical training will question the value of studying an equation for calculating engine thrust when the prime objective is to learn to troubleshoot the fuel control system of a particular jet engine. It is incumbent upon ITS developers to explain to learners why something must be learned.

In a classroom of adult learners, the same people inevitably ask all the questions and thereby place unreasonable demands on both the group's and the instructor's time and resources. A well-designed ITS should be able to cater to the inquisitive learner and permit others to learn at a pace more in tune with their cognitive and learning styles.

Adult learners have additional characteristics that ITS designers should take into account. Adult learners want to perceive immediate transfer of training to the demands of their job. They want reasonable control over the instruction delivered. They are motivated to learn but are occasionally preoccupied with other problems; furthermore, they learn best by integrating past experience and new knowledge with practice problem solving.

The adult learner in the military may be a new soldier learning basic electronic principles or a senior officer practicing decision making in a war simulation. In either case, the training system should be able to adapt to the student first, then monitor and model the student's performance, and finally provide feedback and correction accordingly.

Design Needs for the Technical Training Environment

Anderson (chapter 2) classifies knowledge that can be tutored into three categories: procedural, declarative, and qualitative or causal. For technical training, which usually includes troubleshooting, the ITS must provide tutoring in all of the categories of knowledge. It must do more than the mundane variety of computer-based instruction that merely provides drill and practice or limited tutorial with simplistic branching.

In addition to tutoring all these categories of knowledge, training for a technical system should permit guided exploratory learning. The student should be able to explore how the system works overall and how various components operate or fail to operate. The ITS should permit the user to learn the procedures for operating the system. On a communication system, for example, the student should be able to manipulate controls and observe the effects. That is, the student should be able to try out the system and understand the effect of improper as well as proper operation. In the case of war games, the learner should be permitted to try the "what if" moves and should receive an operationally oriented explanation of how the outcome was derived. As with the technical simulation, such capabilities will enable the learner to understand the consequences of an action. Finally, the ITS should be designed to provide the student with the opportunity to troubleshoot the system, and it should provide tutoring as appropriate.

ITSs must permit errors, but they must also provide appropriate feedback based on the kind of actions the learner chooses. Moreover, this feedback must be provided at the right time. Constant intrusive feedback and advice may be detrimental to instruction (Munro, Fehling, & Towne, 1985). Feedback that is unclear or too narrow in focus may also adversely affect learning (Rouse, Rouse, & Pellegrino, 1980).

The type of feedback that an ITS provides must also be carefully considered. In addition to correcting errors and explaining why an action was an error, ITSs should allow the user to ask, "How am I doing?" The answer can be based on a comparison of the student with other students; a human expert; an information-theoretic model; predetermined criteria; or merely a calculated total of time, actions, and errors. A performance summary that integrates the student's monthly, weekly, or daily progress could also be made available.

Effective integration of ITSs also depends on the quality of the interface between the training device and the users, including instructors and students. The system must be designed so that it is easy to learn and compatible with users' expectations, abilities, and limitations. The issues of learner friendliness, or cognitive ergonomics, are a substantive topic in themselves and are addressed by Miller (chapter 6).

Design Considerations
for Job Site Training

Learning is not limited to the classroom or to the technical training laboratories of industry or the military. In fact, more one-on-one tutoring takes place on the job than in the schools. Therefore, as ITS research continues, considerable attention should be focused on the job site.

ITSs are likely to find their way into the job site as intelligent aids for operations and maintenance personnel. These job aids have taken such names as Intelligent Maintenance Advisors (Richardson & Jackson, 1986) and Maintainer's Associates (National Research Council, 1986). The Integrated Maintenance Information System (IMIS), a U.S. Air Force project, has the potential for providing intelligent job aiding and, eventually, intelligent tutoring. The U.S. Army counterpart to IMIS is called PEAM, the Personalized Electronic Aid for Maintenance.

In the operations area, the Pilot's Associate program, sponsored by the Defense Advanced Research Projects Agency (DARPA), is a notable example of job aiding in the cockpit. A project of the Air

Force Armstrong Aerospace Medical Research Laboratory, called the Designer's Associate, is using expert system technology to provide scientific, technical, and regulatory advice to personnel involved in the specification, design, and acquisition of aircrew training systems. The Designer's Associate project has an additional goal of providing the user with available information in the area of human performance. Other expert systems applications in maintenance are discussed by Richardson, Maxion, Polson, & DeJong (1985).

Intelligent job aids, such as stand-alone devices or those embedded in prime systems, have the potential to provide system instruction, procedural advice on diagnosis and repair, and simulation-based training in the field. As ITS research proceeds, it is imperative that training researchers work closely with job-aiding and logistics researchers. If intelligent job aids and ITSs are developed independently, it is likely that functions will be lost or duplicated when the two systems are integrated.

The integration of training and job aiding in one intelligent device has enormous potential. It could serve to redefine the concept of apprenticeship training. At present, the computer is by no means equal to a human master. However, a well-designed knowledge base and efficient human–computer interface could provide the novice technician with an ever-present, patient, and intelligent mentor. The intelligent maintenance advisor could adapt to the competence level of the user and possibly even enhance the knowledge base from user input.

Meeting the Needs of the Instructor and the Subject Matter Expert

The development of ITSs requires major contributions from the instructors who provide expertise in the subject matter and, often, in technical pedagogy. The importance and role of technical instructors is discussed by Johnson (in press).

If ITSs are to be effective in technical training environments, the instructors will also have to take a leadership role in development. To make their participation possible, tools must be developed to permit technical experts to create a knowledge base without the help of knowledge engineers or artificial intelligence experts. The development of such tools was one of the goals of the Steamer project (Hollan, Hutchins, & Weitzman, 1984) and continues to be a primary goal of the IMTS (Burton, chapter 5; Towne, 1987). Another project that is developing tools for ITSs is Knowledge Acquisition/Intelligent Authoring Aides (KA/IAA). This tri-service project will develop ITS authoring tools and demonstration systems in the domains of satellite control, explosive ordnance disposal, and electronic troubleshooting. A primary goal of this project is to develop tools that subject matter experts who know little about computers can use to develop ITSs.

The development and field use of ITS authoring tools should be a high priority over the next 5 years. An ITS authoring system should be used by content experts and instructors, working first with artificial intelligence researchers and then by themselves. Practical applications will permit researchers to identify problems and new development needs. These field tests of existing technology will permit ITS authoring systems to evolve along with the basic research on ITSs in the laboratory.

ISSUES IN IMPLEMENTING ITSs

Thus far, this chapter has briefly mentioned a few examples of existing ITSs and attempted to identify the design requirements for meeting the needs and expectations of ITS users. It has also described characteristics of ITSs in the classroom and on the job. This final section addresses pragmatic issues related to the implementation of ITSs.

Identifying Candidates for ITS Application

The identification of likely candidates for the application of ITSs may look like the search for a "problem to the solution [the ITS]." That is not the case. Advances in computer technology, in both hardware and software, combined with successful efforts to understand how humans learn, have put researchers and training system developers in a position to improve instruction with technology. Although ITSs are still in their infancy, the time has come to make the transition from the laboratory to the field. It is time to use existing authoring systems and various commercial expert system shells to attempt to build ITSs and try them out.

Candidate application areas for ITSs should be evaluated according to several constraints, or pragmatic considerations, which are discussed in this section. These constraints are formidable, but they can be controlled if handled correctly.

The first consideration is that ITSs will require programming tools and hardware that may or may not exist when the project begins. However, this problem may not be insurmountable.

The second consideration is that the programming environments and hardware capabilities are in a constant state of flux. The particular programming language with which the development of an ITS begins is likely to undergo numerous modifications before the project delivers a product. The hardware is continually changing and offering improvements in memory, storage, and processing speed. Although such changes often cause a minor rewrite of software, they are also likely to increase user capability, thus raising the potential ITS payoff.

A third consideration is that for now and the foreseeable future, the development of ITSs is labor-intensive. It requires an extensive commitment of time from scientists and engineers, computer programmers, knowledge engineers, and subject matter experts. A few ITS authoring environments are emerging, but they will need constant support and improvement from the artificial intelligence experts in universities, industry, and military laboratories. Basic research in cognitive science and various areas of psychology and human engineering will continue to yield new findings that must be incorporated into the development of ITSs. Applications-oriented researchers now must take the existing technology into classrooms and training centers. Subject matter experts should participate in ITS development to evaluate the tools and products of those tools.

The fourth consideration is that thorough formative and summative evaluation of ITSs will in itself require substantial resources.

Characteristics of Candidate Application Areas

The following characteristics describe areas that are suitable for traditional computer-assisted instruction. These characteristics are particularly relevant to candidate application areas for ITSs because the level of resources necessary for their development is so high:

1. High flow of students.
2. Expensive real equipment.
3. Unavailable real equipment.
4. Unsafe real equipment.
5. Critical skill and knowledge must be developed.
6. Training conducted at remote sites.
7. Low availability of instructors.
8. High public visibility.
9. Need for high volume of recurrent training.

To maximize the effective use of resources and to achieve high cost-effectiveness, ITSs should be used for instructional areas that have a high annual flow of students. A high volume of students will also be attained if it is expected that the ITS will be used for many years. Principles of electricity and electronics, turbine engine operation and diagnosis, radar operation and repair, satellite communications operations, and digital computer operation are only a few examples of courses with a high flow of students. Many of these courses traditionally have been the focus of educational technology research and development.

High student flow is not the only way of justifying the cost of ITS development. Prime equipment is often not available or not practical as an instructional device, other than for on-the-job training. This characteristic applies to such examples as training for nuclear fuel–loading equipment, nuclear power plant operations, explosive ordnance disposal, and system troubleshooting on the launch processing system for the space shuttle. These examples also represent tasks where performance must be both error-free and timely.

Technical training is often delivered at numerous remote sites where there may be very few students. Many remote sites do not have an instructor, training equipment, or space designated for training. Also, the demands of the job may not provide a scheduled time for necessary training. In these cases, personnel may be required to perform a critical task that they learned in a technical class 5 years before. A ship, submarine, remote air base, and orbiting space station are examples of remote locations where needed training might best be delivered with ITSs. The ITS does not have to be a stand-alone, dedicated training device. Instructional software can be embedded in the prime system, which can then be used to provide training. This embedded training can be as basic as using a word processor to teach a user to operate the word-processing system or as complex as permitting a fighter pilot to fly simulated battles with training software embedded into the aircraft's avionics and weapons systems.

The unavailability of competent instructional personnel may also drive the decision to develop ITSs in a given area. When this is the case, the expertise of the limited number of instructors can be incorporated into an ITS.

A combination of characteristics such as high student flow, complex or unavailable prime systems, and a low number of available instructors is a reasonable justification for the development and use of an ITS. These characteristics, however, do not necessarily mean that an ITS can be developed. Other questions must be asked about the prime system and organizational resources to determine whether an ITS is feasible:

1. Can the area for expertise be clearly defined?
2. Does human expertise exist in this area?
3. Can human experts communicate their knowledge?

4. Does an ITS authoring system and approach fit the needs of the training system?

5. Do human and computer resources exist to develop, implement, evaluate, and support the ITS?

Given present ITS development tools and strategies, humans must supply a substantial amount of subject matter expertise. In the future, particularly for technical training, it may be possible to extract this expertise from computer-aided design and manufacturing data.

The area of expertise must be clearly defined. For example, an ITS cannot be expected to train a person to be an all-round troubleshooter on all electronic equipment. The work on the TASK and FAULT systems showed that training must be context-specific to maximize transfer to real equipment. An example of a clearly defined area of development is the Intelligent Maintenance Trainer System project at Behavioral Technology Laboratory. The first ITS system developed for that project deals with the rotary blade system of a specific Navy helicopter. However, this specific knowledge base is a by-product of a larger effort to develop generic tools for ITS authoring.

The availability of ITS authoring tools should also be considered. The complexity of writing an ITS from the ground up in LISP, PROLOG, or another artificial intelligence language would far surpass the effort using an ITS development system. But there are two problems. First, ITS designers would be limited to the ITS design constraints imposed by the developers of the authoring system. Second, there are currently no such complete ITS development packages available. The best compromise at this time is an "open" system that would provide authoring tools and also permit the combined use, as needed, of a programming language for artificial intelligence.

Finally, the feasibility of an ITS also depends on the human and computer resources needed to develop, implement, evaluate, and maintain the system. The answer to this question has, of course, a very broad range depending on how ambitious the project is. This author is familiar with estimates of the time it takes to develop simulation-oriented computer-based instruction that range from 200 to 400 hours of development for 1 hour of instruction. Anderson (chapter 2) estimates that development of an expert module may require "hundreds" of development hours per instructional hour. Building the student module and the instructor module are also sizeable tasks that may have ratios of 100 to 200 hours of development per student hour. Using these rough numbers and assuming that much of the work will be done by senior-level researchers means that the early single-copy ITSs are likely to be extremely expensive. The hope is, of course, that the research needed for these early systems will develop concepts and tools that will ultimately be widely used and eventually justify the initial expenditures.

ITS APPLICATIONS AND RESEARCH

This volume describes the scientific, technological, and organizational issues related to ITSs. The previous chapters, for the most part, have described basic research issues and suggested priorities for continued basic research. This chapter has complemented the others by addressing the pragmatic and applied issues related to ITSs. Therefore, this chapter ends with recommendations for research related to ITS applications.

Research Directions
for the Application of ITSs

Near-term research should capitalize on the interim results of research and development in progress and on findings from projects that have recently been completed. The goals of near-term research and development should be the following:

1. Refine existing tools by developing ITSs.
2. Explore the development and delivery of ITSs on microcomputers.
3. Use existing expert system shells for ITSs.
4. Study the cognitive aspects of user interfaces.
5. Commit to evaluation.
6. Integrate intelligent job aiding with intelligent training.

The first recommendation is to move forward from the laboratories to real-world applications. Such efforts will permit researchers and curricula developers to identify software and hardware limitations. Further, these efforts will refine the tools and practices of ITS development. The Navy has funded the Steamer project and, most recently, the Intelligent Maintenance Training System (IMTS). The IMTS project has produced its first demonstration system, a helicopter maintenance and troubleshooting system. The second effort of that project will more closely involve Navy technical personnel in the knowledge development phase. While the second development is underway, the first system will be evaluated in an operational training squadron. Simultaneous development and use will accelerate maturation of the IMTS and other such ITSs.

The Knowledge Acquisition/Intelligent Authoring Aids (KA/ IAA) is another example of research in progress that will result in tools for ITS development. This project will demonstrate an ITS system first in a U.S. Army training environment, although the work is sponsored by the Army, Navy, and Air Force.

In the short term, the efforts of the KA/IAA and IMTS projects can be expanded. If a variety of research and development teams are permitted to use and modify the ITS authoring tools, the results are likely to be improved ITS development systems within 3 to 5 years. In that same time frame, hardware capabilities will improve, thus improving the ITSs.

Not all of ITS development and delivery has to be done on dedicated artificial intelligence workstations. A near-term effort might compare expert system development capabilities of off-the-shelf microcomputers and AI workstations. Such comparison must consider not only capabilities but also costs. The cost trade-offs must incorporate in particular the expected time needed to develop ITS software based on the capabilities of the respective machines and programming environments.

Near-term research should explore the use of personal computers for ITS delivery. When the ITS must be delivered on an AI workstation, its acceptance is hampered because the user organization is not likely to have a reasonable number of such stations in each training center. The abundance and low cost of personal computers make them likely candidates for ITS delivery.

If microcomputers are used as development systems, it may be possible to capitalize on existing expert system shells that are readily available. The off-the-shelf frameworks for expert system development are most likely to provide the expert module as described by Anderson (chapter 2). However, other portions of the ITS system, such as the student module, will have to be developed and integrated with the existing software.

An Air Force example of a small-scale effort implemented on an IBM PC/XT is described by White and Cross (1986). They combined an instructional program written in PASCAL with the M.1 expert system shell by Teknowledge, Inc., to build a small ITS for a war game called TEMPO. Their project selected the low-cost, off-the-shelf hardware to make their ITS available in numerous Air Force locations. Their program can be modified for real-world applications and provides an intelligent computer adversary as a gaming partner. It includes an instructor-expert module to provide advice and a performance critique.

Another near-term research effort should be the integration of ITSs with existing and proven computer-based training systems. This type of project can capitalize on the computer systems already in place as well as on the organizational support for those systems.

Ongoing evaluation is an important near-term research goal (see Littman & Soloway, chapter 8). Evaluation should focus on existing ITS development tools. It should also assess the value of ITSs over conventional computer-based instruction and over nonautomated instruction. These evaluations could determine whether the ITS is instructionally sound and cost-effective. Further, evaluations will help to identify the strengths and weaknesses of current ITSs and provide direction for future research and development. In the near term, research might broaden the scope of evaluation to include new measures that are reflective of the reality of the workplace. In a frenzy to develop new systems the tendency is often to deemphasize evaluation. Ideally, ITS research and development should avoid that temptation.

ITS development must place adequate emphasis on the user interface (see Miller, chapter 6). ITSs must be developed to be easy to use. Research should focus on the learnability of intelligent instructional software. A research effort of this type might focus on "cognitive ergonomics," which refers not to typical human-factor considerations like character, size, color, and contrast but to the extent that the user can easily understand and learn from the system. The result might be a set of guidelines to be used not only by ITS designers but by all personnel involved with the design of prime or training systems.

A previous section discussed the job incumbent and issues related to intelligent job aids and embedded training in real equipment systems. This author believes that researchers in the fields of intelligent job aiding and ITSs should develop a close working relationship. Lack of cooperation between these research communities will result in redundant efforts and difficulties with integrating their work at a later date.

The near-term research and development efforts will support long-term goals as well as define new ones. This chapter has concentrated on the use of ITSs in technical training and has not addressed such areas as tactical decison making, business management, interpersonal communications, or public education.

The near-term recommendations imply that the depth of ITS research can be increased by building and evaluating tools and application systems in various technical domains. Long-term research should emphasize the breadth rather than the depth of ITS development. This research should investigate whether the tools and techniques of ITSs for technical subject matter will transfer to other instructional areas.

SUMMARY

This chapter has answered the following questions: Who will use ITSs? What can each user expect from ITSs? How can ITSs be developed? It has emphasized real-world pragmatic issues related to ITS development. The field of ITSs is in its infancy, and development efforts are likely to be labor-intensive. However, now is the time to develop and test ITSs in a variety of training applications. The science and technology, although not fully matured, are ready to undergo preliminary application.

REFERENCES

Clancey, W. J. (1982). Tutoring rules for guiding a case method dialog. In D. Sleeman and J. S. Brown (Eds.), *Intelligent tutoring systems* (pp. 201–225). New York: Academic Press.

Hollan, J. D., Hutchins, E. L., & Weitzman, L. (1984). Steamer: An interactive inspectable simulation-based training system. *The AI Magazine, 5,* 15–27.

Johnson, W. B. (1981). Computer simulations for fault diagnosis training: An empirical study of learning from simulation to live system performance. (Doctoral dissertation, University of Illinois, 1980). *Dissertation Abstracts International, 41,* 4625-A.

Johnson, W. B. (1987). Development and evaluation of simulation-oriented computer-based instruction for diagnostic training. In W. B. Rouse (Ed.), *Advances in man-machine systems research* (Vol. 3, pp. 99–127). Greenwich, CT: JAI Press.

Maddox, M. E., Johnson, W. B., & Frey, P. R. (1986). *Diagnostic training for nuclear power plant personnel: Vol. 2. Implementation and evaluations* (EPRI NP-3829). Palo Alto, CA: Electric Power Research Institute.

Munro, A., Fehling, M. R., & Towne, D. M. (1985). Instruction intrusiveness in dynamic simulation training. *Journal of Computer-Based Instruction, 12,* 50–53.

National Research Council. (1986). *Isolation of faults in Air Force weapons and support systems.* Washington, DC: National Academy Press.

Newell, A., Shaw, J. C., & Simon, H. A. (1960). A variety of intelligent learning in a general problem-solver. In M. C. Yovits & S. Cameron (Eds.), *Self-organizing systems* (pp. 153–189). New York: Pergamon.

Richardson, J. J., & Jackson, T. E. (1986). Developing the technology for intelligent maintenance advisors. *Journal of Computer-Based Instruction, 13,* 47–51.

Richardson, J. J., Maxion, R. A., Polson, P. G., & DeJong, K. A. (1985). *Artificial intelligence in maintenance: Synthesis of technical issues* (AFHRL-TR-85-7). Brooks Air Force Base, TX: Air Force Human Resources Laboratory.

Rouse, W. B., & Hunt, R. M. (1984). Human problem solving in fault diagnosis tasks. In W. B. Rouse (Ed.), *Advances in Man–Machine Systems Research* (Vol. 1, pp. 195–222). Greenwich, CT: JAI Press.

Rouse, W. B., Rouse, S. H., & Pellegrino, S. J. (1980). A rule-based model of human problem solving performance in fault diagnosis tasks. *IEEE Transactions on Systems, Man, and Cybernetics, SCM-10,* 366–376.

Towne, D. M. (1987). The generalized maintenance trainer: Evolution and revolution. In W. B. Rouse (Ed.), *Advances in Man–Machine Systems Research* (Vol. 3, pp. 1–63). Greenwich, CT: JAI Press.

White, G. B., & Cross, S. E. (1986). TEMPO-AI: Using artificial intelligence concepts in war gaming and professional military education. *Proceedings of the Air Force Conference on Technology in Training and Education* (pp. V-98–V-117). Montgomery, AL: Air University, U.S. Air Force Academy.

Evaluating ITSs:
The Cognitive Science Perspective

David Littman
Elliot Soloway
Yale University

INTRODUCTION

There can be no doubt that evaluating Intelligent Tutoring Systems (ITSs) is costly, frustrating, and time-consuming. In fact, in our own work to build PROUST, one component of an ITS for introductory programming students, evaluation has consumed nearly as much effort as the design of PROUST itself. If evaluation of ITSs is so costly, why do it at all? Wouldn't it be better just to finish one ITS and then build the next one, perhaps letting the marketplace determine survival? On the contrary: Our experience with PROUST has taught us that, far from being a useless burden, evaluation pays off by helping to answer two evaluation questions that are central to cognitive science, Artificial Intelligence (AI), and education:

1. *Evaluation Question 1:* What is the educational impact of an ITS on students?
2. *Evaluation Question 2:* What is the relationship between the architecture of an ITS and its behavior?

Our attempts to evaluate PROUST with the two evaluation questions in mind have proved to be very beneficial. We have learned a great deal that we might not otherwise have learned about how novices learn to program, how to teach programming, and how to build ITSs to actually do the teaching.

As we have gained experience evaluating PROUST, we have found that addressing the two evaluation questions leads to a somewhat different perspective on evaluation from that of traditional educational evaluation. Traditional educational evaluation consists of two main categories, formative and summative evaluation. Designers of educational technology use formative evaluation to define and refine their goals and methods *during* the design process. They use summative evaluation to determine whether a finished educational product is effective *after* it has been built. Because building ITSs is still somewhat an art, and because there are few ITSs that can be called "finished," designers of ITSs are currently more concerned with usefully guiding the development of their systems than with determining whether they are effective educational end products. At least for the time being, then, the idea of formative evaluation seems more appropriate for designers of ITSs than does the idea of summative evaluation. Hence, we have formulated Evaluation Question 1 and Evaluation Question 2 to be much more focused on the development of ITSs than on determining whether they are effective educational end products.

Unfortunately, there is no standard set of evaluation methods for addressing the two evaluation questions—the field of ITSs is too young. However, as a result of our ongoing evaluation of PROUST, we have begun to define two classes of evaluation methods that are useful for this purpose. One class consists of methods based on recent progress in student modeling. From them, researchers can learn how an ITS affects students and changes their knowledge and problem-solving skills. Methods in this case can be used for *external evaluation,* so called because this kind of evaluation assesses an effect external to the ITS, namely the student's learning. External evaluation therefore addresses Evaluation Question 1.

The second class of evaluation methods, adapted from knowledge engineering techniques developed for AI, can be used to construct an accurate picture of the relationship between the architecture of an ITS and its actual behavior. These methods are the basis of *internal evaluation,* which is concerned with the inner workings of an ITS. Internal evaluation therefore addresses Evaluation Question 2.

In this chapter we explore external and internal evaluation and demonstrate how the two classes of methods we have developed have helped us to address the two evaluation questions. In particular, we show how using the methods to evaluate PROUST has made it possible for us to (a) isolate specific aspects of PROUST that have particular effects on students' learning and (b) understand more clearly how the design and implementation of PROUST lead to its behavior. One of the major benefits of external and internal evaluation is that they have greatly enhanced our ability to improve and modify PROUST in a controlled, goal-directed manner as we design and redesign subsequent versions; this is, we argue, a primary goal of current work in ITSs.

Even though our methods of evaluation have been productive, we are aware that we tread new, potentially controversial ground. We are equally aware that, at this time, we cannot present a fully formed theory of external and internal evaluation. Nonetheless, the potential usefulness of the directions and techniques for evaluation identified in this chapter warrant their presentation to the ITS community.

The remainder of this chapter explores the possibility of evaluating ITSs from the perspective of external and internal evaluation. First, we look more closely at external evaluation to see how recent advances in cognitive science have made it possible to perform fine-grained analyses of the impact of an ITS on a student's understanding. These methods are illustrated with examples of evaluations of PROUST, our ITS for novice programming. Next, we describe some of the knowledge engineering methods of internal evaluation we have used to gain insight into the relationship between the architecture of an ITS and its behavior. These methods are also illustrated with examples from our own work with PROUST. Then, we show how methods similiar to those of external and internal evaluation have been used to evaluate several well-known ITSs. Finally, we indicate several issues for future research that are implied by our analysis of evaluation.

EXTERNAL EVALUATION: THE COGNITIVE PERSPECTIVE

Recent progress in cognitive science and AI has provided the field of computer-based instruction with new and powerful tools—namely process-based student models (see VanLehn, chapter 3)—for representing students' knowledge and problem-solving skills. Because these tools were not available to researchers who developed Computer Aided Instruction (CAI), they made the reasonable and pragmatic assumption that students' answers to test questions adequately reflected their mental processes. The goal of evaluating CAI, therefore, has been primarily to determine whether students can correctly respond to test questions. With the advent of process-based student models, however, the goal of evaluating ITSs ought to be much more ambitious. That goal should be to determine how well the ITS teaches students the knowledge and skills that support the cognitive processes required for solving problems in the content domain of the ITS.

This cognitive perspective on external evaluation, made possible by student modeling, is the topic of this section. We first define student models and discuss their potential role in evaluation. We then report on our external evaluation of PROUST; finally we address some anticipated criticisms of applying the cognitive perspective to external evaluation.

Student Models
and Their Use in Evaluation

As an ITS interacts with a student, it builds up an understanding of the student's knowledge and skills, which it uses to interpret the student's behavior and, in part, to guide its own actions. The common name for the ITS's understanding of the student is "student model." In order for an ITS to build a student model its designers must provide it with methods for reasoning about students' problem-solving in the ITS's domain of instruction. There are many kinds of student modeling methods (see VanLehn, chapter 3) but two major types are those that are based on process models of problem solving and those that are not.

Student modeling techniques based on process models solve problems in a supposedly humanlike way. For example, the student modeling component in Anderson's LISP tutor is based on a process model of how students write simple LISP programs and is embodied in their GRAPES simulator (Anderson, Farrell, & Sauers, 1984).

The LISP tutor uses the GRAPES simulator to simulate the problem solving of novice LISP programmers when they write simple LISP programs. The student model is thus represented in terms of what the GRAPES process model did to solve the problem.

Student models that are not based on comprehensive process modeling do not solve problems as humans do. For example, WUSOR, the tutor for the discovery game WUMPUS built by Carr and Goldstein (Goldstein, 1982), has a checklist of skills required for playing WUMPUS. The student model simply consists of the skills that have been checked off in WUSOR's representation of the skills. WUSOR does not try to play WUMPUS as a student would in order to build its student model and, hence, does not use process models.

Whether or not student models actually have process models that simulate students' behavior, they can be used to assess how well the ITS teaches students skills and knowledge for solving problems that are like the problems encountered during learning. First, student modeling techniques can guide the construction of new problems for testing the student. Because these techniques use explicit representations of problem solving knowledge and skills, and possibly the actual processes of problem solving, they can be used to predict how well the student will perform on the new problems and, thus, which problems should lead to effective problem solving and which to ineffective problem solving.

Because student modeling techniques capture *how* students solve problems and not merely that they *can* solve the problems, they can be used to identify problems that the student should be able to solve. Student modeling techniques that are not based on process models can be used to predict some of the knowledge and skills the student will use to solve problems. Process-based techniques can be used to predict the actual process the student will go through to solve problems. Thus, the evaluation of ITSs can be substantially different from the evaluation of CAI. The latter focuses primarily on correct and incorrect answers; the former assesses the *reasons* that students give correct and incorrect answers.

In the foregoing discussion, we have purposely glossed over an important issue: the degree of completeness, or comprehensiveness, of the process model underlying the ITS. For example, Repair theory (Brown & VanLehn, 1980) is a relatively comprehensive process model of how people carry out subtraction. In contrast, the process model underlying PROUST, our system that diagnoses students' buggy programs, is considerably less comprehensive. Although comprehensiveness is desirable, it is not always possible, and it is not even necessary for evaluation. In fact, a student model such as the checklist of skills used in WUMPUS and WEST can still provide insight into the microstructure of the skills and concepts students use when they solve problems. In an external evaluation of an ITS the criterion is not how many of the students' answers are correct but rather the underlying, fine-grained skills that have been learned. To measure these skills during the development of an ITS, it is important to be able to perform external evaluation with models that are not complete. In the next section, we address the problem of external evaluation with incomplete process models by showing how we were able to evaluate the impact of PROUST on a circumscribed aspect of students' programming.

An Example of External Evaluation: PROUST

This section presents our initial attempts to perform an external evaluation of PROUST. First, we describe PROUST and how it works; then we discuss our approach to the problem of external evaluation.

Our external evaluation of PROUST was based on a process model of novice PASCAL programming. We reasoned about the process model to identify skills we thought PROUST should help students learn. Of course, our process model of novice programming is incomplete. Thus, one implication of our successful evaluation of PROUST is that it is not necessary to have a complete process model in order to perform an external evaluation from the cognitive perspective. This result is encouraging because the development and evaluation of ITSs must be done concurrently and because of the unavoidable necessity of making evaluations with incomplete process models.

A Description of PROUST

PROUST is a large LISP program written by Lewis Johnson (1986) that finds the nonsyntactic bugs in students' PASCAL programs. PROUST is especially expert at finding bugs in programs that students write for the Rainfall Assignment, shown in Figure 8.1. The assignment, which is usually given during the fifth week of class, is to write an enhanced "averaging program" that calculates from an input stream of rainfall values the average, the maximum rainfall on any day in the period, the number of rainy days, and so forth. The program also prints out several summary values.

A correct solution to the rainfall assignment is shown in Figure 8.2. Figure 8.3 shows part of a buggy solution that contains three extremely common bugs; Figure 8.4 shows what a student sees as a result of asking PROUST to identify the bugs in the program in Figure 8.3. Notice especially that the output of PROUST is essentially an identification of the student's bugs, sometimes accompanied by a brief statement of how the bug violates the specifications of the assignment. In addition, PROUST makes an effort to tell the student which bugs it thinks are important for various parts of the program (e.g., the "OUTPUT part"). Thus, the first bug that PROUST reports is very common: Students often neglect to consider the case in which

---

The Noah Problem: Noah needs to keep track of the rainfall in the New Haven area to determine when to launch his ark. Write a program so he can do this. Your program should read the rainfall for each day, stopping when Noah types "99999", which is not a data value, but a sentinel indicating the end of input. If the user types in a negative value the program should reject it, since negative rainfall is not possible. Your program should print out the number of valid days typed in, the number of rainy days, the average rainfall per day over the period, and the maximum amount of rainfall that fell on any one day.

FIGURE 8.1   The Rainfall Assignment.

the user does not enter any valid data. If no data are entered, a runtime division-by-zero error occurs and can cause the program to discontinue its run.

To analyze a student's program, PROUST attempts to see how the student's program has attempted to meet the specifications of a problem statement. PROUST understands problem specifications in terms of goals that must be achieved and uses a knowledge base of plans that students know and that can achieve those goals. PROUST's main analytic task is to locate in the student's code the plans for each of the goals in the problem specification. For example, in the rainfall assignment, the main goal is to calculate the average of a series of rainfall values entered by the user. PROUST recognizes that to achieve the averaging goal, an iterative looping plan is required to achieve the subgoals of the main goal. The loop must collect the rainfall values, sum them to calculate the running total, and count the number of days. After the running total and counter have been calculated, the running total must be divided by the counter to obtain the average. PROUST thus sets up an agenda of goals and subgoals and attempts to match each of them to the student's code by using

```
Program Rainfall(input,output);
  Var DailyRainfall,TotalRainfall,MaxRainfall,Average : Real;
     RainyDays,TotalDays : Integer;
  Begin
    RainyDays:= 0; TotalDays:= 0; MaxRainfall:= 0; TotalRainfall:= 0;
    Writeln ('Please Enter Amount of Rainfall');
    Readln(DailyRainfall);
    While (DailyRainfall <> 99999) Do
      Begin
        If DailyRainfall >= 0 Then
          Begin
            If DailyRainfall > 0 Then RainyDays := RainyDays + 1;
            TotalRainfall    := TotalRainfall + DailyRainfall;
            If DailyRainfall > MaxRainfall
               Then MaxRainfall := DailyRainfall;
            TotalDays := TotalDays + 1
          End;
        Else Writeln ('Rainfall Must Be Greater Than 0');
      Read(DailyRainfall)
    End;
    If TotalDaysCounter > 0 Then  Begin
        Average := TotalRainfall/TotalDays;
        Writeln('Average is: ', Average: 0:2);
        Writeln('Maximum is: ', MaxRainfall: 0:2);
        Writeln('Total Number of Days is: ', TotalDays);
        Writeln('Total Number of Rainy Days is: ', RainyDays)
    End;
    Else Writeln('No Valid Days Entered.');
  End.
```

FIGURE 8.2 Sample of a correct rainfall program.

```
01 Program Rainfall(input,output);
02    Var DailyRainfall,TotalRainfall,MaxRainfall,Average : Real;
03        RainyDays,TotalDays : Integer;
04    Begin
05        RainyDays:= 0; TotalDays:= 0; MaxRainfall:= 0; TotalRainfall:= 0;
06        While (DailyRainfall <> 99999) Do
07            Begin
                    .
                    .
                    .
33            End;

    BUG 1: Missing Divide-By-Zero Guard
34            Average := TotalRainfall/TotalDays;
    BUG 2: Missing Output Guard On Average
35            Writeln('Average is: ', Average: 0:2);
    BUG 3: Missing Output Guard On Maximum
36            Writeln('Maximum is: ', MaxRainfall: 0:2);
                    .
                    .
                    .
    End.
```

FIGURE 8.3 Sample of an incorrect rainfall program.

techniques for finding buggy implementations of plans. When all the goals on the agenda have been successfully matched to the student's code, a process that sometimes invokes the techniques for finding buggy plans, PROUST has understood the student's program because it knows how the student achieved, or failed to achieve, each of the goals in the specification. Each of the failures is understood by PROUST as a bug.

External Evaluation of PROUST

Johnson's (1986) analyses show that Proust is also able to understand between 70% and 80% of all programs written by novices trying to solve the rainfall assignment; other evaluations of PROUST's ability to find bugs have been reported as well (cf. Sack et al., 1986). This discussion will not repeat the results covered in other papers. It focuses instead on whether a program that simply identifies nonsyntactic bugs for novice programmers and provides only minimal, noninteractive, tutorial advice can positively affect their programming skills. This evaluation is based on our process model of novice programming. As noted before, although the model is incomplete and somewhat idealized, it nonetheless makes some interesting statements about bugs that should cause novices difficulty.

Boundary condition bugs are in this category. A boundary

condition bug occurs when the programmer neglects to guard some aspect of the program, such as an arithmetic calculation, against an unexpected value. Examples of boundary condition bugs are shown in Figure 8.5. In BUG 1 the student has overlooked the boundary condition in which the user does not enter any valid data. The calculation of the average results in division by zero, which causes the program to crash. The other bugs arise in the same boundary condition and result not in the crash of the program but in the illegal output of a value. For example, BUG 2 permits the average to be printed out even if it was never calculated.

Very generally, the process model of program generation posits that a programmer reads a problem statement, identifies from it goals to attain, and then selects and implements plans to achieve the goals. The model predicts that errors involving boundary condition bugs are easy to make but hard to find because goals for handling boundary conditions do not typically arise directly from the statement of the problem. A programmer must infer that boundary conditions are necessary from knowledge about negative instances; for example, users who do not enter any valid data. The programmer must then create a safeguard to insure that legal values have been entered. According to the process model, novices are deficient in generalized programming knowledge and, therefore, do not identify goals such as safeguarding boundary conditions; moreover, they typically do not have plans for achieving the boundary condition goal even if they identify it. Thus, they frequently make boundary condition bugs.

```
Starting Bug Analysis, please wait ...
NOW BEGINNING BUG REPORT:

Now Reporting CRITICAL Bugs in the OUTPUT part of your program:

Bug 1:   You need a test to check that at least one valid data point has been
         input before line 34 is executed.  The Average will bomb when
         there is no input.


Now Reporting MINOR Bugs in the OUTPUT part of your program:

Bug 2:   The average is undefined if there is no input.  But line 35 outputs
         it anyway.  You should output the average only when there is
         something to compute the average of.

Bug 3:   The maximum is undefined if there is no input.  But line 35 outputs
         it anyway.  You should output the maximum only when there is
         to compute the maximum of.

BUG REPORT NOW COMPLETE.
```

FIGURE 8.4   PROUST output for program in Figure 8.3

```
Program Rainfall(input,output);
  Var DailyRainfall,TotalRainfall,MaxRainfall,Average : Real;
      RainyDays,TotalDays : Integer;
  Begin
    RainyDays:= 0; TotalDays:= 0; MaxRainfall:= 0; TotalRainfall:= 0;
    Writeln ('Please Enter Amount of Rainfall');
    Readln(DailyRainfall);
    While (DailyRainfall <> 99999) Do
      Begin
        If (DailyRainfall > 0) Then
                    .
                    .
                    .
        Read(DailyRainfall)
      End;
BUG 1: Divide-By-Zero-Guard Missing
        Average := TotalRainfall/TotalDays;
BUG 2: No Guard For Undefined Average
        Writeln('Average is: ', Average: 0:2);
BUG 3: No Guard For Undefined Maximum
        Writeln('Maximum is: ', MaxRainfall: 0:2);
        Writeln('Total Number of Days is: ', TotalDays);
BUG 4: No Guard For Undefined Rainydays
        Writeln('Total Number of Rainy Days is: ', RainyDays)
  End.
```

FIGURE 8.5   Some boundary condition bugs.

The process model predicts both how easy it is to make bugs and how hard it is to find them. The bug of failing to include an update for the counter for the divisor in an averaging program is both easy to make and easy to find because its effects are apparent as soon as the program attempts to calculate an average. Boundary condition bugs are easy to make but hard to find because they show up only under specific input conditions. If students do not generate sufficient test data for their programs, they will rarely find their boundary condition bugs. Because effective testing of programs requires extensive generalized programming knowledge, most novices are poor program testers. (J. Spohrer of Yale is currently elaborating the process model based on extensive empirical data about students' buggy programs. This model more fully accounts for the prevalence of boundary condition bugs.)

We focused our initial evaluation of PROUST on how well it could help students manage boundary condition bugs for three reasons. First, boundary condition bugs are some of the most common bugs students make. Second, our process model offers a reasonable account of why they are easy to make and hard to find. Third, PROUST is very good at identifying them so they are prime candidates for an evaluation of how well a bug identification program can help students.

In addition to evaluating boundary condition bugs we also assessed PROUST's impact on students' ability to manage other types of bugs but we do not present those results here.

A Guide to External Evaluation

The goal of an external evaluation of an ITS is to identify properties of the ITS that affect students' problem-solving processes in positive and negative ways. From our experiences in performing external evaluations of PROUST, we have abstracted a pattern of activities that characterizes our approach to the analysis. Figure 8.6 illustrates our approach to assessing the effectiveness of PROUST and, by extension, any ITS. The top portion of the figure, labeled "THEORY," shows the four theoretical components of an external evaluation. The bottom portion of the figure, labeled "PRACTICE," shows the way in which these components were combined in practice in an evalu-

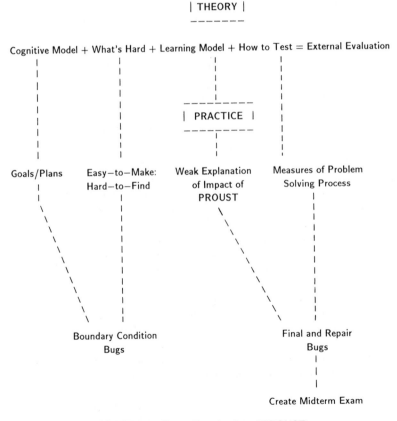

FIGURE 8.6 External evaluation of PROUST.

ation of PROUST. Thus, as the figure shows, construction of an evaluation of an ITS typically follows a well-defined plan. The following description discusses each component of external evaluation in terms of the underlying concept and the application it has to the external evaluation of PROUST.

1. Cognitive Model:

   Concept: Determine which aspects of the cognitive model are relevant to evaluating the effects of the ITS on students' programming skills.

   Application: In the present case we focused on goals that are implicit in problem statements and on the plans that are required to achieve these goals.

2. What's Hard:

   Concept: Identify a class of problems that arise from a task that students have trouble doing.

   Application: In the present case we reasoned that (a) boundary conditions bugs are easy for students to make because they call for specialized knowledge to identify and plan for them and (b) they are hard to find because most students do not know how to generate effective test cases that would detect them.

3. Learning Model:

   Concept: Determine which functional aspects of the ITS should affect students' ability to avoid or correct the target problems.

   Application: In the present case we concluded that PROUST's identification of bugs for students would teach them about the existence of the class of bugs that arise at boundary conditions.

4. How to Test:

   Concept: Identify classes of behaviors that students should demonstrate when the ITS is having a positive or a negative impact.

   Application: In the present evaluation we used students' ability to find and repair boundary condition bugs as measures of PROUST's impact.

5. External Evaluation:

   Concept: Analyze the students' behaviors both individually and in groups. The groups of students are defined either according to (a) some attribute, derived from the process model, that is common to the program generation processes of all students or (b) some response the ITS makes to all the students in the group.

   Application: In the present case, the performance of groups of students who had access to PROUST was compared with that of groups of students who did not have access to PROUST. In addition, to control for PROUST's ability to identify bugs, we assessed the effect of the accuracy of PROUST's identification of bugs for students.

To measure the effect of PROUST's identification of bugs for students, we defined two performance tests that reflected our process theory of programming. From these tests we inferred students' underlying problem-solving processes. One test was the pattern of boundary condition bugs in students' versions of the rainfall assignment. When students do the rainfall assignment, they typically generate 15 versions before submitting one for grading. As noted, we predicted from our process model that students would have difficulty with boundary conditions because they are easy to make and hard to find. We also predicted that if PROUST identified boundary condition bugs for students, they would be less likely either to make as many of the boundary bugs in the first place or to leave the bugs in their final versions.

The second test was students' scores on the midterm examination. We reasoned that because PROUST could help students isolate boundary condition bugs, students would be better able to find such bugs in programs written by other programmers. Therefore, the students' task on the midterm examination was to identify, describe, and fix bugs that had been seeded in the programs similar to the ones the students had been writing in their assignments. Boundary condition bugs, as well as other types, such as performing the wrong arithmetic calculation, were seeded in the midterm. Thus, even though both measures of improvement in students' ability to identify bugs essentially count numbers of correct answers, we arrived at these measures by reasoning explicitly about our process model, and we used the measures to make inferences about the effects of PROUST on students' knowledge and skills.

Briefly, the tests supported the claim that PROUST helps students repair and avoid boundary bugs when they are writing programs to solve the rainfall assignment. Access to PROUST also appears to improve by approximately 16% students' ability to identify seeded boundary condition bugs in programs they did not write. (See Sack et al., 1986, for a full report of these evaluation results.)

In summary, the evaluation of the educational effectiveness of one aspect of PROUST's performance was based on the perspective of cognitive science. The evaluation began with a process model that explains novice buggy programming. We used the model to identify the management of boundary cases as a task in programming that students typically find troublesome. Then we predicted how PROUST's bug identification strategy would affect students' ability to handle boundary cases. We also used the process model to interpret the finding that PROUST is only somewhat helpful for teaching students to find and repair bugs.

Because simply identifying bugs for students is not enough to achieve radically improved performance, the next version of PROUST will have to include stronger tutorial capabilities to help students learn debugging skills. The evaluation also indicates that some aspects of the process model must be changed. We had predicted that if students knew about certain kinds of bugs, they would not make them. The process model requires a more complex mechanism to account for students' failure to eliminate boundary condition bugs after a one-trial learning experience—that is, after these bugs were identified for them. The mechanism that is needed to account for this phenomenon is still somewhat unclear, but evidently it will have to specify the conditions under which students can identify and achieve goals that are not explicitly called for in the problem assignment and that involve specialized programming knowledge.

Lessons Learned from External Evaluation of PROUST

The initial external evaluation of PROUST taught us three important lessons. First, PROUST has some positive educational effects. Second, we learned some important principles for formulating and executing external evaluations of ITSs. Third, and perhaps most important, we were successful in evaluating PROUST with an incomplete process model and then identifying insufficiencies in that model. It is thus quite reasonable to expect that the process of developing an ITS can be integrated with assessing its educational effectiveness. This suggests that by performing evaluations based on student models during development, we can facilitate the development of ITSs.

Possible Objections to the Cognitive Perspective

The foregoing description of the external evaluation of PROUST may seem too clean, and several objections can be raised about both the practicality of and justification for performing such evaluations. Three major criticisms of the cognitive science approach are discussed here.

1. It is too hard. There is no doubt that detailed evaluations of students' cognitive processes will be extremely time consuming and that in many cases, designers will want to build ITSs before they have student models sufficiently powerful for doing definitive evaluations.

However, a central promise of ITSs is that they will make use of the best that cognitive science has to offer. ITSs are most decidedly not just computer-aided instruction with an expert system or two thrown in to generate problem solutions. Rather, ITSs are intended to understand students in a fundamental sense; and one of the goals of the field of ITSs is to produce systems that are as good as the very best human tutors. Of course, once we have achieved that goal, we will want to make ITSs that are better than human tutors. For these reasons the development of effective, cognitively based evaluation strategies must proceed hand in hand with researchers' growing expertise in the field. Thus, although fully realized evaluations are too hard to make now, they are still both a goal to achieve and a measure of our own progress toward truly intelligent tutoring systems.

2. We might use the wrong student models in our evaluations. The ability to perform valid evaluations clearly depends on having powerful student models. If the evaluation suggests that a particular student failed to acquire the skills that the ITS was intended to teach, and if the evaluation was based on an incorrect student model, researchers may conclude that the ITS was not performing effectively.

Avoiding this mistake requires that researchers be sensitive to different ways of representing knowledge and skills. A single model of student knowledge may not be sufficient for evaluation. In fact, it seems naive to expect that a single model would capture all the different ways that students might understand a domain. Researchers therefore should investigate alternative ways that students can adaptively represent knowledge and skills. In addition, they must distinguish between assessing the ability of the ITS to teach students how to solve problems and its ability to teach students a particular way of representing problem-solving skills. In either case, identifying correct student process models for an evaluation is crucial for the field; the problem of identifying the correct student model for any tutoring situation is certainly no easier and just as important. It appears that progress in evaluation will go hand in hand with progress in diagnosing students and identifying appropriate student models.

3. Students' internal representations are irrelevant to education. Proponents of the microworlds approach to intelligent tutoring argue that an educator should not so much teach as provide tools that make it possible to learn. One implication of this view is that student models, and hence process models, are superfluous if not entirely counterproductive. Such models may be used to assess a student's progress or failure, but that is not the business of education.

Our own view is that educational philosophy should be divorced from the philosophy of assessment. Regardless of the advisability of directive tutoring in education, evaluating the effectiveness of intelligent tools for facilitating learning requires having process models of students' problem solving. Building such models in a microworlds context may be difficult because microworlds environments are unconstrained; for just this reason model building promises to be extremely productive.

Thus, although there are several objections to the cognitive approach to evaluation, three of the most interesting can be seen as practical rather than fundamental. Indeed, work on the problems of cognitively based evaluations of ITSs may possibly make significant contributions to the theory of ITSs itself.

INTERNAL EVALUATION:
THE ARCHITECTURE PERSPECTIVE

The goal of internal evaluation is to provide a clear picture of the relationship between the architecture of an ITS and its behavior. To clarify this relationship it is necessary to characterize the ITS in terms of answers to three key questions.

1. *What Does the ITS Know?* It is important to answer this question whenever a revision of the ITS is proposed. Any changes in the requirements of the ITS should be based on a clear understanding of the effort it will take to equip the program with the knowledge necessary for achieving the new requirements. The question is addressed by an analysis of what the ITS can possibly do based on what it knows.

2. *How Does the ITS Do What It Does?* Answering this question assesses whether the program performs in the way the designers intended. It requires analyzing the ITS to determine how the algorithms use available knowledge to produce the observed behavior or the ITS.

3. *What Should the ITS Do?* This question should be asked when a revision of the ITS is proposed, particularly when it seems desirable to increase the teaching ability of the ITS in one area or reduce it in another. This question is answered by clarifying the areas of the tutoring domain, such as programming, that the ITS is responsible for teaching.

Though, we cannot provide a complete plan for answering these questions definitively, we think that they are the right ones to ask.

This section discusses three methods adapted from knowledge engineering that can help to characterize all components of an ITS, including the student model, the curriculum content, the instructional component, the expert problem solver, and the interface. We have found these methods useful for addressing the three questions central to internal evaluation of ITSs. In what follows we describe the methods and show how we have used them to perform internal evaluations of PROUST.

1. **Knowledge Level Analysis** attempts to characterize the knowledge in the ITS and thus answers the first question, *What does the ITS know?* This question is important to ask between versions of an ITS because any changes of the requirements should be made with an understanding of how much effort would be required to give the program the knowledge to achieve the new requirements.

2. **Program Process Analysis** uses focused simulations of the ITS to answer the second question, *How does the ITS do what it does?* This method is intended to provide information about whether the ITS does what it does in the way the designers intended.

3. **Tutorial Domain Analysis** provides a methodology for iteratively adding

and subtracting requirements of the ITS and, therefore, answers the third question, *What should the ITS do?*

Why should all this effort be required to understand an ITS? We often find ourselves saying to each other, "But it's obvious! Why did we have to go through all this analysis to see *that?*" The answer is that ITSs are so complex that it is impossible to know everything about them. We have spent years discovering new, important facts about PROUST. Since each individual finding is obvious once brought to light, it is easy to fall prey to an attitude of 20-20 hindsight. The cure for this is to ponder all the things about PROUST that we do *not* know that are just waiting to trip us up! Because ITSs are so complex and, therefore, hard to understand, designing them is a cyclical process in which a version is built, weaknesses and strengths are identified using the techniques we discuss here, a new version is built, and so on. We hope extended examples from our work with PROUST demonstrate the value of these techniques.

Knowledge Level Analysis: What Does the ITS Know?

Knowledge level analysis provides useful information about whether the program knows enough to perform its intended tasks. It is concerned not with how the program accomplishes the tasks but with what the program can conceivably do and with whether the program has the competence to perform certain tasks. In essence, knowledge level analysis focuses on whether the program has enough of the right kinds of knowledge to meet the requirements that were set for it.

We have carefully analyzed the knowledge PROUST contains. By using these analyses and deriving explicit descriptions of types of knowledge in PROUST, we have discovered certain weaknesses in its representation. Figure 8.7 shows a fragment of a rainfall program that PROUST cannot completely analyze. To us, it is clear that the student intended the variable "MaxRain" to hold the maximum amount of rainfall entered and intended the code "MaxRain := DailyRainfall" to serve as the plan to calculate the maximum. We can infer this because we know what the variable name "MaxRain" probably means. However, PROUST does not know that certain kinds of variable names mean certain things; that is, PROUST lacks lexical and semantic knowledge. It cannot completely understand this student's code and gives the incorrect tutorial advice that the student has failed to include in the program a plan to calculate the maximum amount of rainfall.

```
Program Rainfall(input,output);
  Var DailyRainfall,TotalRainfall,MaxRainfall,Average : Real;
      RainyDays,TotalDays : Integer;
  Begin
         .
         .
         .
    Readln(DailyRainfall);
    While (DailyRainfall <> 999) Do  BUG 1: Should Be "99999"
       Begin
          If DailyRainfall >= 0 Then
             .
             .
             .
          MaxRain := DailyRainfall    BUG 2: Unconditional Assignment
       Read(DailyRainfall)
    End;
       .
       .
       .
  End.
```

FIGURE 8.7   An example of PROUST's need for lexical knowledge.

```
Program Rainfall(input,output);
  Var DailyRainfall,TotalRainfall,MaxRainfall,Average : Real;
      RainyDays,TotalDays : Integer;
  Begin
    RainyDays:= 0; TotalDays:= 0; MaxRainfall:= 0; TotalRainfall:= 0;
    Writeln ('Please Enter Amount of Rainfall');
    Readln(DailyRainfall);
    While (DailyRainfall <> 999) Do          BUG: Should Be "99999"
       Begin
          If DailyRainfall >= 0 Then
             Begin
                If DailyRainfall > 0 Then RainyDays := RainyDays + 1;
                TotalRainfall    := TotalRainfall + DailyRainfall;
                If DailyRainfall > MaxRainfall
                   Then MaxRainfall := DailyRainfall;
                TotalDays := TotalDays + 1
             End;
          Else Writeln ('Rainfall Must Be Greater Than 0');
       Read(DailyRainfall)
    End;
    If TotalDaysCounter > 0 Then  Begin
       Average := TotalRainfall/TotalDays;
       Writeln('Average is: ', Average: 0:2);
       Writeln('Maximum is: ', MaxRainfall: 0:2);
       Writeln('Total Number of Days is: ', TotalDays);
       Writeln('Total Number of Rainy Days is: ', RainyDays)
    End;
    Else Writeln('No Valid Days Entered.');
  End.
```

FIGURE 8.8   An example of PROUST's need for bottom-up analysis.

As a result of discovering several programs that **PROUST** could not understand completely because it lacked lexical knowledge, we altered the specifications for the subsequent version of **PROUST** to require that **PROUST** be able to reason about intended meanings of variables based on their names.

Program Process Analysis:
How Does the ITS Do What It Does?

Program process analysis consists of evaluating whether the program does what it does in the right way. In contrast to knowledge level analysis, which asks whether the program is able to perform certain input–output tasks, program process analysis looks just at how a program uses its knowledge in the process of going from input to output.

For example, we have expended considerable effort understanding traces of **PROUST** to determine exactly how it uses its knowledge. This process analysis has led us to redesign **PROUST**'s overall control structure. Extensive process tracing showed us exactly what kinds of cases **PROUST** could not understand because of its rigid top-down method of analyzing student's programs.

Figure 8.8 shows a program that we can understand very easily. The reason **PROUST** fails to understand it completely is quite interesting. The student has incorrectly typed the sentinel value that controls execution of the main loop. Instead of five 9s, the student has typed only three 9s. One of the consequences of **PROUST**'s strict top-down control structure is that it must anchor its analysis on the main loop in order to proceed with the analysis; that is, it must find the main loop or it cannot find any of the other main pieces of the program. One of the tasks it must carry out to anchor on the main loop is to find the sentinel value that controls the loop execution. It turns out that **PROUST** can recognize a range of sequences of 9s; but the range extends only from four 9s to six 9s. Obviously, **PROUST** could be made to work in this case by extending the range of sentinel values it can detect to any number of 9s, but this solution is bad because it is specific to this bug. The program process analyses of **PROUST** led to a far more general alternative.

Notice that, aside from the 999 bug, the program is perfect. Especially notice that the contents of the loop do exactly what they should do; the counters are updated correctly, the maximum is calculated, a new value for rainfall is obtained, and so on. The correctness of the contents of the loop helps us to understand the program: Because the loop with the three 9s as the sentinel contains everything that a correct loop should contain, we conclude that this loop is the main loop. But PROUST cannot even see that the correct functions are in the loop because it must identify the main loop before it can find the contents of the loop. Once we understood how PROUST performed its analysis, and more important, why it overlooked the contents of the loop, we were led to the general solution of combining top-down analysis with bottom-up analysis. This solution seems obvious in retrospect; however, it was not until we had extensively analyzed how PROUST behaved in this case and similar cases that we felt confident enough to commit ourselves to fundamentally rework PROUST's control structure.

Tutorial Domain Analysis: What Should the ITS Do?

Tutorial domain analysis is a reasoned approach to adding new tutorial capabilities to an ITS. Initial descriptions of the domain to be tutored serve as part of the design specifications for an ITS. Although these descriptions may be generally appropriate, the aspects of the domain that the designers wish to tutor may shift as the program takes shape and as the process of tutoring in the domain becomes better understood. For this reason, ongoing evaluation of the appropriate domain of tutoring can help maintain a clear view of the goals of the ITS.

In our work with PROUST, for example, our notions of what we wanted PROUST to be capable of teaching have slowly evolved over the years. At first, we simply wanted it to identify bugs. Then we felt that it might be possible to augment PROUST just a little so that it could give students some advice about the kinds of test data that might be helpful for tracking down the bugs that it located. We looked at the test-data problem and rejected several solutions because they seemed far beyond the then-current capabilities of PROUST. Finally, we decided to broaden PROUST's domain of tutorial expertise.

When we observed PROUST in action, we saw that we could build naturally on PROUST to provide the student with a wider range of skills than we had originally intended. This ongoing domain analysis has an additional positive impact on the cyclical design process. It prevents us from adding capabilities to PROUST without understanding how such new additions fit with the general requirements and theory for tutoring the domain. Thus, internal evaluation has led to a more coherent ITS than we might have otherwise developed.

Lessons Learned

In summary, it is important, yet difficult to understand the relationship between an ITS's architecture and its behavior. Three questions— What does an ITS know? How does an ITS know what it does? and What should an ITS be doing?—seem relevant to internal evaluation, and three knowledge engineering techniques can be used to explore them. We recognize that our treatment of internal evaluation is preliminary. Nonetheless we have had success with these methods, and we feel that it is useful to begin exploring how they, and others, might be used for internal evaluation of ITSs.

EXISTING EVALUATIONS INTERPRETED

This section of the chapter describes some of the evaluations of ITSs that have been reported in the literature. These evaluations are discussed in terms of the categories of external and internal evaluation that we have used in our own work. The evaluations other researchers have performed do not perfectly coincide with our categories; but at this point external and internal evaluation are only ideals or goals. No one we know, including ourselves, has yet carried out such evaluations in an elegant, comprehensive way. Nonetheless, this analysis of other research strategies clearly shows that efforts to perform external and internal evaluation are worthwhile.

This section begins with two case studies of ITS evaluation. The first focuses on evaluations of WEST that are like what we have called "external evaluation." We have selected WEST as an example because it is widely known and because the evaluations of WEST show how evaluators have begun to grapple with the problem of basing evaluations on process models. The second case study illustrates how William Clancey and his colleagues, using several methods akin to what we call "internal evaluation methods," redesigned the rule base of MYCIN to create NEOMYCIN, a tutorial system that teaches strategies for medical diagnosis.

External Evaluation: WEST

WEST (Burton & Brown, 1982) is a computer coach that helps students learn how to play the two-person adversary boardgame "How the West Was Won" (HTW3). The goal of HTW3 is to beat an opponent to the end of a 70-space board. A student determines each move by combining three arithmetic operands, provided by a random device, with arithmetic operators to compute a number of spaces to move. For example, a student might construct the expression "(4/2) + 3" to move 5 spaces forward on the board. Special moves, such as *bumps* introduce the fun into HTW3. For example, a player can construct an arithmetic expression that lands him or her exactly on the opponent's square, then the player can bump the opponent and make him or her move backward two towns, which appear every 10 squares on the board. Thus, the goal of playing HTW3 is to use the operators and operands not to construct the largest number but the number yielding the greatest strategic advantage.

WEST is called a "coach" because of the tutorial principles it incorporates. The tutor in WEST strongly avoids overadvising the student. It sits in the background looking over the student's shoulder, until it is clear that the student needs some help and the student would benefit from the help that WEST could give. Then, by making a few suggestions, WEST attempts to help the student improve his or her skills.

WEST's general approach to student modeling is of identifying the student's use of skills for constructing arithmetic expressions that achieve optimal moves in HTW3. WEST does not attempt to model the process of the student's construction of arithmetic expressions. Instead, it represents whether the student can apply strategies when they are called for. WEST does this by recognizing which strategies a student used to construct a move. Thus, WEST's student model can be seen as a checklist of skills the student can and cannot use correctly. This type of issue-based tutoring is also discussed by Anderson and by VanLehn (chapters 2 and 3).

In 1978, J. S. Brown and his colleagues performed some initial evaluations of WEST. These evaluations assessed the extent to which students learned to use different move patterns depending on whether or not they were coached by the WEST tutor as they played the game (Burton & Brown, 1982). In essence, the use of move patterns defines the student model of WEST. The initial findings suggested that WEST's student model captured some of the important features of students' strategic arithmetic problem solving. Coached students used a wider variety of optimal moves than uncoached students and also made more effective use of the special moves than uncoached students did. Thus, there is evidence not only that the WEST tutor effectively coached students in skills for strategically constructing arithmetic expressions, but also that WEST's student model was powerful enough to capture some interesting aspects of the process by which students solve tasks such as selecting correct moves.

In 1985 Baker, Feifer, Aschbacher, Bradley, & Herman (1985)

reported a more extensive evaluation of WEST. As Burton and Brown had done, Baker performed a controlled experiment; but her experiment included both (a) extensive assessments of the arithmetic skills of students prior to and following experience with WEST and (b) pretraining for students on skills that might be useful for playing HTW3. The general findings of Baker's study were somewhat equivocal. No large effects were found for pregame math training on game performance, and using WEST appeared to have no major effects on the posttests of math skills

Even though she did not find large general effects, Baker's evaluation was formulated in order to test the impact of WEST on specific skills that WEST is designed to help students learn. The posttest assessment included a measure of students' ability to select or construct appropriate moves in the WEST gaming environment. For example, one question in the posttest presented to students the values of the operands generated by the random process and a target value for an expression combining the operands. Students were asked either to construct the target value or to indicate that it could not be calculated with the given operands. Though the effects of WEST on students' ability to select or construct appropriate moves were not statistically significant as measured by the posttest, the attempt to measure specific strategies shows a concern with the cognitive processes underlying such problem solving.

The major point of the WEST examples is that even though neither group of evaluators explicitly described a method of basing evaluations on process models, both groups appear to have used such a method. That is, the evaluations assessed specific skills that WEST was designed to teach. Both studies used measures other than the number of correct answers to assess the impact of WEST on the pattern of use of the skills. Because the same skill might have resulted in either a correct or an incorrect answer, just counting correct and incorrect answers is not a good indication of WEST's impact on the student's knowledge. The conclusions of the evaluations do not fully clarify the effect of WEST on students' strategic arithmetic skills. However, it is important to keep in mind that the student model underlying WEST is not intended to be a powerful process model. The conclusions that can be drawn from these evaluations must be seen in the light of the process considerations on which they were based.

In summary, both evaluations of WEST contained measures of students' learning that were cast directly in terms of the skills that WEST monitors during the game of HTW3. Rather than focusing exclusively on aggregate effects of WEST on students' arithmetic skills, both evaluations sought to study the effect of WEST on specific skills that it was designed to teach. Because both evaluations attempted to relate students' performance directly to WEST's model of the skills that are important for HTW3, they can be categorized as external evaluations.

Internal Evaluation:
MYCIN and NEOMYCIN

Clancey and his colleagues have the goal of using the MYCIN diagnosis system to teach general skills of medical diagnosis (Hasling, Clancey, & Rennels, 1984). One of the major tasks in teaching diagnosis is to explain why certain hypotheses are being pursued at certain times and how to pursue hypotheses when they are approproate. Unfortunately, MYCIN's knowledge base, which is simply a network of rules linking symptoms and bacteriological diseases, makes its explanations unsatisfactory for this task of tutoring.

When MYCIN consults with a user on a diagnosis, it exhaustively chains backward through its rule base trying to find a connection between a disease and the observed symptoms. MYCIN's explanatory capability is based completely on the goal chains it generates during diagnosis. Thus, if the user asks MYCIN to explain why it is performing a certain action at a certain time, all MYCIN can do is describe its goal stack. For example, suppose MYCIN has just asked a user whether the patient has frequent headaches. Now suppose that the user requests that MYCIN explain why it has asked this question. MYCIN replies by identifying the specific goal it is trying to achieve with the question about headaches; this goal is to determine whether the patient has meningitis. The problem is that for someone trying to learn diagnosis, this reply is far too specific. The novice needs to be told something more general about why the possibility of meningitis should be pursued at this time and why it should be pursued before some other possibility. Thus, the goal of a tutor in diagnosis should be to explicitly teach the process of diagnosis. How to diagnose bacteremias in particular is not useful information when the student is still struggling with the difficult task of learning general diagnostic principles.

Clancey and his coworkers set out to learn how to reshape MYCIN so that it could explicitly teach diagnostic skills. In studying MYCIN's rule base, using methods akin to internal evaluation methods, Clancey and his coworkers discovered that much of the strategic knowledge that controls MYCIN's diagnosis is implicit in the structure of the rules. For example, the order in which MYCIN pursues alternative hypotheses is determined by the ordering of clauses in rules that identify which hypotheses to pursue in the presence of specific evidence. Thus, the real reason that MYCIN asked about headaches was that the meningitis hypothesis was next on its list, not that it was the most likely. The meningitis hypothesis was next on MYCIN's list because the designer of the rule base knew that meningitis was the most likely candidate and that it therefore should be pursued. Thus, Clancey's work has been to identify the kinds of diagnostic knowledge the tutorial version of MYCIN should teach, to understand why MYCIN's knowledge base fails to make this knowledge available for tutoring, and then to express this knowledge as explicit tutorial rules. So, for example, NEOMYCIN, a tutorial version of MYCIN, might have a rule that causes it to respond to the student's query about headaches with a statement of diagnostic strategy. NEOMYCIN could reply that it is pursuing meningitis because (a) it is the most likely hypothesis and (b) if meningitis can be supported as a possible diagnosis then the largest set of alternatives is automatically ruled out. This is just the kind of information a student of diagnosis needs in order to learn diagnostic skills, and it is the kind of knowledge Clancey and his group have been uncovering with their evaluations of MYCIN.

In summary, Clancey and his colleagues have spent several years analyzing in detail why the internal structure of MYCIN leads it to behave as it does. On the basis of these analyses, they have augmented and reconfigured the knowledge base in MYCIN so that it can support tutorial reasoning about teaching diagnosis.

A Sampling of Evaluations

Table 8.1 briefly describes a few of the more readily accessible ITS evaluations reported in the literature. The evaluations are identified as "Internal Evaluation" and "External Evaluation." For example, the first row of the table, corresponding to the WEST tutor, contains brief descriptions of Baker's and Brown's findings. The ordering of the tutors is not completely arbitrary. The first two tutors are "coaches," the second two are programming tutors, and the last tutor teaches medical students.

Summary

The categorization of evaluation into external and internal strategies appears to be applicable to many of the evaluations reported by designers of ITSs. The case studies of WEST and MYCIN and the other evaluations referred to in Table 8.1 support what we have found in our own experience with PROUST and now believe is quite general. Current techniques of external evaluation cannot determine

TABLE 8.1
How Current ITSs Have Been Evaluated

	Internal Evaluation	External Evaluation
WEST	Extensive analysis of tutorial strategies and how to implement them (Burton & Brown, 1978)	Comparison of effects of using WEST on battery of tests of strategic use of arithmetic skills (Baker et al., 1985; Burton & Brown, 1978)
WUSOR	Analysis of WUSOR's understanding of differential difficulties of skills used in playing WUMPUS	No formal evaluation
PROUST	Analysis of which aspects of PROUST diagnose various types of bugs (Johnson, 1986)	Comparison of test scores of students with PROUST to scores of students without PROUST (Baker, et al., 1985; Sack et al., 1986)
LISP Tutor	Extensive analysis of tutorial principles embodied in tutors (Anderson, Boyle, Farrell, & Reiser, 1984)	Controlled experiment to evaluate LISP Tutor's ability to teach recursion (Pirolli, 1987)
NEOMYCIN	Evaluations of what knowledge in a diagnostic system needs to be made explicit to teach diagnosis (Clancey, 1983; Hasling et al., 1984)	No formal evaluation

conclusively whether an ITS is effective. More fine-grained analyses of the effects of ITSs on students are probably required at this point in the development of evaluation methodologies for ITSs. On the other hand internal evaluations of ITSs, even if they are not as intensive as Clancey's analyses of MYCIN, can produce valuable insights into the causes of behavior of ITSs. Thus, although only a few examples of evaluations have been published, and although the process of evaluation is only now beginning to be formalized, basic concepts of external and internal evaluation appear to correspond quite closely with the work already done by several designers and evaluators of ITSs.

DIRECTIONS FOR FUTURE WORK

The evaluation of ITSs is not a new idea, but it has been underemphasized in the past. Because evaluation of ITSs is an issue for both the present and the future, it is appropriate to identify some problems that could lead to progress for the field. Some issues need to be addressed quite soon if credible evaluation methodologies for ITSs are to be developed; resolving these issues seems within reach of current methods. Other issues, which need to be addressed over the long term, concern the possibilities and problems of automating the evaluation and revision of ITSs.

Near Term Issues

Four main issues pertaining to the evaluation of ITSs can probably be resolved and should be addressed in the near future. These issues and some potential directions for exploring them are briefly described in this section. The issues are presented in order of difficulty, but each implies additional, equally difficult problems.

More Examples of Evaluations Are Needed

Perhaps 20 evaluations of ITSs have been reported in the literature. Several of these evaluations are of the same systems (e.g., WEST), and most of them are fairly informal. Many more evaluations are necessary to generate useful abstractions that can guide evaluation efforts. Educational evaluators and designers of ITSs need to work closely together (cf. Baker et al., 1985) to generate intensive, well-founded analyses of ITSs that can be used as models for evaluation. This collaboration should be a major priority for research in the immediate future. The work of designers of ITSs will benefit both from more good examples of evaluations and from the experiences of researchers in education and evaluation.

Analytic Methods for Evaluation

When the field of ITSs has matured, standard techniques should be sufficient for designing educational studies to evaluate the effectiveness of ITSs. In addition, techniques of meta-analysis, which are intended to identify patterns of positive and negative effects across several ITSs (cf. Kulik, 1985), are becoming reasonably well worked out. Currently, because many ITSs are incomplete, evaluation relies on standard statistical analyses, and the problem is simply to appropriately qualify the conclusions from evaluations to reflect the incomplete nature of an ITS.

When statistical methods are not applicable, a much more qualitative approach to summarizing results is necessary. Developing guidelines for summarizing such qualitative results would be a valuable enterprise. One approach is to start with those chapters in this volume that concern a particular dimension of ITSs. If the analyses given in the chapters were viewed as the structure of the dimension, then perhaps informative qualitative evaluations of ITSs could be cast in terms of those dimensions (cf. VanLehn's analysis of the dimensions of student models in chapter 3). Meta-analyses can also be performed to compare different ITSs on the relevant dimensions.

At some point, it may be possible to define statistical inference procedures based on these dimensions, for example by giving an ITS a positive score for each of the positive attributes of each dimension it embodies and a negative score for each of the negative attributes. Then, using procedures such as exact randomization tests, sampling distributions could be generated for the patterns of positive and negative scores. This statistical approach should not be taken too seriously, however. Once two or more ITSs have been well characterized in terms of the dimensions, an evaluation should probably be based on the meaning of the pattern of attributes that characterize each ITS rather than on some inferential statistic derived from the pattern of attributes. This kind of evaluation would help designers decide how to change ITSs that do not fare as well as ITSs with more salutary patterns of attributes. Thus, it seems possible to develop useful concepts of qualitative analysis that can be used even when ITSs are still in the developmental phase.

Partial Process Models

One of the pervasive problems of evaluating ITSs is that external evaluations must often be performed with only partial models of the student and incomplete ITSs. One solution may be to integrate the design and evaluation of the ITS with elaboration of the process model. If work on the process model and the ITS were guided by the requirements of evaluation, then attention would be directed toward identifying and elaborating subcomponents of the process model that can be used to assess the effectiveness of corresponding subcomponents of the ITS. For example, in our evaluation of PROUST, we identified a fairly narrow subset of skills related to managing boundary condition bugs, and we then focused on evaluating a corresponding feature of PROUST, its bug identification strategy. The potential danger of this approach is, of course, failing to construct a system because of paying too much attention to individual components. However, if designers of ITSs keep in mind the near certainty of having only an incomplete process model and an incomplete ITS, then perhaps they can increase the correspondence between the more complete aspects of both.

Developing a Metric
for Hard and Easy Bugs

One of the benefits of the cognitive perspective on ITSs is that it has enriched our concept of bugs. Because, in the cognitive view, bugs are attributable to problems in the student's knowledge and skills, trivial bugs and hard bugs can be distinguished according to the complexity of the student's misunderstanding or knowledge deficit (Brown & Burton, 1978). For example, a cognitive theory of the difficulty of bugs predicts that boundary condition bugs are simple because no deep misunderstanding is likely to be responsible for them. On the other hand, a student who omits a "Readln" statement in the loop for the rainfall assignment, on the assumption that the new value of rainfall is read in automatically by the loop, has a serious bug because the cause is related to a deep misunderstanding of how the PASCAL interpreter operates.

To take advantage of possible similarities in causes of bugs across domains, it may be useful to base a theory of bug difficulty on abstract properties of process models. For example, there may be similar patterns of bugs in different domains and, therefore, similar causes for trivial and hard bugs. It may be that all design tasks have analogous bugs. Identifying such similar patterns could provide the basis for more general, domain-independent, process models for bug generation.

Long-Term Issues

The discussion of long-term issues is not wide ranging. It focuses on one problem, the automation of the process of building and revising ITSs. Automating this process is important because it could lead to useful insights into theories of learning and teaching. These insights are possible because of the three tasks that must be accomplished to achieve automation. First, the impact of the ITS on the student's knowledge and skills must be assessed. This requires being able to reason in great detail about how students learn. Second, the results of the evaluations must be interpreted. This requires determining what aspects of the ITS produce changes in students. Third, the ITS must be revised to produce the desired changes in the student based on the interpretation of the evaluation. This requires understanding exactly what the ITS must do to produce specific changes in the student.

Thus, in order to automate the cycle of evaluation, interpretation, and revision, it will be necessary to automate reasoning about how ITSs cause educational change in students. This section, therefore, discusses the three steps to automating the evaluation process and briefly indicates how successful automation could help designers understand more clearly the relationship between teaching and learning.

Generating the
Evaluation Automatically

As suggested in the section on external evaluation, human evaluators can use process models to design problems for evaluating the impact of the ITS on students. By using process model techniques to reason about the state of students' knowledge and skills, evaluators should be able to predict which of these problems students should be able to solve and which they should not be able to solve. Because the process model is the basis for generating the problems for the external evaluation, it seems possible to write "evaluation generator programs" to construct them.

To produce such evaluation generator programs, designers must understand how humans generate evaluation problems. For example, when we designed the midterm examination to evaluate the impact of PROUST's bug identification strategy, we constructed programs that were seeded with bugs, some of which were boundary condition bugs that we expected students to find if they had used PROUST. In deciding to use seeded bugs in this examination, we actually solved three problems. First, we constructed an appropriate context (the midterm) in which to evaluate PROUST's effectiveness. Second, we identified a task for assessing students' ability to manage boundary cases, namely identification and repair of bugs in seeded programs. Third, we constructed the actual bugs to seed into the programs. We can identify only three of the tasks we performed to devise our evaluation because we are just beginning to understand the process of external evaluation.

A potential starting point for automating the generation of evaluations may be both expert human diagnosticians and the theories of automated tutorial diagnosis that have been built from studies of human experts. Much of tutorial diagnosis involves reasoning about (a) how students should answer particular questions and (b) how to determine whether a student has some particular knowledge or skill. Both of these are basis for constructing evaluations of ITSs. Thus, insight into the problem of automatically generating evaluations may come from exploring the relationship between diagnostic tutorial reasoning to identify causes of bugs and the design of assessment problems for evaluations of ITSs.

Interpreting the
Evaluation Automatically

It may be possible not only to generate evaluations automatically but also to interpret the results automatically. A point of departure for the automatic interpretation effort is, again, human designers of ITSs. For example, when we decided that PROUST's bug identification strategy is insufficient for teaching the kinds of skills for handling boundary conditions that we wanted our students to learn, we concluded that PROUST needs tutorial capabilities for explicitly teaching bug identification skills. That is, we assigned the blame for the students' poor performance to a specific lack of tutorial expertise in PROUST. The point here is not whether the assignment of blame was correct, but how we reasoned about it. Designers need to understand such inference processes more clearly in order to write programs that can reason about the results of evaluations.

Automatically Revising
the ITS Based on the Evaluation

If evaluations can be automatically generated and interpreted, then it may at least be possible to attempt to automate the revision of ITSs. To continue our example of the evaluation of PROUST, after concluding that PROUST lacked necessary instructional strategies, we had to reason about how to modify PROUST to include the strategies.

There appear to be three main cases to consider in reasoning about how to provide an ITS with appropriate knowledge and tutorial strategies. First, the ITS has an appropriate strategy, but it needs to be modified. Second, the ITS may have a class of tutorial strategies in which the new strategy should be placed, and the change to the ITS is an addition of a strategy rather than a modification of an existing strategy. Third, the needed tutorial strategy may be the first exemplar of a new class of strategies. Obviously, these three modifications involve various degrees of difficulty. The first is probably within reach of current methods of artificial intelligence and the third will have to await further progress.

Once again, a promising way to begin investigating the automatic revision of ITSs is to study human designers of ITSs. For example, it could be extremely useful to attempt to codify the ways in which John Anderson's group at Carnegie-Mellon University, or William Clancey's group at Stanford, reason about changing their ITSs. Although it may seem an ambitious undertaking, automating the cycle of generating evaluations of ITSs, interpreting the results, and revising the ITSs could reveal useful abstractions about ITS architectures and the assumptions abut human thought on which they are based. Even if this effort does not entirely succeed it will give designers a clearer view of how to construct ITSs and may improve their ability to teach students to build ITSs.

Develop a Causal Explanation of Learning

One outcome of the effort to write computer progrms that can generate evaluations of ITS, interpret the results of the evaluations, and then modify the ITSs appropriately is what amounts to a causal explanation of learning. A causal explanation of learning specifies the exact features of the learning environment (the cause) that lead to precisely specified changes in the student's knowledge and skills (the effect). If designers can automatically generate problems to use in evaluation, then they have begun to describe the student's knowlege and skills precisely enough to characterize the effect side of the causal explanation. If they can automatically determine what aspects of the ITS are responsible for the changes in the student, then they have begun to precisely describe the cause side of the causal explanation of learning. For example, if we can automatically generate the evaluation problems for PROUST's students to solve, and if we can automatically interpret the results of the evaluation in terms of precise actions of PROUST toward the students, then we will have begun to explain the instructional relationship between students and PROUST in causal terms. Thus, although the task of automating the entire cycle of evaluation, interpretation, and redesign is extremely challenging, progress toward achieving it could have strong implications for theories of learning.

Summary

In summary, this section has raised several issues that impinge on the evaluation of ITSs. Several near-term issues seem both tractable and relevant to progress in the immediate future. The long-term issues seem less immediately tractable, but they appear to have important implications for the theory of ITSs. This treatment of future directions for research is not exhaustive. Nonetheless, it shows that future research in evaluation will be just as exciting as research in any other area of cognitive science.

CONCLUSIONS

This chapter has identified two important questions for evaluators of ITSs. Evaluation efforts so far have shown that evaluators need to take very seriously the problem of assessing incomplete systems. We suggested that external evaluation, or assessing the impact of the ITS on users, should be guided by process models of problem solving in the instructional domain of the ITS. In addition, we suggested that evaluation and development of ITSs should proceed in tandem, and we demonstrated that it is both possible and beneficial to use incomplete process models as a foundation for evaluation. The need for methods of internal evaluation arises because ITSs are so complex; a major problem for designers is just understanding why ITSs behave as they do and how they can be changed so that they behave as desired. We acknowledged the iterative nature of the ITS design process and illustrated several internal evaluation methods that, by providing designers of ITS with information about the ITS and their own goals, could help them productively guide the design process.

We conclude from these initial forays into the evaluation of ITSs that evaluation is challenging, useful, and wide open. In the future, we plan to continue both our current evaluation activities and our efforts to identify the questions and methods that are appropriate for evaluating one of the most exciting possibilities for our culture, namely ITSs. We realize that our approach may be controversial, and if readers have found this chapter intriguing or provocative then we will have achieved one of our major goals in writing it.

ACKNOWLEDGMENTS

We would especially like to thank Eva Baker, who was a main mover behind our evaluation of PROUST. Conversations with and comments from Richard Burton, John Seely Brown, Jeff Richardson, John Anderson, and Lt. Charles Capps were also very helpful in shaping our thoughts on evaluation in general, and their presentation in this chapter in particular.

REFERENCES

Anderson, J., Boyle, C., Farrell, R., & Reiser, B. (1984). Cognitive principles in the design of computer tutors. *Proceedings of Sixth Cognitive Science Conference*, (pp. 2–9). Boulder: University of Colorado.

Anderson, J., Farrell, R., & Sauers, R. (1984). Learning to program in LISP. *Cognitive Science, 8*, 87–129.

Baker, E., Feifer, R., Aschbacher, P., Bradley, C., & Herman, J. (1985). *Intelligent computer-assisted instruction (ICAI) study.* Los Angeles: University of California Center for the Study of Evaluation.

Brown, J. S., & Burton, R. (1978). Diagnostic models for procedural bugs in basic mathematical skills. *Cognitive Science, 2,* 155-192.

Brown, J. S., & VanLehn, K. (1980). Repair theory: A generative theory of bugs in procedural skill. *Cognitive Science, 4,* 379-426.

Burton, R., & Brown, J. S. (1982). An investigation of computer coaching for informal learning activities. In D. Sleeman and J. S. Brown (Eds.), *Intelligent tutoring systems* (pp. 79-98). New York: Academic Press.

Clancey, W. (1983). The epistemology of a rule-based expert system: A framework for explanation. *Artificial Intelligence, 20,* 215-251.

Goldstein, I. (1982). The genetic graph: A representation for the evolution of procedural knowledge. In D. Sleeman & J. S. Brown (Eds.), *Intelligent tutoring systems* (pp. 51-77). New York: Academic Press.

Hasling, D., Clancey, W., & Rennels, G. (1984). Strategic explanations for a diagnostic consultation system. *International Journal of Man-Machine Studies, 20,* 3-19.

Johnson, L. (1986). *Intention-based diagnosis of errors in novice programs.* Palo Alto, CA: Morgan Kaufmann.

Kulik, J. (1985, April). *Consistencies in findings on computer-based instruction.* Paper presented at the annual meeting of the American Educational Research Association, Chicago, IL.

Pirolli, P. (in press). A cognitive model and computer tutor for programming recursion. *Human-Computer Interaction.*

Sack, W., Littman, D., Spohrer, J., Liles, A., Fertig, S., Hughes, L., Johnson, L., & Soloway, E. (1986). *Empirical evaluation of the educational effectiveness of PROUST.* (Working paper). Yale University, New Haven.

Directions for Research and Applications

J. Jeffrey Richardson
University of Colorado at Boulder

This chapter presents a synthesis of the recommendations presented in foregoing chapters for the future development of ITSs. The recommendations are organized under two broad categories, research and applications. The distinction made between research and applications is that reserach is concerned with the additional knowledge and understanding necessary to build ITSs; applications are concerned with building, with the available knowledge, ITSs that can meet the instructional requirements of individuals, and organizations.

The information in this chapter should be of use to directors of research programs, faculty and scientists interested in pursuing research in ITSs, students curious about future directions for the field, and consumers of training. For the practitioner, the applications suggestions provide examples of ITS projects that are feasible and practical solutions to training needs. At the same time, the research suggestions involve some risk and uncertainty, and projects designed to meet practical instructional needs should not be structured around these approaches.

RECOMMENDED RESEARCH

Meta-Theory of Expert Knowledge

State of the art. The subjects taught by ITSs can be divided into two broad categories: those that deal with declarative knowledge (general knowledge about a topic, its vocabulary, relations, and methods) and procedural knowledge (specific knowledge about how to achieve a goal by applying and eventually automatizing general knowledge). An additional type of knowledge and knowledge representation is so new to artificial intelligence that ITSs for this type have not even been implemented; namely, *causal knowledge* (reasoning from first principles). The ITSs in the literature teach specifically either declarative or procedural knowledge and do not take into consideration whether or how these types of knowledge interrelate (see Anderson, chapter 2).

Opportunity. Common sense suggests that any intellectual endeavor involves both knowing about things and knowing how to do things. We know about numbers and their symbols, notation schemes, and kinds of operations on numbers, but we also know how to calculate. Educational psychology has for 50 years argued that rote memorization of procedures is an inferior instructional approach to teaching with meaning. Cognitive psychology has found distinct mixes of declarative and procedural knowledge and associated problem-solving strategies in contrasting expert and novice performance. Early ITSs faced tough challenges, and research efforts had to focus on manageable objectives, such as the declarative aspect of a task only, or the procedural aspect only, but not both. Now that modest successes have been achieved, and now that a considerable body of experience and technique has developed, the field should address intellectual activity in a more comprehensive manner.

Basic research. Further basic research is needed in building a meta-theory of expert knowledge that shows how declarative, procedural, and causal knowledges relate. Pieces of this research have been conducted, such as Anderson's ACT* theory (Anderson, 1983) or studies of differences between experts and novices (Larkin, 1980); but further work is needed to establish a solid foundation in knowledge representation for ITSs to build upon.

Applied research Although a comprehensive theoretical foundation is being built for a meta-theory of expert knowledge, there is absolutely no reason why some initial effort cannot be made in developing ITSs that formally represent and teach both the declarative and procedural aspects of a domain. One approach would be to take an existing ITS that is procedural and augment it with declarative knowledge.

Causal Reasoning
and Qualitative Simulation

State of the art. Only recently has there developed a significant body of artificial intelligence litrature on the subject of causal reasoning and qualitative simulation. One of the classic works in causal reasoning is SOPHIE III, the third and last of the SOPHIE systems (Brown, Burton, & deKleer, 1982) for electronic troubleshooting. The knowledge representation issues were so challenging that SOPHIE III focused on them solely, leaving as future work the job of completing the student modeling and tutor modules of an ITS for this form of knowledge.

Opportunity. No ITS has been developed explicitly to investigate tutoring through the use of qualitative simulation. SCHOLAR had a declarative knowledge representation for rainfall in the form of a semantic net, but it was not a simulation. Because one of the most important training domains is maintenance, where qualitative simulation is the principal form of reasoning, there is a great opportunity here to move the ITS field forward, both in the theoretical and practical senses.

Basic research. Although there is a good artificial intelligence research base in qualitative simulation (Bobrow, 1984), no single representation in artificial intelligence has predominated for this type of reasoning. Qualitative simulation is an active field of research in artificial intelligence, and its furtherance would serve ITSs. Cognitive theories of qualitative simulation are in a similar situation. Descriptive work has been published in the troubleshooting literature (Keller, 1985), and a theoretical foundation for mental models exists (Card, Moran, & Newell, 1983; Gentner & Stevens, 1983). However, further studies need to focus specifically on explicating how people reason with mental models.

Applied models. While basic research is underway in the cognition of causal reasoning, ITSs can be built using artificial intelligence techniques for qualitative simulation in the expert module. The direct cognitive validity of these techniques will not yet have been established, but they will serve as an approximation and afford the opportunity to build ITSs with a representation for expert knowledge that has yet to be utilized.

Natural Language
and Tutorial Discourse

State of the art. Teaching is an act of communication that allows the transmission of culture from generation to generation. We use language for many purposes, but clearly one of the most important uses is teaching. What there is to know about how people use language to teach must therefore be great indeed. However, the educational literature says much more about classroom interaction, questioning strategies, and teaching methods in formal instructional situations than about tutoring.

Opportunity. Builders of ITSs need a knowledge of tutoring that is prescriptive in nature, not descriptive. That is, they need a computational form of the rules of tutorial discourse. Some work in this area has been conducted by Collins and Stevens in SCHOLAR (Collins, 1976) and by Clancey in GUIDON (Clancey & Letsinger, 1981). But these few first attempts merely scratch the surface of this field.

Basic research. A theoretical approach needs to be developed for investigating the linguistic character of tutorial discourse. Empirical, descriptive studies of classroom or tutoring situations need unifying concepts to direct the search for data. Clearly, the vast educational literature should be incorporated from the start in a basic research effort to develop computational models of tutorial discourse, but researchers need to develop an overall strategic approach to this problem. The investigation, as far as ITSs are concerned, should focus on tutorial interactions (one-on-one teaching situations) in preference to classroom situations. A research question of interest is the domain independence (or dependence) of tutorial strategies, as suggested by Halff (chapter 4).

Applied research. Because the goal of the basic research effort is a computational theory, it will be necessary to express this theory as running ITSs and to test this theory by using the ITSs to teach students. This work has begun, notably with Woolfe's Meno-tutor (Woolf & McDonald, 1985), and should be continued and expanded. Researchers should continue to elaborate on the curriculum and instruction part of ITSs, in particular with computational schemes implementing what we already know about tutoring.

Realistic Student Modeling

State of the art. Realistic student modeling in ITSs requires the modeling of the student's cognitive development throughout the course of acquiring expert-level competence in a domain. It must track, in Piaget's terms, the changes that occur as incremental assimilation triggers accommodations in the way the student views the domain.

It should faithfully track and monitor the changes that occur as a novice becomes an expert. That is, it should be able to predict and note when the novice's means-ends, backward reasoning, which is dependent on surface structure, shifts to the expert's pattern recognition and forward reasoning, which is dependent on deep structure.

Opportunity. Student modeling techniques are just beginning to acquire this capability, notably through the use of bug libraries and bug part liabraries (VanLehn, chapter 3). Researchers have little theoretical understanding of the developmental course of knowledge that is prescriptive and procedural rather than descriptive. They can model novice and expert performance in physics, and can even model a few intermediate points; but fully articulated developmental models suitable for ITSs do not exist in physics or in any other domain. The standard student modeling techniques represent student knowledge as a proper subset of expert knowledge (the overlay method) or augment this representation with a library of bugs or bug parts (VanLehn, chapter 3). The beginnings of a developmental theory for the source of these bugs is evident in repair theory (Brown & VanLehn, 1980), but this theory has been worked out only in simple domains such as subtraction.

Basic research. There is a big potential research agenda in modeling the acquisition of expert-level skill. This research would ask what developmental changes occur in the representations and processes used in reasoning about specific domains as expertise is acquired. It would also investigate how these changes occur. One clue to the answer to this last question is that, somehow, qualitative simulation or causal reasoning helps learners convert more and more of their declarative knowledge into procedural knowledge, and that this process somehow causes changes in the way the declarative knowledge is represented.

Applied research. Current techniques for student modeling need to be broadened to account for learning and the changes in representation and process that learning engenders. Some procedural studies have been done, for example in the balance beam (Klahr & Siegler, 1977), suggesting that for a suitably chosen domain some progress could be made in enhancing the way ITSs model students. Physics, perhaps orbital mechanics, might be a good place to start because of the prior work on distinctions between experts and novices in physics.

RECOMMENDED APPLICATIONS

Design Issues

In order to apply what researchers have learned about ITSs, it is necessary to make the design of ITSs somewhat systematic. That is, practitioners will benefit from guidance regarding how their instructional or training requirements map onto ITS design alternatives or architectures. As each preceding chapter has discussed, a number of design alternatives are available within each ITS module. For the expertise module, there are three principal knowledge representations: declarative, procedural, and qualitative simulation. The choice of knowledge representation affects the selection of an appropriate student modeling technique. Instructional environments may vary from microworlds, which support open-ended discovery learning, to tightly controlled simulations, in which immediate, corrective feedback is provided for any deviation from optimal behavior.

This book has made explicit, for the first time, the interplay between the various modules of an ITS and the range of design options available within each module. The information in this book could lead to developing a more prescriptive decision guide for practitioners to use in developing ITSs. Examples of some of the considerations from this volume that are of assistance in ITS design are discussed in this section.

Matching Instructional Objectives
to Knowledge Representation

A key to making decisions about the appropriate ITS configuration or design lies in the instructional or training requirements. The answer to the question, "What form of knowledge must the student learn?" determines the basic knowledge representation for use in the expert module. If the objective is knowledge of facts, concepts, and relations, a declarative knowledge representation is appropriate. If the objective is knowledge of how to execute specific procedures quickly and accurately, then a procedural knowledge representation is appropriate.

Matching Student Model
to Knowledge Representation

The chapter on student modeling (chapter 3) maps out a three-dimensional space of alternatives for ITS student models. One of these dimensions is knowledge type, and hence the choice of knowledge representation will reduce the space of student modeling options to two rather than three dimensions. The instructional or training practitioner will need to make a selection in each of the two remaining dimensions: bandwidth and student-expert differences. Having selected the appropriate type of student model, the practitioner must then determine the diagnostic technique (model tracing, plan recognition, etc.) with which to implement the model.

Matching Instructional Objectives to Tutorial Strategy and Environment

The chapters on curriculum and instruction and on instructive environments outline an array of options the practitioner has in deciding how the ITS is going to interact with the learner. One dimension discussed by Burton (chapter 5) is the degree of abstraction. The literature on ITSs offers at least five examples of troubleshooting simulations, each at a different level of abstraction, from use of actual equipment, to block diagrams faithful to specific equipment, to randomly generated network diagrams representing no specific piece of equipment at all. The selection of an alternative along this dimension depends to a great extent on the instructional objective, and on its place in the curriculum of objectives.

ITS Design Summary

It is impossible to assign to one of the modules of an ITS—expert, student modeling, curriculum and instruction, or instructional environment—the principal design constraint. The interactions between modules are just too numerous and subtle. For example, the choice of instructional environment determines the character of human-computer interaction, which in turn sets the bandwidth available to the student model. Or, as VanLehn states in his chapter, the level of refinement in diagnosis and tutoring should be the same; and thus choices about instructional environment or instruction affect the student model, and vice versa. The best approach to designing an ITS might be to list, for a given domain and instructional application, the range of possibilities available for each of the modules. Then, with the maximum set of possibilities in clear view, the process of eliminating alternatives can be based on the expected interactions among modules. This approach may not be superior to a purely "artistic" one, but it does provide a background against which to judge the merit of each facet of a design.

ITSs for Algorithmically
Tractable Domains

ITSs can now be developed for algorithmically tractable domains, or domains that can be reduced to fairly straightforward procedures. The procedures can be more complex than a recipe or checklist, and indeed many need to be represented as a production system. For a domain to be tractable, the goals must be explicit and well defined, the start state must be known, and all operators and the conditions of their applicability must be known for all states in the problem search space. Topics from elementary and secondary education involving procedural knowledge, such as subtraction, algebra, and geometry, are algorithmically tractable; and examples of ITSs for these domains are given throughout this book. Other examples from the training arena include the use of navigational tools and the maintenance of equipment.

Issue-Recognizer Student Models
for Off-the-Shelf Expert System

If the issue-recognizer method of student modeling is used, ITSs can be built from existing expert systems, as discussed in chapter 2, and it should be possible to augment off-the-shelf expert system shells to serve as ITS development shells. VanLehn (chapter 3) does caution that the more satisfactory approach to the expert module in an ITS will always be the one that has greater fidelity and correspondence to the sequence of mental states people use in reasoning.

Simulation Kits

A simulation kit is an ITS building tool for instructional objectives dealing with reasoning about systems (e.g., troubleshooting). Development of this form of application is already underway with the Navy's Intelligent Maintenance Training System (Burton, chapter 5). If this project is successful, the application of ITSs to simulation-based training objectives will have been proved feasible, and software tools for doing this type of work will have been developed.

Medium-Scale Evaluation
and Empirical Testing

In the chapter on evaluating ITSs, Littman & Soloway make the case for internal and external evaluation of ITSs during their development. They argue that if the final ITS is to be as good as possible, it must be formally evaluated as it is being built from the perspective of its effect on its users and of its internal functionality. That is, formative evaluation of an ITS is a required, integral part of system development.

However, in the applications setting, summative evaluation and empirical testing are of paramount importance in justifying the costs of using an ITS for instruction. To date, most ITS evaluations have focused on supporting the development of a particular ITS research prototype. For ITSs to become viable instructional applications, more summative evaluations need to be done. A pioneering effort in this regard is the medium-scale evaluation of Anderson's geometry tutor now underway in the Pittsburgh public schools. As we develop ITSs for application, as opposed to research, summative evaluation will need to be a part of the overall approach.

Applicability to Traditional Instruction

Spinoffs from ITS research have enriched several other fields. One of the most important spinoffs is the application of the concepts and philosophies, if not the methods, of ITSs to traditional instruction. Richard Burton characterizes in his chapter the new educational philosophy that the ITS field embraces: the concepts of constructivism, the importance of conceptual understanding, the role of preconceptions, the need to connect in-school and out-of-school learning, the importance of self-monitoring and self-management techniques, and the vision of lifelong learning.

The set of ITS modules, and the concepts and approaches each module embodies, suggest ways to improve the development of instruction in any setting, mode, or media. As one example, the basis for all ITS instruction is a coherent, performance-based model of what is to be learned, that is, the expert module. As a second example, instruction should not be delivered unless its effect on the student (i.e., the student model), particularly the way it interacts with students' misconceptions, is understood.

ITSs Outside the Classroom— The Master and the Apprentice

Outside the classroom, education often becomes training. Industrial, business, and commercial training accounts for about half of the total educational expenditure in the United States. In this context, ITSs can play a much greater role than that of classroom tutor—they can become the master in the master-apprentice paradigm of on-the-job training.

When the apprentice joins the guild, he or she knows little and must be told much; but eventually, through the oversight and mentoring of the master, the apprentice becomes a master in his or her own right. By virtue of its expert module, the ITS, as the master, can tell the apprentice what to do or how to accomplish a task. This is the typical mode of functioning of an expert system. But augmentation of an expert system with the other architectural components of an ITS can produce a much more powerful system that is capable not only of telling its user what to do, but of systematically increasing the competence of its user to perform unaided. This capacity to transform the apprentice into a master is what ITSs bring to the field of job aiding and expert systems. The material consequence of ITS technology will extend beyond the classroom.

REFERENCES

Anderson, J. R. (1983). The architecture of cognition. Cambridge, MA: Harvard University Press.

Bobrow, D. B. (Ed.). (1984). *Qualitative reasoning about physical systems.* Cambridge, MA: MIT Press.

Brown, J. S., & VanLehn, K. (1980). Repair theory: A generative theory of bugs in procedural skills. *Cognitive Science, 4,* 379–426.

Brown, J. S., Burton, R. R., & deKleer, J. (1982). Pedagogical, natural language, and knowledge engineering techniques in SOPHIE I, II, and III. In D. Sleeman & J. S. Brown (Eds.), *Intelligent tutoring systems* (pp. 227–282). London: Academic Press.

Card, S. K., Moran, T. P., & Newell, A. (1983). The psychology of human–computer interaction. Hillsdale, NJ: Lawrence Erlbaum Associates.

Clancey, W. J., & Letsinger, R. (1981). NEOMYCIN: Reconfiguring a rule-based expert system for application to teaching. *Proceedings of the Seventh International Joint Conference on Artificial Intelligence* (Vol. II, pp. 829–836). Los Altos, CA: Morgan Kaufman.

Collins, A. M. (1976). Processes in acquiring knowledge. In R. C. Anderson, R. Spiro, & W. E. Montague (Eds.), *Schooling and the acquisition of knowledge* (pp. 339–363). Hillsdale, NJ: Lawrence Erlbaum Associates.

Gentner, D., & Stevens, A. L. (Eds.). (1983). *Mental models.* Hillsdale, NJ: Lawrence Erlbaum Associates.

Keller, R. A. (1985). *Human troubleshooting in electronics: Implications for intelligent maintenance aids* (AFHRL-TP-85-34). Brooks Air Force Base, TX: Air Force Human Resources Laboratory.

Klahr, D., & Siegler, R. S. (1977). The representation of children's knowledge. In H. Reese & L. P. Lipsitt (Eds.), *Advances in child development* (Vol. 12, pp. 61–116). New York: Academic Press.

Larkin, J. H. (1980). Expert and novice performance in solving physics problems. *Science, 208,* 1335–1342.

Woolf, B., & McDonald, D. D. (1985). Building a computer tutor: Design issues. *AEDS Monitor, 23,* 10–18.

Appendix I
Selected Intelligent
Tutoring Systems

This appendix gives a brief description and overview of selected ITSs discussed in this volume. Abbreviated references are followed by the number of the chapter in which those references are first cited in full.

ACM: Automated Cognitive Modeling
DPF: Diagnostic Path Finder

The **ACM** system is an approach to automating the construction of cognitive process models. Two underlying psychological assumptions are made: (a) cognition can be modeled as a production system and (b) cognitive behavior involves a search through a problem space. The system starts with a set of overly general condition–action rules, adds appropriate conditions to each of these rules, and then recombines the more specific rules into a final model. By inferring a solution path through the problem space, the system produces a set of productions that model the cognitive behavior.

    DPF was developed to improve the path-finding capabilities of the original ACM system. The domain for testing both systems was subtraction errors. (Langley & Ohlsson, 1984: 3; Ohlsson & Langley, 1985: 3)

Algebraland

Algebraland is a workbench for algebra that can be used to study the acquisition of problem-solving skills. The system provides a set of algebraic operators (e.g., combined terms, distribute) that can be successively applied to an equation until it is solved. As these operators are applied, a search tree is dynamically created and displayed, thereby providing a trace of the problem-solving steps taken to find a solution. This problem-solving trace can be used by students, both during problem solving to keep track of their progress, and afterward, to study the consequences of their errors and to make comparisons with optimal solution paths. (Brown, 1985: 5; Foss, 1987: 5)

BIP, BIP II: Basic Instructional Program

BIP applied knowledge-based planning techniques for dynamically sequencing problem exercises in a stand-alone, on-line programming course. Knowledge about the exercises curriculum is represented in a Curriculum Information Network (CIN) that links exercises to underlying coding skills. In **BIP II** the coding skills are represented in a semantic network that describes their interrelations. Student learning is modeled by mapping performance on exercises onto the skills. Exercises are selected dynamically by applying teaching heuristics to the student model to identify skills to teach and then to determine an exercise that best involve those skills. The system was used and evaluated in several introductory programming classes. (Barr, 1976: 2; Westcourt, Beard, & Gould, 1977: 2)

Bite-Sized Tutor

This ITS authoring system, still being developed at the Learning Research and Development Center at the University of Pittsburgh, is based on a three-layered hierarchical architecture. The lowest layer, the Knowledge Layer, contains mixed declarative and procedural knowledge represented in grouped nets of concepts connected by predicators. Above the Knowledge Layer is the Curriculum Layer, which contains the knowledge about the sequencing of the curriculum in terms of prerequisite knowledge. The Aptitude Layer or Metacognitive Layer, the uppermost layer, is concerned with individualizing the instruction to suit different students' capabilities. The architecture is based on an object-oriented programming language. (Bonar, 1985: 6; Bonar, Cunningham, & Schultz, 1986: 5)

BUGGY
DEBUGGY
IDEBUGGY

These systems are some of the most frequently cited examples of using "bug" libraries to diagnose student errors. **BUGGY** is a multi-function system built by Burton and Brown as a framework for modeling misconceptions underlying procedural errors in arithmetic. Students' errors are conceived as the products of "bugs" or errors in an otherwise correct set of procedures. **DEBUGGY** is an off-line version of a diagnostic system based on the BUGGY framework. The knowledge base in DEBUGGY contains a library of both primitive and common compound bugs. DEBUGGY uses the pattern of errors from a set of problems to construct a hypothesis concerning bug or a combination of bugs from the library that has generated the errors. **IDEBUGGY** is an interactive version of the system that generates problems to successively narrow the set of hypotheses under consideration. (Brown & VanLehn, 1980: **2**; Burton, 1982: **2**; Brown & Burton, 1978: **3**, **5**; VanLehn, 1982: **3**; VanLehn, 1983: **3**)

Geometry Tutor
LISP Tutor

These tutors are two of a series of tutors from John Anderson's laboratory. The tutors are based on either the ACT*, (Adaptive Control of Thought-star) production system or its successor PUPS (Penultimate Production System). The systems consist of a tutorial component, an interface, and a set of ideal and buggy rules. Using the expert rules, the expert module is capable of solving the problems being tutored. Students' errors are diagnosed by means of the buggy rules.

A notable feature of the **Geometry Tutor** is the use of the proof graph to communicate to the student the logical structure of the problem-solving process by which a proof is generated.

The **LISP Tutor** has the seldom-used name of GREATERP (Goal-Restricted Environment for Tutoring and Educational Research in Programming). The ideal model of LISP programming in the LISP Tutor is implemented in GRAPES (Goal-Restricted Production System). A salient feature of the LISP tutor is its immediate correction of errors. As soon as the student makes an error, the system attempts a diagnosis and gives a hint as to the correct solution. (Anderson, in press: **2**; Anderson, 1983: **2**; Anderson, Boyle, & Yost, 1985: **2**, **5**; Anderson, Corbett, & Reiser, 1986: **2**; Reiser, Anderson, & Farrell, 1985: **2**; Anderson, 1981: **5**)

GUIDON
GUIDON-2
IMAGE

GUIDON, an ITS for medical diagnosis, is an example of a tutoring system that was built to interface with an existing expert system. **GUIDON** is based on MYCIN, a rule-based expert system for diagnosing certain infectious diseases such as meningitis. MYCIN was reconfigured to consist of two separate parts: EMYCIN, a domain-independent shell for inferencing, and so forth, and the medical knowledge base. GUIDON was constructed to interface with EMYCIN and to interactively present the rules in the knowledge base to a student.

Because the rules in MYCIN often combined diagnostic rules and medical facts in such a manner that the reasoning process was not clear, MYCIN was reconfigured in a system called NEOMYCIN, in which diagnostic strategy was separated from medical facts. HERACLES is the domain-independent shell for NEOMYCIN. These systems became the basis of the tutor **GUIDON-2. Image** is the student modeler subcomponent of GUIDON-2. GUIDON-WATCH is the graphic interface for all these components and is the mechanism for interacting with the system for instruction, running consultations, and editing the knowledge base. (Clancey, 1982: 1; Clancey, 1984: 4; Clancey & Letsinger, 1981: 4; London & Clancey, 1982: 3; Richer & Clancey, 1985: 5; Shortliffe, 1976: 2)

IMTS: Intelligent Maintenance Training System

IMTS was developed by the University of Southern California in cooperation with Search Technology, Inc. It consists of simulation-based software tools that can produce system behaviors from a deep model of the system. IMTS, designed for use in training troubleshooting skills and for conducting research in intelligent tutoring, contains a generalized model of an expert diagnostician and domain-independent editing tools to construct graphic simulations of equipment systems. The initial application was for a Navy SH-3 helicopter rotor head braking and folding diagnostic training system. IMTS operates on a XEROX 1186 AI Workstation. (Towne, 1987: 5)

Kimball's Calculus Tutor

This ITS was developed for the domain of symbolic integration. The goal of symbolic integration is to find a set of transformations that will transform a given symbolic expression into an expression for which the integration is "known" and automatic. The tutor can either pose problems or use problems submitted by the student. The student then indicates an approach for solution such as substitution, integration by parts. When queried, the tutor responds with its estimate of the best approach. The estimate is based on a prioritized test of choices among approaches, not on the known solution to the problem. The expert module is not actually capable of solving the problems being tutored. The student diagnostic module maintains a knowledge base of approaches known to the student to guide suggestions for approaches. The knowledge base is updated as successive problems are solved. (Kimball, 1982: **3**)

LMS: LEEDS MODELING SYSTEM
PIXIE

The **LEEDS MODELING SYSTEM (LMS)** is a diagnostic model for determining sources of error in algebra problem solving. Errors are assumed to be due to incorrect procedural rules or "mal-rules." The underlying concept is similar to the "buggy" rules for arithmetic in BUGGY. The LMS system is not designed for remedial teaching, only for diagnosis of the incorrect rules. **PIX** is LMS's new name now that Derek Sleeman has left **LEEDS. PIXIE** is an on-line ITS and is based on the LMS system. (Sleeman, 1982: **3**)

MACSYMA Advisor

MACSYMA Advisor is an automated consultant for MACSYMA, an interactive system designed to help professionals perform symbolic manipulations of mathematical expressions. The MACSYMA Advisor uses plan recognition as its underlying methodology for diagnosis of misconceptions that are causing errors when students attempt to use MACSYMA. The Advisor accepts a description of violated expectations from its user, tries to reconstruct the user's plan, and if successful, generates advice tailored to the user's needs. (Genesereth, 1982: **2**)

Meno-tutor

This domain-independent tutoring shell is designed to manage tutorial discourse. The system contains (a) tutoring component, which contains knowledge bases and reasoning mechanisms for planning the text, and (b) a surface-level language generator, which produces the syntactically correct utterances. Meno-tutor was implemented with two different knowledge bases, one concerning rainfall and one concerning Pascal programming. (Woolf & McDonald, 1985: **4**)

PROUST

This ITS, which is a system for diagnosing nonsyntactic student errors in Pascal programs, is an example of an off-line tutor that has access only to a final product or state on which to base its diagnosis of student errors. The completed student programs are submitted to **PROUST,** which provides a printout of the diagnosis. This system is discussed in some detail in chapter 8. (Johnson & Soloway, 1984a: **3**; Johnson & Soloway, 1984b: **3**)

SCHOLAR

One of the earliest ITSs, **SCHOLAR** is a mixed-initiative system for tutoring declarative knowledge. The original system was developed with a knowledge base about South American geography. The knowledge base is represented as a semantic net of objects or concepts. It uses a Socratic style of tutoring, first attempting to diagnose the underlying misconception in the student's knowledge, then posing a problem that will force the student to discover the errors. (Carbonell, 1970: **1**; Carbonell & Collins, 1973: **3**; Collins, Warnock, & Passafiume, 1975: **2**; Stevens, Collins, & Goldin, 1982: **2**)

SOPHIE I, SOPHIE II, SOPHIE III

The three SOPHIE (Sophisticated Instructional Environment) systems are successive generations of a system for tutoring electronic troubleshooting. For **SOPHIE I,** the underlying "expert" or simulation of the device (a regulated power supply) is implemented with a general purpose electronic simulator called SPICE (Simulation Program with Integrated Circuit Emphasis). Faults can be inserted in this simulation, and the student then diagnoses them. In addition to the simulation, the system contains a natural language interface which permits students to pose questions. **SOPHIE II** extends the basic environment of SOPHIE I with the addition of an articulate expert based on a prestored decision tree for troubleshooting the power supply and annotated with schema for producing explanations. **SOPHIE III** contains three modules, the electronic expert, the troubleshooter, and the coach. SOPHIE III is a radical departure from SOPHIE I in that the underlying expert is based on a causal model rather than a mathematical simulation produced by SPICE. (Brown, Burton, & deKleer, 1982: **1, 5**; Brown & Burton, 1975: **2, 5**; Brown & Burton, 1987: **5**; Brown, Burton, & Bell, 1974: **4**)

SPADE

The tutoring environment of **SPADE** is designed to teach higher level concepts, such as styles, strategies, and organization techniques, that underlie efficient planning and debugging of computer programs. Implemented for the programming language LOGO, the system contains a model of the design process which it uses on line to communicate with the student during the construction and debugging of programs. Based on the expert planning module, the system suggests alternative designs to the student by means of menus. (Miller, 1982: **2**)

Steamer

This simulation of a steam propulsion plant consists of a graphical interface to a mathematical model of the plant. The interface allows a user to select from a library of views of the propulsion system and to interact with a selected view to change the state of the underlying simulation model. Several levels of detail of the propulsion plant can be depicted in different views. The level of detail can vary from gauges and dials to schematic diagrams. One instructional advantage of Steamer is the ability to show global views of systems that are physically dispersed in a real power plant. (Hollan, Hutchins, & Weitzman, 1984: **1**; Hollan, Hutchins, McCandless, Rosenstein, & Weitzman, in press: **5**)

WEST

An example of an ITS with issue-based tutoring, **WEST** provides on-line coaching for a mathematics game first developed on the PLATO computer-assisted instructional system. The object of the game is to move a player across an electronic gameboard by a number of moves equal to the value of an algebraic expression that the student formulates. The coach compares a student's performance with that of a computerized expert, constructs a model of the differences and uses the model to suggest alternative equations or strategies that would have given better performance. (Brown & Burton, 1982: **2, 5**)

WHY

This system is another example of a tutor for declarative knowledge. **WHY** tutors not just factual knowledge but the principles of rainfall as well, correcting students' misconceptions concerning the causal models underlying rainfall. A follow-up of the Scholar system, it also uses mixed-initiative dialogue and a Socratic tutoring heuristic. Based on an extensive analysis of tutorial dialogue, an effort was made to characterize the global strategies used by human tutors to guide the dialogue. (Collins, 1976: **2**; Collins, Warnock, & Passafiume, 1975: **2**; Stevens & Collins, 1977: **2**)

WUSOR

WUSOR I, II, and **III** are coaches developed for the electronic game WUMPUS. The object of the game is to locate and destroy the WUMPUS without being entrapped by the many dangers that lurk in the maze of caves surrounding the hidden lair. WUSOR has a rule-based expert representation and uses plan recognition for diagnosis. (Goldstein, 1982: **2**)

Glossary of ITS Terms

Advancement. The use of an algorithm to determine whether to advance the student to the next curriculum topic.

Authoring system. A domain-independent component of an ITS that allows the developer to enter specific domain knowledge into the tutor's knowledge base.

Bandwidth. The amount of the student's activity available to the diagnostic model. The three categories of bandwidth in ITSs, from low to high are: final states, intermediate states, and mental states.

Black box expert system. A procedure that generates correct behavior over a range of tasks in the domain, but whose mechanism is inaccessible to the ITS. (See *glass box expert system*.)

Bug catalog. See *bug library*.

Bug library technique. A student-expert difference model that represents misconceptions. It augments an expert model with a list of bugs.

Bug part library. A student-expert difference model that generates bugs from fragments of valid rules.

Bugs. Student misconceptions in declarative or procedural knowledge.

Coarse-grained student model. A student model that does not describe cognitive processes at a detailed level.

Cognitive fidelity. The measure of correlation between the cognitive model and actual human problem solving strategy.

Cognitive model. A representation of human cognitive processes in a particular domain.

Condition induction. A diagnostic technique used in the student model for constructing buggy rules for bug part libraries, a student-expert difference model. (See *bug part library*.)

Constructivism. A pedagogical philosophy that views learning as *constructing* knowledge, rather than *absorbing* it.

Curriculum module. The component of an ITS that selects and orders the material to be presented to the student.

Curriculum selection techniques. Techniques that deal with selecting problems to exercise those areas in the curriculum where the student is weak.

Decision tree technique. A diagnostic technique used in the student model that creates a tree of paths. Each diagnosis corresponds to a path from the root to some leaf.

Declarative knowledge. Knowledge represented as basic principles and facts of a domain. It is usually contrasted with knowing how to use facts, that is, *procedural knowledge*.

Deep-level tutoring. Tutoring that can provide explanation of the internal reasoning of its expert module.

Diagnostic module. The component (a process) of an ITS that infers and manipulates the student model. The selection of a diagnostic algorithm is dependent on the bandwidth of the system.

Direct manipulation interface. See *first person interface*.

Divergence principle. A curriculum principle that states that there should be a broad representative sampling of exercises and examples in curricula for procedural tutors.

Enabling objectives. An instructional objective's immediate prerequisite.

Environment. The component of an ITS that specifies or supports the activities that the student does and the methods available to accomplish those activities.

Expert module. The module of an ITS that provides the domain expertise, i.e., the knowledge that the ITS is trying to teach.

Expert system. A computer program that uses a knowledge base and inference procedures to act as an expert in a specific domain. It is able to reach conclusions very similar to those reached by a human expert.

Expository tutor. A tutor that is concerned with declarative knowledge. Usually interactive dialogue is the instructional tool used in this type of tutor.

External evaluation. Evaluation of an ITS that focuses on the impact of the ITS on students' knowledge and problem solving.

External–internal task mapping problem. A problem in the human–computer interaction component of an ITS. It is a gap between what the user wants, the goal of the interaction, and the actions the user must make to achieve the goal.

Felicity conditions. Principles of instruction that facilitate ease of learning, such as presenting only one new step in a procedure per lesson.

Fidelity. A measure of how closely the simulated environment in an ITS matches the real world. There are four kinds of fidelity: physical, display, mechanistic, and conceptual.

Fine-grained student model. A student model that describes cognitive processes at a high level detail.

First-person interface. A type of user interface where the actions and objects relevant to the task and domain map directly to actions and objects in the interface. With this interface the user has a feeling of working directly with the domain. An example of this type of interface is the icon.

Flat procedural knowledge. Procedural knowledge that is not organized by subgoals, i.e., an undifferentiated set of production rules.

Generate and test. A diagnostic technique used in the student model that generates bug combinations (sets of bugs) dynamically and tests these for validity against student performance.

Glass-box expert system. An expert system that contains human-like representation of knowledge. This type of expert system is more amenable to tutoring than a black box expert system because it can explain its reasoning.

Goal-factored production system. A rule-based system that makes explicit references to goals in the conditional part of its rules.

Grain-size of diagnosis. The level of detail used by the diagnostic technique for processing student models. Closely related to *bandwidth*.

Hierarchical procedural knowledge. Procedural knowledge with subgoals.

Increasingly Complex Microworld (ICM) framework. A pedagogical technique of exposing the student to a sequence of increasingly complex microworlds that provide intermediate experiences such that within each microworld the student can see a challenging but attainable goal.

Individualization. A curriculum principle that states that exercises and examples should be chosen to fit the pattern of skills and weaknesses that characterize the student at the time the exercise or example is chosen.

Instruction. Actual presentation of curriculum material to the student.

Instructional Environment. See *environment*.

Instructional Systems Design (ISD). A systems engineering approach to the analysis, design, development, delivery, and evaluation of instruction.

Intelligent Computer Assisted Instruction (ICAI). Synonym for Intelligent Tutoring System.

Intelligent Tutoring System (ITS). A computer program that (a) is capable of competent problem solving in a domain, (b) can infer a learner's approximation of competence, and (c) is able to reduce the difference between its competence and the student's through application of various tutoring strategies.

Interactive diagnosis. A diagnostic technique used in the student model that does not use a fixed list of text items.

Internal evaluation. Evaluation of an ITS that focuses on the relationship between the architecture of the ITS and its actual behavior.

Issue-oriented methodology. A methodology for building an ITS that relies on access to intermediate states of cognitive processing. These intermediate states are used to identify instructionally useful issues characteristic of differences between expert and student performance.

Issue-oriented recognizers. Methods that note in student behavior the presence or absence of issues or characteristic traits of expert performance.

Issue-oriented tutoring. A type of tutoring that bases instruction on patterns of differences in the intermediate cognitive processes underlying student and expert behavior.

Issue tracing. A diagnostic technique used to construct a student model. A variant of model tracing that relies on access to intermediate states of student performance rather than on access to a highly detailed cognitive process model.

Knowledge level analysis. An internal evaluation method; it attempts to characterize the knowledge in the ITS and thus answers the question: *What does the ITS know?*

Manageability. A curriculum principle that states that every exercise should be workable and every example should be comprehensible to students who have completed previous parts of the curriculum. Manageability applies to procedural tutors.

Matching principle. A curriculum principle that states that both positive and negative instances of concepts, procedures, or principles should be presented.

Misconception. An item of knowledge that the student has and the expert does not have. A type of student-expert difference. A *bug*.

Missing conception. An item of knowledge that the expert has and the student does not have. A type of student–expert difference. See *overlay model*.

Mixed Initiative Dialog. An ITS environment that accepts and responds in natural language to both solicited and unsolicited natural language input from the student.

Model-tracing. A diagnostic technique used to build a student model. It uses the student's surface behavior to infer the sequences of rules fired in a rule-based model of performance; that is, the student's actions traced a path through the rule base.

Overlay model. A student–expert difference model that represents missing conceptions, usually implemented as either an expert model annotated for those items that are missing or an expert model with weights assigned to each element in the expert knowledge base.

Path finding. A diagnostic technique used to find a path from one state to the next, which is a chain of rule applications. This is a way of representing the student's mental state sequence. The path is given to the model tracer.

Plan recognition. A diagnostic technique used in student models that represent hierarchical procedural knowledge. It is similar to path finding in that it is a front end to model tracing.

Procedural knowledge. Domain-dependent knowledge about how to perform a specific task.

Procedural tutor. A type of tutor that teaches procedural knowledge, i.e., skills and procedures. Usually exercises and examples are used by procedure tutors.

Process model. A model that reveals the *mechanism* behind behavior.

Production rule. A rule of the form *condition(s) imply action(s),* used in modeling cognitive behavior. A set of production rules and an interpreter for processing them is termed a *production system.*

Program process analysis. An internal evaluation method; it attempts to answer the question: *How does the ITS do what it does?*

Propaedeutics. Knowledge that is needed for learning but not for proficient performance.

Qualitative process model. A type of cognitive model, concerned with reasoning about the causal structure of the world; the simulation of dynamic processes in the mind. It is an important facet of troubleshooting behavior.

Repair theory. A generative theory of bugs; a method of deriving bug libraries directly from correct procedures, reducing the need to collect bugs through empirical observation.

Rule-based model. An expert module of an ITS that is implemented with a rule-based (production) system. (Also called a "production model.")

Second-person interface. A type of user interface where the user gives commands to a second party. Examples of this type of interface are command languages, menus, and (limited) natural language interfaces.

Step theory. A theory that states that curriculum should be divided into discrete lessons, each of which adds a single decision point or step in the procedure to be learned. See *felicity conditions.*

Structural transparency. A curriculum principle that states that the sequence of exercise and examples should reflect the structure of the procedure being taught and should thereby help the student induce the target procedure.

Student–expert differences. The difference between the expert's knowledge and the student's knowledge. There are two basic types of student–expert differences; missing conceptions and misconceptions. The three models used to represent student–expert differences are: overlay model, bug library technique, and library of bug parts.

Student model. The component (a data structure) of an ITS that represents the student's current state of knowledge (mastery) of the domain, i.e., a detailed model of student cognition.

Surface-level tutoring. Tutoring that can be implemented with issue-oriented recognizers. Access to the internal reasoning of the expert module is not available.

Target knowledge type. The type of knowledge that is represented in the expert and student model modules. Knowledge representation can be categorized into three types: procedural (both flat and hierarchical), declarative, and qualitative process model.

Tutorial domain analysis. An internal evaluation method for iteratively adding and subtracting requirements of the ITS design.

User Interface Management System (UIMS). A strategy that attempts to separate the interface component of an application program from the computational part.

Web teaching. A curriculum approach where selection of materials is guided by two principles: relatedness (priority is given to concepts that are closely related to existing knowledge), and generality (discuss generalities before specifics). Web teaching applies to expository tutors.

Wizard-of-Oz system. Semiautomated tutors where a human tutor replaces some or all of the instructional functions of an automated tutor. Used in research and development of ITSs.

Author Index

Subject Index